HOW IT ALL BEGAN

Selected Works by W. W. Rostow

Essays on the British Economy in the Nineteenth Century, 1948
The Growth and Fluctuation of the British Economy 1790–1850
(with A. D. Gayer and A. J. Schwartz), 1953; Second Edition 1974
The Process of Economic Growth, 1952; Second Edition 1960
The Stages of Economic Growth, 1960; Second Edition 1972
The United States in the World Arena, 1960
Politics and the Stages of Growth, 1971
The Diffusion of Power, 1972

W. W. Rostow

HOW IT
ALL BEGAN
Origins
of the
Modern
Economy

McGRAW-HILL BOOK COMPANY

New York   St. Louis   San Francisco
Düsseldorf   Mexico   Toronto

Book designed by Stan Drate.

123456789BPBP798765

Library of Congress Cataloging in Publication Data

Rostow, Walt Whitman, date
  How it all began.

  Includes bibliographical references.
  1. Economic history—1600–1750. 2. Economic
history—1750–1918. I. Title.
HC51.R66   330.9′03   74-18062
ISBN 0-07-053897-2

To my mother

The author is grateful to the following for permission to quote from copyrighted material:

Cambridge University Press for Phyllis Deane and W. A. Cole, *British Economic Growth 1688–1959*, copyright © 1962; for Alexander Gerschenkron, *Europe in the Russian Mirror*, copyright © 1970; and for Joseph Needham, *Clerks and Craftsmen in China and the West*, copyright © 1970.

Economic History Review for an article by M. I. Finley, "Technical Innovation and Economic Progress in the Ancient World," in Second Series, Vol. XXVIII, No. 1, August 1965.

Journal of Economic History for an article by François Crouzet, "Wars, Blockade, and Economic Change in Europe 1792–1815," pp. 567–588 in Vol. XXIV, No. 4, December 1964.

Methuen & Co., Ltd. for an excerpt by François Crouzet, "England and France in the Eighteenth Century: A Comparative Analysis of Two Economic Growths," from R. M. Hartwell's *The Causes of the Industrial Revolution in England*, copyright © 1967; and for a chart excerpt by Ralph Davis, "English Foreign Trade, 1660–1700," from W. E. Minchinton's *The Growth of English Overseas Trade in the Seventeenth and Eighteenth Centuries*, copyright © 1969.

Oxford University Press for T. S. Ashton's *The Industrial Revolution 1760–1830*, copyright © 1948.

Stanford University Press for Mark Elvin, *The Pattern of the Chinese Past*, copyright © 1973.

University of Kentucky Press for Shelby T. McCloy, *French Inventions of the Eighteenth Century*, copyright © 1952.

Preface

This book is a preliminary chapter to a larger work that burst its bounds.

I am engaged in an effort to set down the story of how the world economy has evolved over the past two centuries and, interacting with it, how the various nations of the world have moved through the stages of economic growth. As we enter an era when the common economic task will be to reconcile the imperatives of balance between man and his physical environment with the determination of the latecomers to achieve affluence, it seemed to me a good time to put the remarkable tale of what has happened since the late eighteenth century into coherent perspective, and then to peer ahead at the problems we shall all confront in the times ahead. I have for long taught economic history in these terms, but had never tried to put this way of looking at things between covers.

But it was first necessary to account for where the world economy stood at the end of the eighteenth century and how it got to the point where the British could break through the technological barriers that had constrained man and his civilizations for all of prior recorded history. As I addressed myself to a first chapter on how it all began, I found that no wholly satisfactory answer to the question existed either in my own mind or in the distinguished literature bearing on the theme. I concluded this was the case because that literature is fragmented in three distinct ways which make synthesis difficult. First, the evolution of early modern Europe, from the fifteenth to the eighteenth centuries, is, with a few notable exceptions, recorded and analyzed in national terms; and, as the primal success story, the economic history of Britain has understandably been accorded disproportionate attention. Second, and more important, those elements in the equation that determined the outcome are fragmented: the struggle for the domestic sinews of war, which largely shaped mercantilist policy at home; the struggle for power and profit, which shaped the commercial revolution; and the interweaving of all this with the scientific revolution. The literature on these themes has tended to separate into specialist fields, with some of the best work on the first, for example, done by political rather than economic historians. Third, conventional theory tends to separate the generation of technology from the workings of the economic system. Moreover, its reigning propositions are misleading with respect to the link between commercial expansion and the introduction of new technology, and they do not adequately illuminate the connections among science, invention, and innovation. It is a simple fact that, from Adam Smith to the present, the structure of formal economic theory has not absorbed satisfactorily the process of technological change. This combination of specialist fragmentation and lack of a sufficient framework of theory makes it difficult to account in an orderly way for the manner in which each element contributed to the rather odd outcome: an explosive expansion in British cotton textile production based on machines largely created as substitutes for the skill of Indian hands that Europeans could not match.

In economists' language, the end product is a case of increasing returns yielding the first leading sector in self-sustained economic growth. The path to that result, out of the whole tangled web of early modern history, is not simple. This has long been recognized. Herbert Butterfield, for example, in writing about the scientific revolution, warned against trying to disentangle the great bundle:

> . . . the scientific, the industrial and the agrarian revolutions form such a system of complex and inter-related changes, that in the lack of microscopic examination we have to heap them all together as aspects of a general movement, which by the last quarter of the seventeenth century was palpably altering the face of the earth. The hazard consists not in putting all these things together and rolling them into one great bundle of complex change, but in thinking that we know how to disentangle them—what we see is the total intricate network of changes, and it is difficult to say that any one of these was the simple result of the scientific revolution itself.*

Ultimately, this complexity arises because man is a many-faceted being whom we imperfectly understand. It is much easier for us to describe one of his activities than to relate his activities to one another and to the complexities of his mind and heart as he goes about his various kinds of business.

But in seeking to account for the beginning of the great saga of two centuries of uninhibited growth, I could not accept Butterfield's dictum. I had to try, in degree at least, to separate the strands, to show how they had their impact not only on the individual countries of Europe but on the regions beyond. I then had to relate this historical analysis to the theorist's case of increasing returns and to what I call the preconditions for takeoff into sustained economic growth and the takeoff itself. I also found it necessary to come to a conclusion on another great issue: Why ancient civilizations and mediaeval Europe failed to generate sustained growth. It turned out that all this required, even if tersely done, five chapters, not one. And so a preliminary chapter became a preliminary book.

*Herbert Butterfield, *The Origins of Modern Science, 1300–1800* (New York; Macmillan Co., 1952), p. 145.

In this effort, as the quotations and footnotes make clear, I have been sustained by the scholarship, insights, and wisdom of many others who have sought to illuminate aspects of this remarkable phase in human history.

In addition, I would thank François Crouzet, David Kendrick, Nathan Rosenberg, M. M. Postan, and Elspeth Rostow who offered observations on early drafts. Mrs. Vera Anstey, Tomasson Januzzi, and Jagdish Mehra were helpful in providing bibliography on Indian economic history and the history of Indian science and technology. Miss Pamela Grisham cheerfully typed and retyped the various versions of the text as it evolved, and Miss Lois Nivens, as on many other occasions, was an invaluable aide.

Portions of the argument were published in the *Journal of Economic History,* September 1973, and are used here with the kind permission of the editors.

The dedication of this book to my mother reflects a professional as well as human debt. She typed my first undergraduate essays in economic history, read them, and urged me to go on.

W. W. ROSTOW

Austin, Texas
May 1974

Contents

1

Why Traditional Societies
Did Not Generate
Self - Sustained Growth

I

The premodern world is worth study for many reasons: to satisfy our curiosity; to extend our knowledge of the human condition and of human creativity; to help us understand the long shadows the premodern world cast on modern civilizations and cultures. For the limited purposes of this book, however, there is a narrow, almost mathematical reason for beginning with the premodern world: It did not generate self-sustained growth. If we can establish which factors were present and which absent in premodern as opposed to modern societies, we may help identify the specific elements that brought about the two centuries of self-sustained growth that began in the late eighteenth century. Was self-sustained growth blocked in premodern societies by a lack of interest in material things, religious beliefs, systems of slavery and feudalism, excessively narrow and impoverished markets, scientific ignorance, the lack of a commercial middle class, or what?

II

In one sense, the answer is simple and obvious: What distinguishes the world since the industrial revolution from the world before is the systematic, regular, and progressive application of science and technology to the production of goods and services. This is how and where I would draw the line in the famous debate whether the ancient world was "primitive" or "modern."[1] It was neither; it simply lacked a more or less regular flow of technological innovation. In the modern world, this flow has been an additional factor of production which is, so far as we know, infinitely expansible. The organized creativity of the human mind appears thus far to be of a productivity capable of compensating for limitations of land and natural resources. Thus for two centuries have societies, which organized themselves to exploit the technological stock and flow, fended off Ricardian diminishing returns to land and the Malthusian spectre. Only now have the rate of population increase, potential limits on natural resources, and threats to the environment challenged the efficacy of the scientific and technological revolution, although science and technology will surely play a decisive part if man succeeds in coming to dynamic equilibrium with his physical environment.

The premodern world was not without scientists, inventors, and innovators, as well as philosophers, politicians, administrators, artists, and creative writers of great sophistication, but at any given period of time men and societies lived within technological limits, because innovation was sporadic. The ceiling could be lifted—and was—by elements of technological advance and innovation, but it could not be lifted regularly. Therefore, constraints operated on the levels of agricultural production, output and employment in urban industry, population that could be sustained, taxable income, and on the consequent capacity of governments to carry forward their objectives.

To assert these propositions, however, is to pose, not to answer, the question that is the main subject of this chapter; that is, why technological innovation was not a regular flow in the premodern world. Before getting at that central question, we may find it useful to consider how a relatively fixed technological ceiling caused the life of the premodern world to assume the form of cycles.

Consider first a model of what might be called a small-scale traditional society—say, an African tribe.

The small-scale traditional society is one whose economic life is bound quite rigorously by a relatively fixed area of arable or grazing land and by a narrow, or relatively stable, trading environment. It is mainly taken up with producing for local consumption. Its political and social organization is also tied intimately to the region and does not strain to enlarge the area of its political and economic power, although it may be drawn, from time to time, into offensive or defensive military activities on its borders. Production functions may change with chance discoveries or the occasional intrusion of knowledge from outside, such as knowledge of a new crop, but these are, essentially, one-time changes to which the society adjusts, moving to a new plateau.

The model, however, is not static; the small-scale traditional society does not ride smoothly along its plateaus. Within its existing production functions and acreage, population and income are likely to exhibit fluctuations of relatively short duration, determined by the size of the harvests and the incidence of disease and war. By routes of considerable complexity, these factors yield birth and death rates that, in turn, cause population to move in a roughly cyclical way, quite aside from a year-to-year sensitivity to the availability of food. The pattern that Heckscher was able to present for eighteenth-century Sweden is likely to prove general for small-scale traditional societies; that is, "Nature audited her accounts with a red pencil," with a rise in the death rate roughly, and fairly promptly, cancelling a population surge induced by intervals of peace, absence of epidemic, and good harvests.[2]

History also offers cases that suggest a somewhat different model. Large political trading units are permitted, as well as the possibility of substantial increase in acreage. The scale of allocations to military activities fluctuates over a much wider range than in the small-scale case, allowing for protracted intervals of peace and for wars yielding, directly and indirectly, greater economic damage and more profound political and social consequences than in the model of the small-scale traditional society. Here we are probing at the dynamics of the empires and dynasties of Asia and the Mediterranean world.[3] Although history offers us no pure cases, not even the tempting case of the undulating sequence of Chinese dynasties, the most appropriate model appears to be a cycle of greater length than the relatively short compensatory adjustment of the small-scale model.

The abstract cycle of the traditional empire begins with the establishment of political order over a reasonably large area by strong purposeful administration that concentrates a high proportion of its energies and resources on the domestic scene. It comes to power at the trough of a previous cycle when war and epidemic have driven down the population, freed acreage, and disrupted trade. In this special sense, idle capacity exists.

Within the framework of peace and order, agriculture revives; the routes for domestic, and sometimes international, trade are opened or reopened, and kept open and reliable; and, where appropriate, the irrigation works are built, or rebuilt, and maintained. Agricultural output not only expands but shifts in its composition to exploit the possibility of trade with the expanding cities in commodities of higher value than the basic grains. The taxes are collected with tolerable efficiency and honesty by the government, and the expanded outlays of a prosperous government, as well as those above the ranks of the peasantry, stimulate various forms of handicraft manufacture. Processing and handicraft manufacture—and, in general, higher degrees of specialization—are stimulated as well by an increase in interregional and, perhaps, international trade. Efforts may be made not only to repopulate the old acreage but to bring new lands under cultivation. In this environment, women are married younger, more of their children survive the early precarious years, reasonably provident government combines with reasonably efficient transport to make food available to regions suffering poor harvests, and population expands.

As time passes, however, three factors tend to set a limit on economic progress: first, the pressure of expanding population against good land; second, the built-in difficulty of maintaining over long periods of time efficient, honest and purposeful administration; and, third, the likelihood that the state will become embroiled in wars whose cost outweighs their return either in expanded trade, booty, or in acquisitions of good land. At some stage these factors might yield bad harvests arising from land pressed too hard, excessive taxation, epidemics, peasants' revolts or other forms of civil strife, and the decay of central administration.

Proximately—operationally—the downturn is caused by a fiscal crisis: the government cannot generate the taxes required to meet the security and welfare obligations that have accumulated, and its own efforts to deal with the situation may exacerbate an underlying constitutional crisis caused by the disequilibrium between resources and objectives.

After this upper turning point, economic, social, and political life retreats to narrower limits, within which the society conducts its affairs on a less productive, more self-sufficient basis, a process usually accompanied by a decline in population.[4]

The fundamental technical reason for the abortive character of these expansions, in both small-scale and imperial cases, lies in the fact that economic invention and innovation in traditional societies were not regular features of their life. For reasons that are examined later in this chapter, these societies did not regularly allocate a substantial proportion of their creative talent and other resources to breaking economic bottlenecks.

To understand the nature of modern economic growth, we must, therefore, begin by accepting Postan's challenge ". . . to lay bare the essential processes of a society held in by physical or, if the term is used in a broad sense, Malthusian checks."[5] And, from what we know, his tentatively expressed insights have a meaning beyond the late Middle Ages. In the history of traditional empires, we can, indeed, ". . . find explanations of later decline in the conditions of previous growth." It is not only in fourteenth-century Britain that "the honeymoon of high yields was succeeded by long periods of reckoning when the marginal lands, no longer new, punished the men who tilled them with recurrent inundations, desiccations and dust storms."[6]

The premodern world poses, then, two questions: What forces account for the periods of economic expansion and what characteristics of premodern societies yielded the technological ceiling which set limits on expansion and, sooner or later, sent them into decline? We shall deal with these questions under three headings: politics; trade and industry; and science, technology, and innovation.

III

In talking about traditional, premodern societies we are, of course, generalizing the experience of many cases of great variety. In his study, *The Political Systems of Empires,* for example, S. N. Eisenstadt summarizes his findings on thirty-two premodern societies in tables set out in an appendix of about one hundred pages. These tables array his cases against many structural and functional standards, primarily drawn from Parsonian sociology. One's first impression is that there is almost impenetrable variety among them. Moreover, there is change over time within these premodern societies; for example, in the succession of Chinese dynasties and the evolution of Rome and the Byzantine Empire. Nevertheless, for our narrow purposes, a few generalizations about the politics of these societies are possible.

Like their predecessors and successors throughout history, the primary aim of their rulers was, of course, to stay in power. But in so doing they were caught up in one or another version of the three eternal tasks of government: to preserve or advance their interests against other political systems; to provide an acceptable standard of welfare for the people in terms of the cultural norms of their day; and to conduct their constitutional business, notably the maintenance of unity and the provision of justice.[7] Like their successors down to the present day, these rulers lived in a competitive arena of power, which always threatened and often yielded war. Similarly, their constitutional business —the unity and tranquility of the state, the quality of justice, and the presence or absence of corruption in the court and bureaucracy—reflects criteria which extend into modern times. With respect to welfare, the situation was different. Their cultures, in the widest sense, set a relatively static standard. There were norms for good times, often drawn from the memory of golden eras of the past when the frontiers were quiet, crops ample, taxes modest, state granaries full, the roads free of bandits, and, where relevant, the irrigation works well maintained. Rulers were assessed, in part, against such standards, but the society was not expected to yield a regularly rising standard of life for the people as a whole. This was not because people lacked interest in material things and worldly goals. From top to bottom, from courtiers to peasants, the desire for more was evident, be it luxuries, money, land, or additional food for the village family to eat. And, narrow as they sometimes were, there were channels for vertical mobility in these societies that individual men exploited with vigor. But the expectation for the society as a whole was that, although it might suffer good times or bad at the whim of the harvests, the vicissitudes of war, or the quality of rule, there would not be regular overall progress.

In political aphorisms, the reality of the three functions of government was recognized and, sometimes, a priority asserted among them. Confucius, for example, is quoted as follows:

> Tsekung asked about government, and Confucius replied: "People must have sufficient to eat; there must be a sufficient army; and there must be confidence of the people in the ruler."
> If you are forced to give up one of these three objectives, what would you go without first?" asked Tsekung.
> Confucius said, "I would go without the army first."
> "And if you were forced to go without one of the two remaining factors, what would you rather go without?" asked Tsekung again.
> "I would rather go without sufficient food for the people. There have always been deaths in every generation since man lived, but a nation cannot exist without confidence in its ruler."[8]

And from the Middle East came this less discriminating prescription:

> A ruler can have no power without soldiers, no soldiers without money, no money without the well-being of his subjects, and no popular well-being without justice.[9]

The rulers of such societies sought to reconcile these often conflicting objectives in the face of complex restraints and dilemmas. These were present, in one form or another, within city states, tribes, and relatively simple state structures, but they are most dramatically revealed in the larger empires, consolidated and maintained for substantial periods of time.

The great rulers of such empires were inherently modernizers. They came to power in times of disarray or fragmentation, sometimes by conquest from outside. They sought to establish unity and order over wide areas, and they sometimes asserted new objectives or visions of the society's mission. Their initial enemies, moreover, were usually the traditional landowning (or landholding[10]) aristocracy, and they had to look to new, more flexible men to win their victories, consolidate their rule, and administer their large domains. But they soon found themselves hedged about.

Let us look first at their relations to the landowning aristocracy. The rulers might displace at least some of the existing aristocracy and reallocate land to their own supporters, but these supporters, in turn, soon generated familiar vested interests in local power and in retaining payments from the land for their own purposes rather than those of the central ruler. Moreover, the landowning aristocracy was needed to help administer, often to collect revenues, and to mobilize troops and corvée labor.

Their second problem arose in relations with the bureaucracy. The rulers initially built or enlarged bureaucracies with men loyal to them, but with the passage of time the bureaucrats sought to consolidate a quasi-independent position and to perpetuate the position of their families by the acquisition of land.

The third relationship of the rulers was with the peasantry. They were needed to generate food for the cities, taxes for the rulers, and to serve in the armies and on large public projects. Moreover, they could not safely be driven to such desperation as to yield revolt—a subject of constitutional anxiety of rulers that can be traced from antiquity down to the freeing of the Russian serfs in the nineteenth century.[11] There is a tendency for the rulers to reach over the heads of the large landowners and try to establish a direct relation of mutual confidence with the peasants, but a true alliance between rulers and peasants could not be consolidated, because the rulers needed a viable, even if sometimes tense and competitive, relation with land owning aristocrats.

The fourth group, the merchants and bankers, played a substantial role in many of the premodern empires. They were needed to supply the rulers with loans and taxes as well as to assure to the cities the necessary supplies from home and abroad. If pressed too far, however, their interests conflicted with those of the aristocracy and bureaucracy. Sometimes they were foreigners or otherwise socially degraded.

Finally, the rulers' connection with religious groups and institutions was of great importance. The rulers often claimed legitimacy in terms of their link to divinity as well as their performance of other regal duties in ways the culture required. There is wide variety in the relations that evolved between rulers and religion, the clergy, and their institutions. The relation was never without some ambiguity, and, even when the rulers' control over religious institutions was most direct and straightforward, the maintenance of such institutions laid a substantial claim on scarce resources.

Pervading the whole political and social structure—as well as the international arena in which these empires found themselves—was the assumption that resources, as well as land, were finite; what one man, family, or state gained had to be at the expense of what another lost. This proposition was a daily working reality to rulers struggling endlessly, and against great resistance, for resources they needed to maintain their courts and administrations, to erect the monuments that their assertion of legitimacy required, and, above all, to maintain or generate the armed forces necessary to defend their realm and its unity or to pursue abroad their ambitions.

It is within these political, social, and resource constraints that the premodern imperial rulers presided over periods of expansion and prosperity as well as crisis and decline. On the upswing of their cycles we can observe many of the elements that we would now recognize as pre-industrial modernization:

- an improvement of communications, tending to unify and lower costs within domestic markets, and an enhanced sense of nationhood
- an expansion in agricultural output and intensified exchanges with the cities
- an enlargement of external, as well as internal, commerce
- an expansion in manufacturers within the limits of existing industrial technology
- a rise in the number, confidence, and political influence of men of commerce and industry, of bureaucrats, and of technical and professional groups associated with modern urban activities
- an emergence of governmental structures with important degrees of specialization and even some subgroup autonomy within the framework of imperial rule
- a spreading through the society, during the phase of prosperity, of secular standards for judging the performance of men and the increasing pursuit of secular objectives by the people

On the upswing, such societies enjoyed the advantages, as it were, of the previous downswing; that is, there was often unused land to be colonized or recolonized, trade to be revived under reestablished conditions of unity and order, and, sometimes, long intervals of peace. So it was, for example, between Augustus and Marcus Aurelius, in the Mogul Empire after its consolidation by Akbar down to the coming of Aurangzeb, and in China during the century after Manchu rule was fully consolidated (circa 1683).

But, sooner or later, these periods of expansion and prosperity gave way to decline. As noted before, the most typical proximate cause of decline was war. While the possibility of war and, sometimes, limited military engagement encouraged policies that tended to modernize the society, large and protracted wars led the rulers to grasp for more resources than the society could generate, and self-reinforcing processes of economic, social, and political decline ensued. The rapid decline of Athens in the fifth century B.C. and the slow grinding decline of the Roman Empire in the West are, of course, classic examples of this process. It can be seen also at work in the fall of some of the Chinese dynasties and elsewhere.

As Eisenstadt perceives, the inner mechanism of decline is the struggle of the rulers for inputs of resources to meet demands beyond the system's capacity to supply. He sees the decline of the bureaucratic empires as "characterized by a shrinking supply of the free economic and manpower resources available. . . . This diminution of free resources was usually initiated by the excessive demands of the rulers and by the conflicts between the more flexible and the aristocratic groups, and created a vicious circle in the political and social processes of these societies."[12]

But protracted peace and prosperity could also put such societies under strain. As China's predecessor of Malthus, Hung Liang-chi, concluded: ". . . during a long reign of peace Heaven and Earth could not but propagate the human race, yet their resources that can be used to the support of mankind are limited. During a long reign of peace the government could not prevent the people from multiplying themselves, yet its remedies are few."[13] Both Ch'ing China and Tokugawa Japan ultimately came under this kind of Malthusian pressure, as did, earlier, England in the late Middle Ages.[14]

Declines induced by the excessive claims of war or by population pressure had the same root: The traditional societies did not generate inventions and innovations as a regular flow into the economy. Therefore, they ultimately strained and broke against a technological ceiling that set limits on the inputs of men and resources governments could generate for war, or on the population that the land could support. Neither could wide-ranging commerce, highly sophisticated handicraft manufacture, virtuosity in civil engineering, a lively urban life, and large and sometimes competent and dedicated bureaucracies lift these economies into takeoff. Rostovtzeff's ultimate questions about the Roman Empire could be asked of a good many other societies that experienced golden years of expansion and prosperity: "The problem remains. Why was the victorious advance of capitalism stopped? Why was machinery not invented? Why were the business systems not perfected? Why were the primal forces of primitive economy not overcome? They were gradually disappearing; why did they not disappear completely?"[15]

One answer to Rostovtzeff's question lies in the nature of politics in these premodern societies. Their cultures and religions did not set for the rulers the objective of regular growth. This is more than a tautology. When times were peaceful, the harvests good, and the rulers' revenues honestly collected, surpluses would generate. Culture and tradition prescribed how these surpluses should be used: to build public monuments, for private luxury, or, occasionally, to ease the burden of revenue payments on the peasantry. There were positive norms for good rulers and good societies but they did not include the notion that surplus, when it existed, should be invested to yield a progressive expansion in per capita income. This is one fundamental reason why modern growth did not happen in traditional societies. Rulers, ancient and modern, have had an unambiguous incentive to enlarge the output from which their scarce tax revenues could be drawn, and, in later times, when regularly increasing output emerged in men's minds as a realistic option, the rulers played a central role in encouraging invention and innovation.

Another part of the answer to Rostovtzeff's question belies Adam Smith's famous dictum: "The division of labour is limited by the extent of the market." The widening of domestic and foreign markets in premodern societies did not cause fundamental and regular changes in industrial or agricultural technology by private entrepreneurs.

IV

In *The Wealth of Nations*, Adam Smith observes that ". . . in manufacturing art and industry, China and Hindostan, though inferior, seem not to be much inferior to any part of Europe."[16] Although he later deprecates China's view of foreign trade as "beggarly commerce," he notes its large and vital domestic trade and can only conclude that its technology would be still more refined if ". . . this great home market added the foreign market of all the rest of the world," including knowledge of ". . . all the different machines made use of in other countries."[17]

But the lesson of history is that Smith's powerful insight, relating the scale of the market, specialization, and technology in manufacture, is incomplete. Dwight Perkins puts it well: "There is no natural or irresistible movement from commercial development to industrialization. The experience of China alone is testimony to this."[18] In fact, the general lesson of economic history is that periods of substantial expansion in foreign and domestic trade did not automatically foster radical or cumulative improvements in technology. Nevertheless, this conclusion about Athens in the fifth century B.C. might hold, with commodities and sources suitably altered, for many times and places over the subsequent twenty-two centuries: "An Athenian citizen of the Periclean age might enjoy not only Attic olive-oil and wine but also the corn and the dried fish of the Black Sea, the dates of Phoenicia and the cheeses of Sicily; he might wear slippers from Persia and lie on a Milesian bed with his head resting on a Carthaginian pillow."[19]

The simple fact is that such phases of trade expansion led to capital widening, not capital deepening; that is, to expansion of output without significant technological change. There was some invention and innovation in the two mass industries where substantial trade was normal in the premodern world—food-growing and textiles—but they occurred slowly and sporadically. When, for example, Adam Smith came to illustrate in woolen textiles the "Effects of the progress of Improvement upon the real price of Manufactures," he noted that there was no substantial change over the previous century, but there were three "very capital improvements" since the end of the fifteenth century: the spinning wheel, machines for winding yarn and arranging the warp and woof before they are put into the loom, and the fulling mill.[20]

There were also slow changes in agriculture, accelerated in both Europe and Asia by contacts with the New World. But, as Moreland notes about India: ". . . in Akbar's days there were no men of science investigating the peasant's problems, no skilled engineers designing implements to meet their needs, and no financial talent devoted to organising their markets or facilitating the supply of capital."[21]

Given the critical importance of the food supply to both popular welfare and the ruler's revenues, one might have expected a more energetic policy in India and elsewhere. But aside from the maintenance of irrigation works (notably in China, Egypt, and Central America, but also in parts of India) and an insistence that the peasant cultivate the land to which he was in one way or another attached, efforts to increase the size of the crops were sporadic at best.

It was in areas where the market was narrower that one can perceive some effective pressure for invention and innovation in the tools of warmaking, shipbuilding and navigation, mining, jewelry, luxury textiles, the construction and ornamentation of public buildings, and the construction of roads, viaducts, and irrigation works. The demands of the state and the wealthy were real enough, but they were also inelastic. Moreover, there was, by and large, an ample supply of cheap labor. These societies did not generate the explosive interaction between cost-reducing innovation and elastic demand embraced by the case of increasing returns.

One is strongly tempted, in the face of this phenomenon, to seek a straightforward economic explanation; that is, to attribute to an elastic labor supply and/or inelastic demand for its products the failure of invention and innovation to emerge as a regular flow. Why assume the pain of creation if labor is cheap and abundant and the market is narrow and relatively fixed?

As for the labor supply, Samuel Lilley[22] has made some effort to find a systematic connection between periods of labor abundance and shortage in the ancient world and phases of greater or lesser technological change, but his correlations are not wholly persuasive. The periods of relative labor shortage (e.g., the late Roman Empire and the late Middle Ages) do not appear to have yielded a marked acceleration in technology. The spread of the water mill is the best case in both instances, but its diffusion is slow and incomplete. And, as will later emerge, labor shortage does not appear to have been a decisive factor in the germinal inventions of the late eighteenth century: cotton spinning machinery, coke metallurgy, and the steam engine. Speaking of the abundant supply of cheap labor in Greece and Rome, Finley concludes:

> This is obviously a key fact, but its implications are complex and often elusive. It is not often that one can point to slaves and say, simply and with confidence, "There lies the explanation for a static technology and a static economy." An occasional one-for-one relationship seems likely, as in the hauling of ores or draining of water from the mines. Mechanical devices were sometimes used for these purposes, but normally ore continued to be brought from the mines in leather bags on the backs of slaves and water to be removed by hand-bailing, also by slaves. On the other hand, it was in the Spanish mines (where the exploitation shocked even contemporary writers) that the Archimedean screw was employed, and it was on the Roman latifundia, with their notorious *ergastula,* that most progress was made with farm machinery.[23]

As for demand, the vast majority of the populations in these societies was poor peasants, servants, handicraft workers, or slaves. The surplus above minimum consumption levels was systematically concentrated in the hands of the ruler, his court and administration, and the landed aristocracy. The middle class of men in commerce and the professions was small. Craftsmen's wages were relatively low. As Moreland says of Akbar's India:

> ... we have seen that the only career open to men of ability and enterprise was the service or the bounty of the State, and that the dominant note of this career was consumption rather than production of wealth. A wealthy upper class may render substantial economic services if they use their wealth wisely, and direct a steady flow of savings into productive channels, but there are no

signs that such services were rendered in the India of Akbar's time, and where savings were accumulated they took the useless form of stores of gold and silver and gems. In the aggregate, a very substantial proportion of the income of the country was spent on waste and superfluities, the cost of which fell in the long-run on the producing classes, the peasants, artisans, and merchants. . . .[24]

His recurring theme is the narrowness of the Indian market for goods and services.

In short, one can draw an economic portrait of the typical traditional society which suggests persuasively that its structure—above all, the poverty of the peasant and the concentration of all income in the hands of landowners and the state—would inevitably damp or destroy any incentive for invention or innovation arising from the expansion of commerce. But, in fact, landholding systems varied among these traditional societies and the size of the effective market. On such straightforward economic grounds China, for example, would appear a quite promising candidate for leadership in modern industrialization as compared, say, to India under the Moguls. By the twelfth century A.D., China had moved beyond a system of feudal land tenure. As in India, land had been viewed, in theory (in the seventh century A.D., for example), as "the property of the state and was only parcelled out to those who farmed it during their productive lifetime (age eighteen to sixty)."[25] But a protracted struggle ensued between the state and a semifeudal aristocracy which sought to build up large estates. The state won, yielding a system of family landownership without primogeniture. Rural life contained a wide spectrum, from large landowners to tenants and agricultural workers with about 70 percent of the families owning some land, their holdings expanding and contracting with the vigor of successive generations, including their capacity to earn income outside rural life, notably, in the bureaucracy and commerce. Mobility was heightened to a significant degree by the method of recruitment for the imperial civil service through competitive examinations.[26] Here one is clearly dealing with a potentially wider market, but innovation was still limited and sporadic.

Contemplating the failure of regular technological innovation in China, Joseph Needham concludes: ". . . the merchants were always kept down and unable to rise to a position of power in the State. They had guilds, it is true, but these were never as important as in Europe. Here we might be putting our finger on the main cause of the failure of Chinese civilisation to develop modern technology, because in Europe (as is universally admitted) the development of technology was closely bound up with the rise of the merchant class to power."[27]

There are three things wrong with Needham's explanation. First, it implies a weaker position for the Chinese merchant than in fact existed. The conventional view of the merchant as "a despised profession" in Chinese, and Indian, society has apparently been overdone.[28] Second, while guilds did help protect the merchant and craftsmen's interests in traditional societies, they were not, as Postan notes, a good vehicle for generating and rapidly spreading new technology.

> In most towns of the later Middle Ages there were regulations to secure fair prices, to maintain wages, to lay down standards of quality, and above all, to protect individual masters from competition. But, however necessary or commendable these objects may have been, they made technical improvement very difficult. For bye-laws were as a rule based on the technical methods in existence when they were framed; and once framed they were to stand in the way of all subsequent change.
>
> What is more, so deeply ingrained was the spirit of protection that in every local trade the technical methods were treated as a secret.[29]

When innovations were introduced, they spread slowly: the machine for throwing silk was invented in Bologna in 1272, but it remained unknown outside Bologna until 1538, and it was not copied and put to work in England until the seventeenth century. In short, the guild in traditional societies was not generally an instrument for the encouragement and diffusion of inventions. Third, as our argument in later chapters suggests, the increase in technological innovation in Europe during the eighteenth century is related to factors other than the expansion of trade and the rise of merchants, although merchants played a role, and, in many nations (e.g., Japan, Russia, and Turkey), technological innovation was later set in motion primarily from the top—by bureaucrats, soldiers, and modernizing politicians—rather than by merchants. In short, Needham's proposition about China —and his implied view of the coming of systematic technological progress in the West—is too simple and would not be "universally admitted."

In a lively and original review of the long sweep of Chinese history, Mark Elvin[30] arrives at quite a different explanation for China's failure to generate an industrial revolution. Focusing on the period of Chinese economic expansion and prosperity, notably during the seventeenth and eighteenth centuries, he examines the hypothesis that an industrial revolution was forestalled by any one or all of the following factors: inadequate capital, restricted markets, political obstacles to growth (including the status and power of businessmen), and an alleged incapacity of the Chinese to develop large-scale and long-lived enterprises. He adduces convincing evidence for rejecting all these "conventional explanations."

His argument comes to rest on the notion that Chinese technology in agriculture and water transport had moved into a "high-level trap." It had progressed to a point where large discontinuous leaps in technology would have been required to permit substantial increases in output in the one case, and radical cost reductions in the other. In effect, chemical fertilizers and steam power (for both pumping irrigation water and transport) were needed to go forward. To these circumstances, he adds low per capita income resulting from population pressure on limited arable land, rising raw material costs, and a partially related shortage of domestic cotton supplies. Finally, he notes little pressure for laborsaving machinery in an overpopulated society progressively moving toward the Malthusian crisis which came in the mid-nineteenth century.

I would take a somewhat different view. The steam engine presented as great a technological discontinuity to seventeenth- and eighteenth-century Europe as it did to China. Although per capita income in eighteenth-century China was (or became, under population pressure) lower than that in western Europe, the price elasticity of demand for textiles was high and a cost-reducing technological revolution of the kind that occurred in late eighteenth-century England would have generated its own markets. Indeed, cheap European manufactured cottons did find a market in impoverished China of the nineteenth century. Finally, the critical inventions of eighteenth-century Europe were not primarily addressed to labor saving. Put another way, China's "high-level trap" of the late traditional period did not differ significantly from the situation of other great traditional empires, which had experienced prior periods of economic expansion without undergoing a technological revolution.

What appears lacking in seventeenth- and eighteenth-century China is the gathering scientific, philosophical, inventive, and innovative ferment which marked Europe of the same period—a ferment described in Chapter 4—and which suffused the courts, the universities, the scientific societies in capital cities and provinces, the coffee houses, and the workshops, coming to focus on the bottlenecks that had to be broken, the opportunities for increased power and profit that might be seized by the state or private entrepreneurs.

The following passage from Elvin's study indicates the similarities and the difference between his view and that developed here:

> Almost every element usually regarded by historians as a major contributory cause to the industrial revolution in northwestern Europe was also present in China. . . . Only Galilean-Newtonian science was missing; but in the short run this was not important. Had the Chinese possessed, or developed, the seventeenth-century European mania for tinkering and improving, they could easily have made an efficient spinning machine out of the primitive model described by Wang Chen. . . . A steam engine would have been more difficult; but it should not have posed insuperable difficulties to a people who had been building double-acting piston flame-throwers in the Sung dynasty. The critical point is that nobody tried. In most fields, agriculture being the chief exception, Chinese technology stopped progressing well before the point at which a lack of basic scientific knowledge had become a serious obstacle.[31]

Our formal, analytic difference lies in how basic science is believed to relate to invention. Elvin assumes that the relation of basic science to invention was direct, that there was sufficient science to permit invention to go forward in China, and that it was the lack of economic incentives which prevented the necessary "tinkering and improving." In short, the failure was on the demand side. The argument of Chapter 4 is that the scientific revolution—in his phrase, Galilean-Newtonian science—was the critical factor in the industrial revolution of Western Europe, but its multiple role, affecting the supply of inventions, the demand for them, and the will to innovate, was indirect.[32]

V

There were, then, scientists at work in Greece and Rome, the Arab world, mediaeval Europe, India and China.[33]

There were inventors and inventions, and some of the inventions were applied in agriculture and industry, construction, shipping, and navigation. The problem to be explained is why these three distinct but related human activities—the analysis of the physical world, the creation of new technology, and the introduction of new technology into the working round of life—did not yield a regular flow of innovations.

In one sense, the problem is quantitative. There were simply not enough men at work on scientific problems to achieve great breakthroughs. Postan's observation about the Middle Ages has its analogue in other traditional societies: ". . . on the whole the persecution of men for their scientific ideas was very rare: rare because men with dangerous ideas, or indeed with any scientific ideas at all, were themselves rare; and it is indeed surprising that there were any at all. This does not mean that there were not intellectual giants. All it means is that in an age which was one of faith, men of intellect and spirit found the calls of faith itself—its elucidation, its controversies, and its conquests—a task sufficient to absorb them. To put it simply, they had no time for occupations like science."[34]

There is in man, however, an innate compulsion to seek a rationale for the physical world around him. As Giorgio de Santillana said: ". . . man very much wants the universe to make sense. . . ."[35] In a society where some men believe their observations and reflections can make sense of the universe—or even small parts of it—and where such men can find ways to subsist, the supply curve of scientists can be highly inelastic with respect to economic or other incentives. But despite the role of men of genius, scientific progress is the cumulative result of many minds, interacting, building on each other's work with the passage of time. The traditional societies left a place for men of scientific bent, but they did not generate steady, strong incentives to draw such men in large numbers into the work of science.

Nevertheless, the ancient Mediterranean world generated, as we all know, a rich body of observations and reflections in many fields, and scientists in mediaeval Europe revived and preserved this heritage. Joseph Needham and his colleagues have demonstrated that, on an essentially independent basis, Chinese science and technology at least matched that of the ancient Mediterranean world.[36] In India, it is clear that a number of scientific fields were pursued systematically, in terms of a sophisticated concept of the scientific method.[37] It is also evident from the quality of Indian craftsmanship in textiles and metals, the scale of mining, and the routes of trade that a considerable body of technological skill was accumulated. There is much evidence of sophistication in Indian medical practices.[38] In general, contacts with China made its technological achievements available to India as well as to the Arab world, and it may have been a two-way street. Needham notes, for example, that "the personal contacts between scientists from the ends of Asia in those days have not been sufficiently appreciated."[39] Among his examples is an Indian scholar of the seventh century A.D. who informed the Chinese of the properties of certain mineral acids.[40] Although Needham leans to the view that the Chinese gave much more than they received, he also underlines that the problem is complicated by difficulties in dating the important scientific texts of India.[41]

By modern standards this impressive body of scientific material—East and West—was, of course, incomplete and often wrong. But it lacked something else. It did not project to men beyond the world of science a new vision of the physical world to challenge the religious, philosophical, and mythical explanations which rationalized the inescapable phenomena men confronted from morning till night, from season to season. The pursuit of science was an accepted but minor part of the life of traditional societies. No scientist in the premodern world—not even Aristotle—produced results which permitted others to proclaim credibly an equivalent to Edmund Halley's lines in his prefatory ode to Newton's *Principia:*

> Here ponder too the laws which God,
> Framing the universe, set not aside
> But made the fixed foundations of His work.[42]

What we would now call basic science, in the traditional world, did not inspire in political rulers or merchants, bureaucrats or landowners a view of their physical environment that led them to believe it was comprehensible and subject to systematic, creative, and profitable manipulation.
   Traditional science suffered another narrower weakness: by and large its practitioners did not link their work to the tasks of technology.[43] Aristotle, for example, drew the line between science and practical technology on grounds of "good taste":

> The aim of ancient science, it has been said, was to know, not to do; to understand nature, not to tame her. The proposition is true, even if it is commonplace, and attempts to challenge it, which seem to be rather fashionable at the moment, are in my view misguided and certain to fail. Aristotle's verdict holds. At the end of the first section of the *Politics* (1258b 33ff.), he wrote as follows (in Barker's translation): "A general account has now been given of the various forms of acquisition: to consider them minutely, and in detail, might be useful for practical purposes; but to dwell long upon them would be in poor taste. . . . There are books on these subjects by several writers . . . anyone who is interested should study these subjects with the aid of these writings." Aristotle was the greatest polymath of antiquity, a tireless researcher, and the founder of any number of new disciplines in science and philosophy. His curiosity was unbounded, but "good taste," a moral category, interposed to put beyond the pale knowledge in its practical applications except when the application was ethical or political.[44]

This separation denied scientists the tools for experiment which inventive men from the practical world might have provided, and it denied inventors and potential inventors the stimulus and inspiration that might come from regular contact with the scientists. Postan's dictum about mediaeval Europe explains a good deal of the sterility of premodern science: "Mediaeval technology and mediaeval science each kept to their carefully circumscribed spheres."[45]

As for the inventors, they, like the scientists, are a distinctive breed. Their creative contriving and tinkering capacity—like other inborn gifts—seeks expression. They evidently derive satisfaction from solving practical problems in new ways, quite aside from the economic and social rewards success might bring. As nearly as we know, such talent is distributed at random. Also, as in the case of scientists, the number of men of talent engaged on tasks of invention is significant. Progress in technology is generally the cumulative result of the work of many hands and minds, struggling over a period of time to solve a clearly defined problem, building on each other's work. Breakthroughs occur, associated with the name of an individual, and occasionally—but rarely—an invention is, indeed, like Eli Whitney's cotton gin, the work of a single man. But, in the end, the scale of the inventive effort going forward in a society is likely to determine, broadly, the pool of technology available for application.

This means, in turn, that we must ask questions about both supply and demand. Did the traditional societies make it easy for men of potential inventive talent to become inventors? Were there strong incentives, from the demand side, for men to invent and bring forward their inventions for application?

On the side of supply it is evident that the structure of traditional societies could tap only a small proportion of the potential creative talent of their populations. A very high proportion of the total population was caught up from childhood in a grinding round of life associated with agriculture, with virtually no access to education, the world of ideas, or even the stimulus of the diverse and differentiated life of the cities. Undoubtedly low-born men and women of innate talent—rural as well as urban—not only absorbed the traditional methods in textiles, metalworking, and the decorative arts but also devised creative variations and refinements beyond the capacity of historians to trace. When one adds to these workers of irrepressible talent those of higher status engaged in medicine, organizing and designing the tasks of construction and civil engineering, shipbuilding, navigation, weapons manufacture, mining, and the working of basic metals, one emerges with an impression that the absolute size of the pool from which inventors might have been drawn was not so small as inherently to frustrate a cumulative process of technological development. After all, India and China of the seventeenth and eighteenth centuries contained very large populations by European standards: perhaps 100 million in India, 150 million in China around 1700. Even if the proportion of the potential inventive talent brought to a position to exercise it as a realistic option was low, the absolute numbers must have been vastly higher than in a Britain of, perhaps, 7 million or a France of 25 million. And from the pool of talent in traditional societies there was a flow of inventions, thin as it may appear by later standards. Finley observes: "Paradoxically, there was both more and less technical progress in the ancient world than the standard picture reveals. There was more, provided we avoid the mistake of hunting solely for great radical inventions and we also look at developments within the limits of the traditional techniques. There was less—far less—if we avoid the reverse mistake and look not merely for the appearance of an invention, but also at the extent of its employment."[46] It is precisely this paradox that emerges from Needham's portrait of Chinese technology and from the parallel literature on traditional India and the other great civilizations of the premodern world.

I am led, therefore, to conclude that the decisive formal weakness in traditional societies was on the demand side: in the lack of innovators, of men moved by economic or other incentives or perceptions actively to seek changes in technology.

We come back, then, to rulers and the bureaucracy, landowners and merchants, for these were the potential sources of innovating initiative.

There is first a strictly economic question to be dealt with: Did the potential private entrepreneurs lack capital and credit institutions to finance innovations? Finley argues, for example, that in the ancient world "private capital . . . would not have been readily available for the promotion and utilization of many of the possible technical innovations. . . . There were no proper credit instruments—no negotiable paper, no book clearance, no credit payments."[47] But the point is too narrow. In traditional societies there were merchants, moneylenders, and landowners who commanded great concentrations of wealth, and, indeed, the rulers relied on them or forced them to disgorge resources when public expenditures were high. Moreover, the pools of capital required to start innovation in industry are generally not great, and when innovation succeeds, expansion can be largely financed from the plowback of profits. As Finley concedes: "There were enough individuals who possessed the resources, but not among the men whose interest lay in production (other than agricultural)."[48] And in agriculture, as well as industry, a fundamental question is why those who might have benefited greatly from an expansion in production did not organize talent and resources to increase productivity.

Whatever the situation might have been for potential private innovators, certainly the rulers commanded the resources to encourage and finance innovation in agriculture and industry, as they did from time to time in the tools of warmaking. It simply did not occur to them to do so.

One is thus driven to the view that the fundamental answer to the question posed in this chapter lies primarily in the world of ideas. The impulse to study and understand the physical world was there, in Euripides' evocative phrase, to contemplate "the ageless order of immortal nature, how it is constituted and when and why. . . ."[49] But, beyond weaponry, the links of science to technology and productive invention were few; this was so because traditional cultures lacked the Baconian perception that there might be advantage, to state and man, in forging that linkage. The impulse to do things better and more efficiently was also there—the impulse to tinker, to contrive, and to invent. One can find lying about in the traditional societies many of the inventive insights that were to yield the germinal inventions in textiles, metalworking, and the steam engine that initially sparked the industrial revolution in Europe. They were simply never brought to maturity and to effective application. Those with command over resources were by no means lacking in a desire for more. Whether kings or courtiers, bureaucrats, merchants, or moneylenders, they exhibit all the public and/or private avarice for additional resources that one needs for a system of modern growth. But, in Cipolla's phrase, their "mental and cultural attitude"[50] did not lead them to perceive that the total pool of resources available to them and to all might be systematically expanded by the encouragement of new technology.

The argument must come to rest, above all, in the minds of the rulers in traditional societies. They certainly had a vested interest in breaking through the ceiling on resources available to them as they struggled to conduct the business of state, including costly wars. After all, landowners, bureaucrats, merchants, and moneylenders could usually go on living in relative affluence without the challenge of changing the order of society, unless caught in the vicious circle of a downward spiral in the society's affairs, and even then they could usually live out their lifetimes in comfort. But the challenge to the rulers was stark and inescapable. The rulers commanded the resources and power to instigate processes of technological innovation, but they did not conceive this course as a realistic alternative. Neither scientists nor inventors nor philosophers nor men of religion—nor all together—generated a vision that systematic progress was possible and a potential solution to the rulers' central problem.[51] As R. V. Jones tersely put it: "They could ably govern . . . any situation that their minds could contemplate; but they could not legislate for anything that they could not imagine."[52]

To assert that it was a failure of concept and vision that blocked the coming of modern growth is, of course, to raise a deeper question: What, specifically, in the cultural patterns of traditional societies stood in the way? Some have tried to answer that question with respect, for example, to the cultures of ancient Greece and mediaeval Europe. It has been argued that Greek humanism shied away from the machine[53] and the power of the mediaeval Church over men's minds and institutions stifled invention and innovation. But the central fact is that widely differing traditional cultures yielded the same result; that is, they lacked the notion that man had it in his hands to produce regular economic progress by systematically manipulating nature. Indeed, in the whole sweep of human experience, the most natural image of man's fate as a social animal—in the life of families or great empires—is a cycle around some relatively static norm. As Anaximander expressed it: "It is necessary that things should pass away into that from which they were born."[54] The real problem to be explained is how men came to the rather odd and probably transient notion of regular progress. As we enter a phase of history when the central economic task will gradually come to be the achievement of a dynamically stable balance between man and his physical environment, the remarkable two centuries of uninhibited growth that began in the 1780s (and the perhaps three previous centuries of European history that generated it) may well appear as the great exception in human experience.[55] And so, when trapped, as they periodically were, by conflict between the resources they needed and the resources they could generate, the rulers of traditional societies either sought to squeeze more taxes out of the economy than the economy and social structure could tolerate, or they looked abroad to booty or tribute. Neither proved capable of fending off for long the downward side of the cycle, which was the fate of the traditional empires.

VI

We conclude, then, that the critical failure of the traditional societies was conceptual: science—lively and irrepressible as it was—did not teach those with access to or power over resources that the physical world could be understood in ways that permitted it systematically to be transformed to their advantage. More passive and fatalistic views of man's relation to the physical world, therefore, prevailed. Inventors, too, were irrepressible, but the structure of traditional societies did not permit or encourage the two-way fertilizing ties of the inventor to scientist and entrepreneur. So many inventive experiments were not pushed to fruition; many inventions were not effectively introduced; and inventions, once introduced, diffused only slowly through the traditional economies. Finally, there were potential public entrepreneurs who had an incentive to increase production from a given piece of land or a given corps of workers. They commanded the resources that would have been needed to finance the introduction of new technologies, but they did not do so because they did not conceive this as a realistic option, except for the recurrent introduction of new weapons. Lacking a concept of regular economic progress, the structure of traditional societies made sense. The rulers provided to those ruled an environment of order and the means to settle their disputes. They exacted a high price, as did the landowners and others who helped them rule, but there was a logic to it all in a world where resources and technologies were judged to be, essentially, fixed.

What, then, of the economics of these systems in which peasants were held close to the margin of subsistence; courts and landowners geared to lives of vast luxury expenditures; merchants and moneylenders, who lived well and hoarded, supported and made the best terms they could with the rulers, but did not engage their capital in activities incorporating technological innovation? This was, clearly, not an environment that set up strong economic incentives for invention and innovation. But the question is: Were societies with structures of income distribution and expenditure of this kind capable in themselves of giving birth to societies geared to the possibility of regular technological change and economic progress?

The answer is: Yes, they could and did when mental and cultural attitudes changed. In describing how this change came about we shall proceed as we have in this chapter: first, the role of the political process; then, commerce; finally, science, invention, innovation.

2

The Politics of Modernization

I

In an essay on the links between European and Chinese science, Joseph Needham produces the rather dramatic historical portrait incorporated in Chart 1. He plots his impression of the level of scientific achievement in the two regions from 300 B.C. to the third quarter of the twentieth century. The Chinese curve reflects the notion of slow but relatively steady progress of science within a continuous culture. The European curve catches the falling away from the peak achieved in the ancient Mediterranean world, the slow, uphill recovery of scientific knowledge during the Middle Ages, and the arrival of a phase of unparalleled acceleration in the late fifteenth century. The scientific revolution in the West, in its various branches, then crosses the Chinese curve and, later, under its impact, scientific knowledge fuses, yielding an oecumenical result dated as follows:

Branch of Science	Transcurrent point	Fusion point	Lag (yrs.)
Mathematics Astronomy Physics	1610	1640	30
Botany	1700	1880	180
	or 1780	1880	100
Medicine	1800, 1870, or 1900	not yet	?

SOURCE: Needham et al., *Clerks and Craftsmen*, p. 415.

Needham's bold, broad-brush chart is, evidently, meant to symbolize rather than measure a most complex process in the West, in China, and in relations between the two regions. His curve for mathematics, astronomy, and physics in the West begins to rise about the time of Copernicus, born in 1473, whose revolutionary achievement both reflected and gave thrust to a period of intense study and revision of thought about the physical world. However, in the fifteenth century, much more than the beginning of the scientific revolution was happening that bears on the modernization of Europe and, indeed, on the course of the scientific revolution itself.

Granted forty years of almost unbroken peace in the second half of the century, the Italian Renaissance, rooted in an earlier humanism, produced its remarkable contributions to civilization. Also, at that time, the three inventions Francis Bacon recognized as fundamental to an emerging modern way of life, printing, the compass, and gunpowder, were vigorously put to work. In the fifteenth century, the Germans not only built a good many of their great cathedrals and set up their academies, they also gave to the West printing by metal type—an invention that diffused with

CHART 1

SCHEMATIC DIAGRAM TO SHOW THE ROLES OF EUROPE
AND CHINA IN THE DEVELOPMENT OF OECUMENICAL SCIENCE

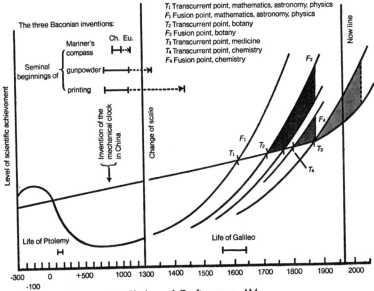

SOURCE: Needham et al., *Clerks and Craftsmen*, p. 414.

NOTE: Mark Elvin (footnotes 30 and 32, Chapter 1) would challenge the notion of
a steady incremental advance of Chinese science implicit in Needham's curve. He
argues for a marked deceleration in the Chinese curve (possibly excepting
agriculture) after the surge from the tenth to the fourteenth centuries.

remarkable speed. It was in that century that the fall of
Constantinople to the Turks helped move the Portuguese
and others out onto the high seas, where they began the
voyages of discovery that brought the Western Hemisphere
and the Far East into the daily life and consciousness of
Europe. In the middle of the century, the cannon came into
its own, making cheap the destruction of the feudal castle

and opening the way to the more economical consolidation of larger political units, despite a subsequent improvement in fortification against artillery attack. By the end of the fifteenth century, Spain had been cleared of the last enclave of Moslem rule and had achieved a reasonable degree of unity. The English were out of a France where Louis XI had consolidated a national state, and, with the coming of Henry VII in 1485, England had reestablished the power of the crown after the bloody, exhausting duel of the Yorkists and Lancastrians. In Russia, Ivan III had refused to pay the annual tribute to the divided Golden Horde, had consolidated the position of Moscow, and had emerged, in effect, as the first national sovereign of Russia.

As the sixteenth century began, nationalism was gaining in power against both fragmented feudal authority and the old concept of a united Catholic Europe. The competitive attraction of colonies and trade routes beyond Europe increasingly shaped the policies of governments along the Atlantic coast. A new kind of science and sense of man's capacity to design his destiny were slowly gathering strength. And these influences were steadily to persist, but their impact was interwoven with and distorted by the religious struggles that emerged in the sixteenth century, partly as a result of these new influences on the mind and behavior of men. The religious struggles continued to shape Europe down to the eve of the eighteenth century—struggles within men's minds, within the nations, and across the frontiers. Each of these strands—including the issue of religion—leaves definable marks on the story of how modern economic growth came to the West.

The concern of this chapter is with one facet of this process: the domestic economic policies of the contending national states and the extent to which their policies, often lumped together under the rubric of mercantilism, helped create the preconditions for takeoff. In two subsequent chapters the expansion of international trade and the acceleration of technological innovation are examined in this context, including the role of governments in those domains.

II

The domestic economic policies of the nation states and principalities of Europe did not derive wholly from objectives of public welfare or economic growth. They arose primarily from the increased assertion of power by the central governments in two other directions: in the constitutional relations between rulers and ruled, including the relative power of the nobility, the towns and the church vis-à-vis the crown; and in the dealings of the states with one another, by war and diplomacy.

As always, the exercise of welfare, constitutional, and security functions partially converged and partially conflicted. For example, the British system for dealing with the poor, which evolved during the sixteenth century and crystallized in the Poor Law of 1597, represented an exercise of the welfare functions of the state, but it also reflected a constitutional concern for tranquility and order in the realm. To take a famous example of conflict, the constitutional settlement between the French monarchy and the nobility yielded a tax system that, we are all taught with some exaggeration, gravely inhibited the state in mobilizing resources for purposes of security, welfare, and growth. Perhaps most important of all, there were short-run conflicts between the objectives of security and those of welfare and growth. It was easy for mercantilist administrators devoted to strengthening the economic foundations of their sovereign's military power to begin to regard that means as an end, to concentrate on expanding the nation's wealth and to resist its dissipation in war. The concern for the indigent in England of the seventeenth and eighteenth centuries was, in part, a moral or constitutional concern, although touched by state interests in higher production. It is, thus, not accurate to view the governments of this period as dominated by a single objective. Like their predecessors and successors in history, they faced multiple tasks and evolved variegated, often conflicting, policies in trying to deal with them. Nevertheless, the central theme of policy was the enlargement of the power of the state, and that impulse was mightily strengthened by the fact that Europe of this period was an arena of endemic struggle for power.

The arena had one notable characteristic: power was so diffused within it that no single nation or grouping proved capable of gaining and holding hegemony. This outcome was, in part, a result of geography, the distribution of population, and limited technologies of communication and warfare. In part, it resulted from limitations on the capacity of the imperial states to administer effectively domains they acquired. Charles V came nearest to such hegemony in the sixteenth century, but he could not firmly consolidate the loosely knit Hapsburg domain at its maximum reach. Above all, however, the result emerged from the nationalist resistance and the instinctive pursuit of balance of power diplomacy conducted by those who felt the weight of the more powerful. Coalitions emerged—fragile, transient, and opportunist though they were—to oppose those who threatened to dominate, be they Turk or Spaniard, Dutchman or Frenchman, Swede or Prussian, Austrian, Russian, or Briton. Between the fifteenth and eighteenth centuries, in one part of Europe or another, the states governing these peoples presented a sequence of threats that united those who feared their excessive success. These coalitions frustrated the dreams of extended power that seized one capital after another.

More directly significant for economic history, the European nation states, caught in a competitive trap they could not escape, learned from each other. At the top of page 528 of volume 5 of *The Cambridge Modern History,* this heading, referring to Petrine Russia, can be found: "The Civilizing Effects of the Great Northern War." To capture the paradox of this heading, one must recall the strain of madness in both young leaders, Charles XII, twenty-seven, and Peter, thirty-eight, at the Battle of Poltava in 1709. For virtually the whole first quarter of the eighteenth century they bled their peoples white, but in his passionate struggle to establish and hold a place on the Baltic, Peter not only learned a great deal about war from the initially more proficient Swedes, he also created a new administration based substantially on the Swedish model, built a navy and an armaments industry, reformed the currency, simplified the alphabet, laid the foundations for a modernized education system, brought to Russia a large number of technicians to strengthen industry, and introduced a wide range of social reforms, which began slowly to close the gap between Russia and the West.

This was the general pattern as Spain, the Dutch Republic, France, and Britain succeeded one another as a force to be feared and a model to be emulated. In part, they learned from each other's guns and ships and military tactics. But, as in the case of Petrine Russia, the methods and policies adopted did not, by any means, always relate directly to military affairs. French as well as Swedish administrative methods crossed borders, as did the example of Dutch banking and agriculture, industrial mechanics and architects, and breeds of sheep and horses, turnips and clover. The process of pre-industrial modernization was thus diffused by essentially the same process that was later to diffuse the industrial revolution beyond Britain; that is, by a reactive nationalism which led the less advanced to accept new methods and policies in an effort to fend off the intrusions or feared intrusions of the more advanced. But war and the expectation of war played an even larger role in shaping policy between, say, 1500 and 1815 than it did in the subsequent century. Military concerns were the primary claim on resources the state could mobilize for public purposes. How much they could mobilize depended on the power of the sovereign vis-à-vis landowners and the powerful towns and guilds of the West; on administrative efficiency; and on the pools of income and wealth generated by agriculture, commerce, banking, and industrial activity to which the sovereign could, in one way or another, gain access. Moreover, soldiers could be hired across frontiers as well as raised at home, and allies could be subsidized if not wholly bought. The "free economic resources," whose mobilization lay at the heart of the ruler's policy in traditional empires, remained central to the problems of rulers in the early modern history of Europe.

There was, thus, some logic to the mercantilist concern for building reserves of bullion through favorable trade balances or by other means. A strong executive like Charles XII—with a commercial base, a sustaining export capacity, and a good administrative system—could make Sweden a formidable military power, on a population base of some 3 million (including non-Swedes), which was forced to withdraw from Baltic hegemony only by Russia, whose population, though poor and ill-organized, was almost five times as great as Sweden's. Even more strikingly, the Dutch Republic, with perhaps 2 million population, converted its fishing, shipping, and commercial possibilities into an example of profit and power that directly goaded both seventeenth-century England and France into great competitive exertions, including the whole Colbertian system. Seventeenth-century England contained more than twice the population of the Dutch Republic, France about six times, but these were more agrarian societies, as of 1650, and the mobilization of a central pool of resources for military purposes required greater effort. As Wilson notes: ". . . Holland was raising a public revenue larger than that of England. The average Dutchman was paying nearly three times as much in taxes as his equivalent in England or France."[1] Moreover, the Dutch achieved this transient preeminence under a system of diffuse political power and economic organization, which, nevertheless, proved capable of generating an adequate defense as well as massive colonial enterprises. As one moved to the East, the task of mobilization was even more difficult. In H. A. L. Fisher's evocative phrase, Prussia had to be "manufactured" out of a diffuse and intractable agricultural base, and it required the strong and sustained leadership of the two great Hohenzollerns to build and defend it. At the polar extreme from the Dutch— in terms of geography, population, readily accessible resources, and politics—were the Russians, dragged into the state system and cultural life of Europe by the visionary barbarism of Peter.

III

In the short run, wars were costly for all these states. The stimulus afforded by the increased demand for cannons and uniforms, ammunition and ships, was clearly outweighed by its depressing effect on foreign trade, construction, and the king's revenues available for nonmilitary purposes. There was in addition, of course, direct and indirect physical and human destruction caused by the Thirty Years' War and some other devastating engagements, including the British civil war of the seventeenth century, the struggle of the aging Louis XIV against the coalition William of Orange had raised against him, and the Great Northern War.

In a set of difficult calculations, Richard Bean has sought to measure the increased scale and cost of military activities in the strengthened nation states which crystallized by the end of the fifteenth century.[2] There is clearly some substantial increase in the proportion of full-time soldiers to the population. He finds, for example, the English figure rising from, say, .2 percent in the period 1200–1500 to a proportion as high as .5–1.0 percent during the sixteenth century. The French, Turkish, and Spanish-Hapsburg data show also a doubling or tripling during the sixteenth century.[3]

With respect to the mobilization of real revenues per capita, Bean's data show an increase for England in the sixteenth century of about 60 percent over the fifteenth century. For France, the increase is about 90 percent when the first half of the fifteenth century is compared with the average for the period 1460–1597, the latter period chosen to embrace the sharp rise in revenues and military outlays under Louis XI (1461–83). There was another sharp increase in taxation in the second quarter of the seventeenth century, when France was under Richelieu and Mazarin. By the eighteenth century, data permit a somewhat more confident evaluation of the short-run impact of war, notably in the case of Britain, which was at war for more than 40 percent of the time during that century.

As Table 1 indicates, the four major wars before 1783 cut the volume of total trade by about 5 percent compared to prewar levels, despite the rising trend in British foreign trade in the eighteenth century. In the first five postwar years, the foreign trade level rose some 13 percent above the prewar average. British timber imports, a fair reflection of construction, fell about 12 percent during the war years and rose about 8 percent over prewar levels in the first five postwar years. With respect to industrial production as a whole, the apparent effect of war was deceleration rather than absolute decline. Hoffmann's overall index rose during the war years an average of 4 percent relative to prewar figures; the first five postwar years saw an average surge of

TABLE 1
WAR AND THE BRITISH ECONOMY: THE EIGHTEENTH CENTURY

	Exports	Re-exports (in £ millions)	Imports	Timber Imports (in £ thousands)	Industrial Production (Hoffmann total index, 1913 = 100)
War of Spanish Succession, 1701–14					
Prewar peak	4.6 (1701)	2.2 (1700)	6.0 (1700)	68 (1700)	1.59 (1700)
Wartime average (1702–13)	4.5	1.6	4.6	58	1.61
Postwar average (1713–18)	5.1	2.2	5.9	60	1.86
War of Austrian Succession, 1740–48 (Jenkins' Ear, 1739)					
Prewar average (1734–38)	6.2	3.3	7.4	70	2.08
Wartime average (1739–48)	6.2	3.5	7.3	55	2.21
Postwar average (1748–52)	8.6	3.5	7.9	60	2.42
Seven Years' War, 1756–63					
Prewar average (1751–55)	8.4	3.5	8.3	68	2.48
Wartime average (1755–63)	9.6	4.0	9.3	63	2.51
Postwar average (1763–67)	10.1	4.6	11.2	80	2.67
American War of Independence, 1775–1783					
Prewar average (1770–74)	10.0	5.6	12.6	114	2.96
Wartime average (1775–82)	9.3	4.4	11.3	106	3.23
Postwar average (1783–87)	10.7	4.2	14.4	145	3.97

SOURCES: Foreign trade data compiled by Elizabeth Schumpeter, reproduced by T. S. Ashton, *Economic Fluctuations in England, 1700–1800* (Oxford: Clarendon Press, 1959), pp. 183, 184, 188. Industrial production index from Walther G. Hoffmann, *British Industry, 1700–1950*, W. H. Chaloner and W. O. Henderson, trans. (Oxford: Basil Blackwell, 1955), facing p. 330.

19 percent over prewar levels.[4] There is every reason to believe that the short-run, overall impact of war was similarly negative elsewhere in Europe.

As compared with the more brutal struggles of the seventeenth century, which were touched by religious passions, those of the eighteenth century were more limited in objective and liability. Nevertheless, Britain had more than 100,000 men under arms for thirty-nine years during the century. Armed forces of similar or larger size were mobilized for long periods and fought for the rulers of France, Prussia, Austria, Spain, and Russia. The traditional view (which, I suspect, requires modification) would not regard the diversion and loss of manpower as economically significant. The military are viewed as the dregs of the working force in these societies marked by chronic underemployment, but the financial burden of war was patently heavy. In Britain, peak wartime expenditures ran about three times the prewar normal levels, and apparently ranged somewhere between 15 percent and 25 percent of GNP. The French proportions were lower, but in the same general range.[5] For what we would now call underdeveloped nations, these were massive diversions of scarce resources away from consumption and civil tasks. By 1782, Britain had accumulated a public debt larger than its GNP—£220 million versus an estimated GNP of £150 million, while the French debt figure was of the same order as its GNP (£215 million).[6] In Britain this kind of burden was mitigated by a banking and credit system (including foreign borrowing) that permitted annual interest charges as low as 3 percent. In France, the interest burden, about twice as high, finally helped detonate a revolution. In Russia, where the burden of the state's military and other efforts came directly to bear on the bodies and diet of the serfs, as well as on any source of taxation ingenious men could perceive, a generation of fighting and striving under Peter the Great left the people, in Kliuchevskii's phrase, "leaner and leaner."[7]

But Kliuchevskii also noted that "the State grew fatter and fatter," and, as a matter of trend, this proved to be so almost irrespective of the outcome of military conflict, whose objectives were calculated in relative rather than absolute terms, since the primary objective of policy was to increase the power of the state vis-à-vis others. The belief that regular progress was a realistic possibility was slowly gaining ground, and, long before Adam Smith, some men came to understand that one nation's prosperity might be enhanced, not diminished, by the prosperity of others. But geography was not as expansible as national income. The dominating assumption of national policy was closer to that of the ancient world and traditional empires: geography and resources set a relatively fixed total on power as a whole. What one nation gained, another lost. The costs of war, therefore, had to be reckoned not in terms of loss in national income and wealth but whether the nation, at the end, had gained relative to its adversaries. In such terms, Britain, Prussia, and Russia, for example, clearly gained from the European wars of the eighteenth century, down to 1793. But even when the accounts of success and failure, thus reckoned, were negative—as for France between, say, 1667 and 1783—the imperatives of struggle set in motion policies which, on balance, helped create the setting from which modern industrial growth emerged.

IV

The headings of mercantilist policy at home constitute a package rather typical of modernizing activities in a pre-industrial society, down to the present day:

- improvements in internal communications
- the direct and indirect encouragement and protection of handicraft industry and mining
- special efforts to achieve an autonomous economic base for the armed forces (guns, explosives, uniforms, ships, etc.)
- measures to assure an adequate supply of food
- measures to expand the supply of public revenues
- measures to improve the quality of public administration

To set out these bare, antiseptic headings raises immediately the need for a host of qualifications.[8] For one thing, the period embraced by mercantilism is so long that national policies often changed within it. Indeed, mercantilism as a doctrine came under increasingly explicit attack in northwest Europe in the eighteenth century. Moreover, the policies pursued were by no means uniform among the states of Europe. In each case, they were shaped by peculiarities of geography; by prior political and social history; by the special imperatives of military policies and events; and, in some cases, by the accident of unique personalities who held, for a time, the reins of power. But despite the complexities, the fact remains that an important array of initiatives was undertaken by the states of Europe—primarily to expand the revenues in the monarch's hands and otherwise to assure their power—which contributed also to the long-run modernization of their economies.

V

Take, for example, the unity of the domestic market and transport costs. Here England was aided by the possibilities of coastal shipping and by a strong tradition, reaching back to mediaeval times, that road tolls should be strictly related to services rendered, rather than be considered a monopolistic source of revenue for local authorities. The policy was carried forward when the transport system was strengthened by the new toll roads and canals sanctioned by Parliament in the eighteenth century, although, as Adam Smith noted, it was not without some monopolistic abuse. Like Sweden, England enjoyed, in effect, a national customs system, but England faced complex problems in its relations with Scotland and Ireland whose orientation affected the strategic position as well as the economy. Scotland finally became a part of the national market in 1707, and Ireland, after some forty years of quasi-colonial commercial status, only in 1800.

In France, the effort to unify a fragmented internal market centers on the efforts of Louis XIV's Controller-General of Finance, Jean Baptiste Colbert. As in many other domains, his achievement, built on earlier precedents, was partial and incomplete. Nonetheless, he succeeded in radically reducing river and road tolls, and his tariff of 1664 substantially simplified and unified customs in the *cinq grosses fermes,* which embraced roughly the northern half of France. The full legal unification of the French market awaited the Revolution. Colbert's initiatives also yielded a marked improvement in roads and river navigation as well as two major canals, one linking the Loire and the Seine, the other, the Atlantic and the Mediterranean via the province of Languedoc.

Compared with France's limited success, the German states in general failed to override the mediaeval inheritance of fragmented markets, with Austria and portions of the Prussian-Brandenburg complex a limited exception. The reason lay not merely in the lack of central authorities sufficiently powerful to suppress local vested interests, but also in the reliance on tolls for revenue by the German princes. As in France, however, the development of canals, notably under Frederick the Great, cut transport costs significantly and widened the market. Canals were con-

structed between the Elbe and Oder, Elbe and Havel, and
Havel and Oder, thus strengthening the economic position
of Berlin. But the mediaeval toll system was not abolished
until 1818.

In Russia, Peter also failed to resolve the question of
internal duties, which were abolished after his time in 1753,
but he did set in motion important projects which began to
overcome some of the inherent awkwardness of Russian
geography:

> The Baltic Sea was linked with the Caspian by a system that hit
> the River Volga rather far upstream, but still provided an essential
> connection with the eastern tributaries of the Volga and, by the
> same token, with the mines and mills of the Ural Mountains. The
> project to connect the Baltic with the Asov and Black seas by a
> Volga-Don canal was begun, but remained unfinished; but the canal
> around Lake Lagoda was started as the first step to other and more
> effective inland waterways between the Neva and the Volga basin,
> although its construction took longer than anticipated and its
> completion did not occur before 1732.[9]

In Spain, the coming of the House of Bourbon in 1700
reversed the decline of the previous century and launched a
wide-ranging process of unification and modernization in
Colbertian style and image.[10] In establishing political and
administrative uniformity, the internal customs barriers
were formally eliminated. Efforts were made, in particular,
to break through the famine-induced regulations (beginning
in the early sixteenth century), which confined cereals
within the district where they were produced, and to
generate a free national grain market. But, notably in
Castile, the effort did not fully succeed in an environment
of chronicly insufficient harvests and storage facilities, and
a quasimonopolistic grain marketing system. In the second
half of the century, a good many canals were built, some
designed for irrigation as well as transport, but, as in the
cases of Russia and Germany, France and the United

States, the railroad was required to overcome fully the fragmenting effects of geography on the Spanish market.[11]

As in many other matters, the Dutch are something of an exception and a paradox. Internal communications were not a major próblem in this small republic, generously supplied with transport by rivers and by the canals required also for draining the land. In addition, its mediaeval history, on a frontier fringe of the Carolingian Empire, largely exempted its agricultural life from conventional feudal institutions. The settlers on the drained peat bogs of central Holland, western Utrecht, and central Friesland enjoyed from the beginning a quasi-independent landowner's status as well as a voice in the operation of the hundreds of water boards that managed the complex hydraulic problems of the region: "The urban communes, or cities, elsewhere in mediaeval Europe existed as legal islands in a rural sea of feudal jurisdictions. In the maritime Netherlands, on the other hand, the rural areas possessed institutions which granted at least a measure of juridical autonomy and taxing authority to the population."[12] DeVries persuasively links the special character of Dutch rural life and institutions, shaped during the Middle Ages, to the precocious political and economic liberalism of the Dutch Republic. Although its example during the seventeenth century proved a major if not dominant stimulus to British and French mercantilist policies, the Dutch Republic is in many respects to be viewed not as a conventional nation of the period but as an enlargement and extension into modern times of a complex of mediaeval trading towns, centered on Amsterdam, with a congenial agricultural hinterland.

VI

The rise of the national states led in a straightforward way to efforts to consolidate the regulation of industry on a national basis and to stimulate manufactures believed relevant to state interests. Like a great deal of mercantilist policy, the initial approach to manufactures was an elaboration of mediaeval practice on a larger stage. Functions previously performed in the towns by the guilds came under more or less effective national control in England and France. There was a consensus that this should be so. As L. A. Clarkson notes:

> One idea that pervaded practically all thinking before 1750 was that the government had the right, even the duty, to regulate the economy in the national interest. . . . Everyone shared these aims: the governed as well as the government, poor farmers clamouring for protection from exploitation by avaricious landlords and landlords seeking freedom to use their land as they pleased. All proposals from pressure groups for particular policies emphasized that the suggested course of action would make the realm secure and prosperous.[13]

Classic illustrations of English industrial regulations are the consolidating Cloth Act of 1552 and the more famous Statute of Artificers of 1563, the former laying down detailed standards for twenty-two varieties of woolen cloth, the latter setting maximum wage rates and apprenticeship rules for the nation. But the flow of English government interventions, touching in one way or another every facet of industry and agriculture, is marked by three characteristics that alter the image of a static, nationally regulated system. First was a responsiveness to changing situations in particular markets. When the wages of textile workers were judged to be too low, for example, the government did not hesitate to set minimum rather than maximum wages. Policy toward agriculture varied with the abundance or dearth of particular harvests and with periods of sustained shortage or grain surplus. Second was a looseness of administration, including the overworked, unpaid justices of the peace, which permitted common sense, sensitivity to the uniqueness of local conditions, and market forces a great deal of play. Except, perhaps, for a period under the Stuarts, effective power was so shared by the Privy Council, Parliament, the courts, the guilds, and the justices of the peace that a rigid, consistent system of regulation was impossible. Third, there was, notably in the sixteenth century, a certain opportunism in granting monopolistic privileges as a source of revenue. The power to grant monopoly privileges was used by the Crown for policy as well as revenue purposes, particularly to strengthen military and industrial capacity: to assure the mobilization of saltpeter as a source of gunpowder; to foster the manufacture of soap, alum, glass, paper, brass and copper, the latter related to ordnance and a reduced reliance on imports. Wide-ranging measures, including the Navigation Acts, were also undertaken in the seventeenth century to expand the supply of ships, sailors, and naval stores. The government operated the naval dockyards at Chatham, Woolwich, Portsmouth, and Plymouth to build naval vessels.

The control over industry in France was, at least formally, more systematic than in England. The powers of the Crown were absolute; they were translated into industrial policy with zeal by able civil servants; they were projected out over the nation by the salaried *intendants* whose offices were, almost uniquely, not for sale; and the guilds were embraced from the past—and extended—as agents of national policy, although they paid a handsome price to the state for their privileges. The series of controls and *règlements*, built up by his predecessors and consolidated and extended by Colbert, constitute a formidable system. In textiles they aimed to determine precisely both method and quality at every stage of manufacture. In fact, the regulations were widely disobeyed or the inspectors bought out. Nevertheless, the system, while fostering luxury products of high quality, lent itself to widespread corruption, endless litigation, and, on balance, probably slowed up the pace of innovation in France, although its effects have often been exaggerated.

The administrative energy of French mercantilists was not wholly exhausted in trying to make this enlarged mediaeval system work. Starting with Louis XI, there were increasingly systematic efforts to encourage as well as to regulate French manufactures. In part, the motive was to strengthen the trade balance by supplanting imports and expanding and maintaining the quality of exports. In part, the enlargement of industry was seen as a source of increased domestic revenues: the guilds paid fees and the office of inspector was up for sale.

In 1601, Henry IV gave Laffemas the opportunity to press forward his mercantilist ideas from the post of Controller-General of Commerce. His Commission of Commerce sought to foster the manufacture in France of the best products of Europe and the Mediterranean: "Milan gold thread, Piedmont type steel, Turkish carpets, Bruges satins, Flemish tiles, Italian glass, Spanish leather, Venetian crystal glass, Persian and Egyptian rugs. . . ."[14] Among his major successes were a successful acceleration of silk-worm production and the founding of the Gobelins tapestry workshops. This strand in policy was carried forward over a wide front with great vigor by Colbert during his twenty-two years in authority. His efforts included not only the building of a great navy in support of colonial policy but also the fostering of self-sufficiency in all branches of armaments manufacture: mines and anchors, cannon, small arms, gunpowder, and naval stores. The grant of monopolistic privilege and other forms of subsidy to private firms was used primarily to expand such manufactures, but there were many more government-owned and operated installations than in England.

The Colbertian example, supplying as it did the foundations for the emergence of French power under Louis XIV,
profoundly influenced economic policy throughout continental Europe. This was nowhere more clear than in Spain
after Philip V, grandson of Louis XIV, came to the throne
at the cost of fourteen years of European war. Eighteenth-
century Spain was ready for a concerted effort to move
forward as part of Europe after the dramatic sequence of
the previous three centuries: the linkage in 1469 of Castile
and Aragón through the marriage of Ferdinand and Isa-
bella; the final elimination of Moorish sovereignty and the
expulsion of the Jews; the extraordinary achievement of
establishing the Spanish Empire in America, accompanied
down to the mid-sixteenth century by economic expansion
and the primacy in Europe of Charles V; the reaching of
Spain beyond its underlying economic capacity, on the
basis of the chimerical flow of American bullion and
compounded by the expulsion of the *moriscos* in 1568,
which yielded the economic decline and social disintegration of the seventeenth century. During that century the
arbitristas sought the cause of Spanish economic enfeeble-
ment and offered with little result a flow of recommenda-
tions to the Hapsburg rulers. To a degree, the Bourbon
dynasty brought proven remedies: "Using methods that
ranged from direct intervention in the production process
to subtle encouragement of private enterprise, they [the
Bourbons] created royal factories, chartered joint stock
companies, imported foreign artisans and technology, at-
tacked the monopoly power of craft guilds, reformed the
internal tax structure, reorganized tariffs and commercial
arrangements, and removed a host of other barriers to
industrial growth."[15] The royal textile factories, impressive
in scale, vertical integration, and in the stubborn support
granted to them, were not generally paying propositions,[16]
but in the environment Bourbon policy helped to create the

private textile industry in Catalonia and Valencia flourished. The royal stimulus produced more straightforward results in a large effort to expand the industrial base for naval and land armament. A host of government arsenals stimulated the demand for Biscayan iron, Asturian coal, timber from the Pyrenees, as well as copper from Peru and Mexico.

The encouragement of manufactures in Brandenburg-Prussia was also along familiar Colbertian lines, although the German Cameralists evolved their own mercantilist formulations in the wake of the Thirty Years' War. The German rulers from 1640 to the death of Frederick the Great in 1786 concentrated more on the economic requirements for their ground forces than did their counterparts with larger colonial ambitions. As in France, the guilds were used, even strengthened, but were brought under central regulation. Silk, woolen, and even cotton industries were encouraged, yielding by the latter part of the eighteenth century a significant contribution to the balance of payments. The silk worm and the potato were implanted in German soil. In a succinct formulation of mercantilist doctrine, Frederick the Great asserted his guiding principle to his officials: "Two things are conducive to the welfare of the country: (1) To bring money in from foreign countries. This is the function of commerce. (2) To prevent money from leaving the country unnecessarily. This is the function of manufactures."[17] Hohenzollern policy, along with a rigorously administered fiscal system, supplied the war chests that permitted Prussia to emerge and survive on the vulnerable northern plain of central Europe. Prussia's military capacity was greatly strengthened by the seizure of Silesia in 1741 and the subsequent further development of its metallurgical resources. The achievement of a self-sufficient base for support of the army remained steadily a prime object of state policy. The whole of Prussian policy over the century and a half from the accession of the Great

Elector to the death of Frederick the Great was underpinned by a willingness to bring in talented and knowledgeable men from abroad, including Huguenots and Jews.

VII

In the story of the pre-industrial modernization of Europe, there were, in each country, phases of special, intense
effort that left significant marks on the structure of policy
and on the economy itself. These can usually be associated
with the role of particular men; for example, Lord Burleigh,
who shaped policy for forty years in Elizabethan England;
Laffemas and Colbert in seventeenth-century France; Gustavus Adolphus, who in partnership with Axel Oxenstierna,
laid the foundations for Sweden's transient primacy in
northeast Europe; the Great Elector and Frederick the
Great in Germany; and Charles III, who designed purposeful policies in his twenty-nine years of power in Spain
(1759–88). Nevertheless, these men and the phases in policy
and action they represent were building on older precedents, and what they accomplished was carried forward by
successors as part of a more or less continuous stream of
history.

In degree, but only in degree, Peter the Great's role in
Russia is somewhat different. His predecessors had brought
to Russia, for example, a great Italian artillery expert,
Greek architects, German engineers, English men of commerce. As Muscovy pushed back the Poles in the seventeenth century, the army and administration were modernized, the landowning nobility paid for their power over the
serfs by commitment to military and other public service,
and foreigners were brought in both to strengthen the
military establishment and to build factories. In fact, from
the sixteenth century forward, the Romanovs had sought to
move beyond simple handicraft production and to in-

troduce industrial technology which the West had generated in the late mediaeval period but which geographical isolation and Tatar dominance had largely blocked from Russia. Their motives were wholly conventional for the period: to increase the self-sufficiency of the military establishment, to expand exports, and to reduce the level of (mainly luxury) imports. Fuhrmann summarizes the statistical outcome as follows:

> Fifty-seven manufactories of Western European type were built in Russia from the early 1500's to the mid-1690's. Although seven of these enterprises appeared during the sixteenth century and two between 1600 and the 1620's, the systematic and extensive development of Russian industry did not begin until the 1630's. The notable achievement of that period, of course, was the construction of the four Tula iron mills and the Coyet glass factory at Dukhanino. Nine more iron manufactories and three other enterprises were built during the next two decades, suggesting a steadily rising (if not dramatic) line of industrial growth. The 1660's saw the addition of only a small iron works, a glass and leather factory, and two paper mills, but from the 1670's to the mid-1690's Russian manufacturing was strengthened by thirteen new iron factories and twelve other enterprises. In summary, seven manufactories (12 per cent of the total) were built during the sixteenth century, two (4 per cent) between 1600 and the 1620's, twenty-two (39 per cent) from the 1630's to the 1660's, and twenty-six (45 per cent) during the last three decades of the seventeenth century.[18]

The import of foreign technicians was an endemic characteristic of European states in this period, but foreigners played a larger role as both entrepreneurs and technicians than elsewhere, organizing about 60 percent of these enterprises at the behest of the Russian state which directly set in motion about 20 percent. Although iron production and munitions manufacture comprise the largest sector, copper, silk, cloth, leather, rope, gunpowder, sawn timber, glass, and paper plants were also put into operation.

These included factories in the Tula-Moscow area, which

produced armaments exported to the West. From the late 1630s to the turn of the century, Russian annual pig iron output may have increased from something like 450 tons to 4,500 tons.[19] This purposeful but erratic industrial effort was conducted by the state not to westernize Russia but to provide the technical capacity to permit it to persist in a world of more advanced hostile or potentially hostile nations.

The results of this policy were uneven. When Peter assumed effective authority in the 1690s, Russia was still not self-sufficient in armaments, and the technological gap with the West had by no means been closed. Nevertheless, his efforts form part of a gathering trend in Russian history, and despite some relaxation in the state's pressure, the modernization of Russia continued beyond Peter's death in 1725. Some slackening in the direct demands of the state and in the creation of state enterprises was taken up and more by private enterpreneurs whom Peter's successors encouraged, granting among other things legal access to serf labor.[20] The momentum of Russian industrialization, within the limits of eighteenth century technology, was, clearly, maintained. In a still overwhelmingly rural society the urban population it helped bring about more than quadrupled between 1722 and 1796, from .3 to 1.3 million.

Nevertheless, there is a special quality to Peter's era. Commenting on the tension between the allocation of resources for development as opposed to military outlays, symbolized by the famous feud between Colbert and Minister of War Louvois, Gerschenkron has defined vividly his view of the uniqueness of Petrine Russia:

> . . . it is precisely at this point that something *sui generis* becomes visible in the Russian experience. For the impression that one receives, particularly from actions during the first part of the reign, say until 1715, is that the answer to the problem was not a calculated allocative decision, but the daimonic feeling that development was a

function of will power translated into pressure and compulsion. The result was the simultaneity of effort in all directions: constructing and equipping the navy; building harbors; creating a new capital in the swamps of the Neva estuary; prospecting for minerals, opening mines and erecting blast furnaces and building factories . . . and at the same time reorganizing and re-arming the army and reshaping the administrative machinery of the government. . . .

The very magnitude of the effort, its vigor, amplitude, and persistence endow the Petrine reign with unique features. Nowhere else in the mercantilistic world do we encounter a comparable case of a great spurt, compressed within such a short period. Nowhere else was the starting point so low; nowhere else were the obstacles that stood in the path of development so formidable. And along with differences in the vehemence of the process were the differences in its character. Nowhere else was the State to any comparable extent the demiurgos of economic development. Nowhere else was it so strongly dominated by the interests of the State. Hence came the composition of the nascent industry with its concentration above all on production and working of metals as well as on plants producing uniforms for the army, sails, ropes, and timber for the ships, and powder for the guns. Hence it came that the large-scale plants were established and run—at least for some time—by the State; that for those plants the State supplied everything: land and entrepreneurship and management, capital and labor. . . and, finally, the demand.[21]

Peter operated on an otherwise almost empty stage of power. The land and the people were, virtually, under his direct control; the nobility and military were his servants, despite his initial troubles with the *streltsi* and the resistance of conservatives, who felt he was violating Russian tradition; the church proved malleable; since the end of the fifteenth century, when Pskov, Rostov, Novgorod, and Tver lost their relative independence, there were no towns with heavily encrusted privileges; and there was no serious challenge from the small if expanding class of tradesmen and bankers. It was with the absolute power of the tsar, working, as it were, with his bare hands, that Peter molded the people and natural resources of Russia into more modern form, although it must be added that, in addition to the foreigners he freely imported, he found among the nobility and others Russians who could learn to build and administer and lead men successfully in battle.

In their technical content, the industrial measures undertaken in Petrine Russia conformed closely to those initiated elsewhere on the European continent, as well as to his seventeenth-century predecessors. Again, at the center is the object of providing a manufacturing base for the armed forces: uniforms and cannon, ships, naval stores, and gunpowder. There was a similar husbanding of foreign exchange by limiting imports and stimulus to exports, and, in the Urals, Peter found a base which not only supplied his military and other domestic needs for iron, but moved Russia rapidly forward into a position of major exporter, as Sweden restricted the number and output of its iron forges. As of 1800, Russia probably stood second only to Britain with iron production of about 100,000 tons[22] and its output probably exceeded Britain's in 1780, before the rapid British expansion of the last two decades of the century.

Peter set up some eighty-six factories. Many were inefficient; some (foreshadowing the policy of Meiji Japan in the 1880s) were sold out to private interests; some foundered, lacking efficient management, skilled workers, and a sufficient domestic market beyond the state's military requirements. On balance, however, he left behind a significantly expanded and diversified industrial establishment.

Peter confronted no guild structure equivalent to that to be bypassed, as in Britain, or used and controlled, as in France and Prussia. He had to exploit his inherited control over the serfs to mobilize workers for his new mines and factories, as for the building of canals, St. Petersburg, and other public works. As we have noted, Russia at the end of the seventeenth century did have an entrepreneurial class and it was growing. But it was not of a size or competence to serve by itself as an instrument for Peter's large enterprises, which were being urgently pressed forward. He continued to rely, like his predecessors, on imported foreigners and on the more talented and strongly motivated members of the nobility, committed as they were to public service as the price for their control over land and serfs. There were some who rose high in Peter's time who came from lower orders. Gerschenkron observes: "It was not class power relations that created the State. The obverse was true: it was the State that was creating the classes: labor, and even the entrepreneurs."[23] With appropriate variations, this proposition is partially true of Colbertian France, Hohenzollern Prussia, and Bourbon Spain where the exigencies of the state's requirements also reshaped the economy and altered the character and relative power of various social groups, but it is even more true of Petrine Russia.

What was truly unique about Peter in the mercantilist era was his traumatic objective of changing Russian culture as well as technology. And what was truly unique about Russia was the system of serfdom. Inherited not from a long feudal past but from the process of creating Russian statehood, it was established by the Romanovs and fully consolidated by 1649, to tie the nobility to the sovereign and the peasant to the land and to state service. It was a system strengthened, not weakened, by Peter's modernizing policies. And as the eighteenth century moved forward, Peter's successors confronted a less pliable nobility determined to maintain their privileges. Like slavery in the American South, but unlike the agricultural policies and trends at work in the rest of Europe, Russian serfdom, created and strengthened at an early stage of modernization, proved a formidable barrier to the full modernization of the economy and the society as a whole.

VIII

The largest industry in mercantilist Europe (exempting food production and housebuilding) was, of course, textiles. Textile production went on in villages as well as towns, for local consumption as well as domestic and foreign trade, by handicraft methods of ancient lineage. Peasants and artisans as well as courtiers had to be clothed. It was in this deeply rooted industry that mercantilism came to confront its greatest but most creative dilemma. The dilemma arose from the widespread popularity of the printed Indian cotton goods that began to come into Europe in increasing volume from about 1670. Trade with the Indies, East and West, was meant, in mercantilist theory, to provide raw materials, foodstuffs, and bullion to be exchanged for European manufactured exports. Here was a manufactured product of great attraction coming from a region that wanted little from Europe except bullion.

India commanded an old primacy in the manufacture of cotton textiles. The unique skill of Indians made their cloth a familiar part of life in ancient Egypt, Babylon, Persia, Greece, and Rome, Japan and China, as well as in the Arab world of the Middle Ages.[24] The skills and traditions of design which made Indian cottons so light and elegant were preserved by guilds and passed from generation to generation.

In Europe, some effort to imitate Indian cotton production was made in the Mediterranean, and in the fourteenth century raw cotton came to Flanders, via Venice.[25] Antwerp became a small center for cotton spinning and weaving, and after the siege and capture of Antwerp in 1585, a number of workmen emigrated to England and probably began cotton manufacture there.

But, as we know from one of the stories on which we are

all brought up, it was the East India Company's imports of Indian cotton goods in the seventeenth century that set forces into motion that were to transform the West and East, in turn. The woolen industry protested with vigor the increasing sale of these imports, a sale expanded by the 1678 prohibition on imports of French silks and linens. The British turned to calico rather than to woolens, and the fashion spread out over the continent as well. The East India Company had thus acquired a reexport as well as an import interest.

As cotton imports expanded rapidly in the last two decades of the seventeenth century a great debate occurred in England, foreshadowing the later clash between the doctrines of free trade and protection. The wool and silk manufacturers and their friends argued that the imported Indian cottons caused unemployment and depleted the kingdom of bullion.[26] The East India Company and its supporters had to produce a more sophisticated case of which two points consonant with mercantilist doctrine proved initially persuasive: the printing of plain Indian calicoes in England provided employment; the reexport of Indian textiles was profitable and strengthened the balance of payments. The legislation of 1700 prohibited only the sale in England of painted or printed Indian cotton textiles.

The argument was settled for the time being in terms of a balancing of interests recognized as legitimate in a mercantilist world, rather than through a direct confrontation with the case for free trade. But the debate produced one distinguished elaboration of the general case for free trade in the pamphlet, "Considerations upon East-India Trade." Its author anticipates and then goes beyond the Smithian proposition relating specialization of function to the widening of the market to argue that Indian imports would induce capital-intensive, cost-reducing inventions and innovations:

The *East-India* trade is a no unlikely way to introduce more Artists, more Order and Regularity into our *English* manufactures, it must put an end to such of them as are useless and unprofitable; the People employ'd in these will betake themselves to others; the most plain and easie, or to the single Parts of other Manufactures of more variety. . . . The East-India trade procures things with less and cheaper labour than would be necessary to make the like in *England*; it is therefore very likely to be the cause of the invention of Arts, and Mills, and Engines, to save the labour of Hands in other Manufactures . . . and therefore may abate the price of Manufactures.[27]

But such long-sighted economic statesmanship did not carry the day. It required intensive lobbying (and possibly some bribery) by the East India Company and those who processed and sold its products to achieve the mitigations of pure protectionism incorporated in the Act of 1700. The formal loopholes and violations of this legislation kept the woolen and silk industries under pressure in the first two decades of the eighteenth century. The English calico printing industry expanded on the basis of imported Indian white calicoes, there was smuggling of Indian manufactures from Holland, and Indian reexports from England competed with English textile manufactures. Meanwhile, Englishmen set about stubbornly to try to learn how to manufacture cotton cloth rather than fustians made of linen warp and cotton weft. Cotton was too weak, in the hands of English artisans, to serve as warp, and it was to solve this problem with machines that a succession of men struggled and finally succeeded.

Before they were to triumph, however, the discontent of the manufacturers and workers in wool and silk succeeded in persuading Parliament to pass, after a protracted struggle, the Act of 1720. It forbade the use or wear in Great Britain after December 25, 1722, of foreign "printed, painted, stained and dyed calicoes" in any garment or apparel whatever or their use for bedcovers, cushions, etc.

But again there were loopholes. The coarse muslins were excepted, as were the mixed fustians, and calicoes dyed all blue. When Norwich weavers of wool tried to claim that domestically produced fustians were illegal, the rising industry succeeded in inducing Parliament in 1735 to exclude explicitly from the Act of 1720 printed goods of linen yarn and cotton wool manufactured in Great Britain. And the fustian manufacturers did not rest easy until they could produce a pure cotton textile.

Thus it was the British woolen industry at least as much as the cheap but skillful labor of India that forced the pace of innovation in British cotton textiles. Those who lobbied successfully against Indian cotton imports helped produce, in effect, the first takeoff rooted in import substitution, a process that was to have many successors.

The French story is similar but not quite identical. The passion for Indian printed calicoes seized France about 1670, and a local industry promptly grew up to print plain imported cloth. [28] The French market was not merely a luxury market: there is every evidence that there was a mass market for calicoes in late seventeenth- and eighteenth-century France.

As in Britain, the imported printed cloth and other Indian fabrics cut sharply into the market at home and abroad for the French textile industry—woolens, linen, and silk. Also, as in Britain, the French authorities faced a dilemma, for the powerful French East India Company had a strong vested interest in the rapidly developing import trade. The government acted more promptly than the British Parliament. On October 26, 1686, it prohibited the importation of calico prints and the printing in France of white calicoes. This sweeping decree came fourteen years before the English Parliament acted in 1700. It may be that the numbers employed in selling and printing Indian textiles had not built up by 1686 to the impressive stature of their

English equivalents who fought shoulder-to-shoulder with the East India Company against protectionist legislation down to 1700. Moreover, a good many of those engaged in the calico printing trade were Huguenots. The revocation of the Edict of Nantes had taken place in 1685, and the calico printers had somewhat less political leverage in Paris than in London. The decree of 1686 heightened the incentive of many Huguenots to leave France for the Netherlands, Germany, and England.

The decree of 1686, however, was not the end of the story. The French East India Company struggled to keep a foot in the door. Arguing on the grounds of balance of payments, it secured permission in 1687 to import white calicoes for printing in France and reexport for two years. During this interval, there was extensive smuggling and the regulations designed to keep calico off the domestic market proved impossible to enforce. In 1689, therefore, the printers were ordered to break their blocks. This they did not do; rather they began printing fabrics of linen and hemp, which was also forbidden. After vacillating through the 1690s, the government issued a decree in 1700 which, in effect, prohibited possession and use of calicoes. All banned textiles found were to be burned. The East India Company was restricted to the reexport business in calicoes.

The enforcement of this policy was notoriously inefficient but disruptive and, occasionally, bloody. Heckscher states: "On one occasion in Valence, 77 were sentenced to be hanged, 58 were to be broken upon the wheel, 631 were sent to the galleys, one was set free and none were pardoned."[29] The more usual punishments were the burning of illicit stocks and heavy fines. Nevertheless, smuggling and printing continued, although the French industry was set back to a degree by the movement abroad of Huguenot printers.

As noted, the British Parliament in 1722 also forbade the

use of printed calicoes. Aside from the British lag in moving against the offending innovations and its greater laxity in enforcement, a critical difference in policy emerged over mixed fabrics. Like other Europeans, the French could not weave a pure cotton cloth, but they did develop their own version of English fustians, made of cotton or linen and silk floss. When printed, they constituted a respectable imitation of calico. They were banned by acts of 1701–02 on the grounds that their continued manufacture and sale would keep alive the French taste for printed calicoes. The British did not allow themselves this elegant piece of logic. They counted employment in fustians as valuable as employment in woolens, even though some imported raw cotton was involved. And in 1735 they formally confirmed, in the face of pressures to ban, the legitimacy of the de facto situation that had emerged; namely, that the manufacture and printing of fustians were permitted. A substantial industry grew up, into which was built a strong incentive to invent machinery that would permit a true cotton cloth to be manufactured. Thus, the French had fallen well behind in this branch of textiles by 1759, when the import of calico was again permitted.

Prussia and Spain also legislated against Indian textile imports, but Holland (after a brief ban) and Switzerland did not. Both enjoyed a lively and substantially illicit export trade, strengthened by the presence of printers who had left France after the decrees of 1685 and 1686, continued illegally to supply the French market, and quickly returned to France when the ban was lifted in 1759.

IX

In a brief survey of policy toward land and agriculture in the mercantilist period, it is useful to begin with a quick summary of available population data.

Population movements and agriculture are interwoven in several significant ways. At certain times and places, population increase put pressure on food supplies and led to changes in agricultural policy. Eighteenth-century Spain is such an example. In other cases, the availability of empty arable land led to migrations, policy-inspired or otherwise, which in turn yielded population increases. Prussia, Russia, and the North American colonies are examples. In at least one case, that of France, the land tenure system, without primogeniture, led to spontaneous population limitation in agricultural areas.

The population figures set out for the eighteenth century in table 2 are, as the note indicates, subject to considerable uncertainty. Data for China and Japan are included to widen the perspective on population dynamics at this time and because, in different ways, the relative prosperity of eighteenth-century China and the relative withdrawal of eighteenth-century Japan from the world economy had some significance for Europe. For the seventeenth century and earlier periods, one is generally dealing with even grosser approximations, when such approximations have indeed been made. But we are reasonably confident that the population trends in table 2 reflect in a number of cases a rebound from prior setbacks. The depression of Spain in the seventeenth century may have caused a decline of 25 percent in population from, say, a little less than 10 million in 1600 to 7.25 million in 1700. The Thirty Years' War reduced the population of central Europe until 1648. There were heavy casualties in the English civil war, including those in Ireland and Scotland. Famine, plague, and a succession of wars damped French population increase in the late seventeenth and early eighteenth centuries. The population of Denmark fell by more than a fifth between 1650 and 1660. The Great Northern War must, similarly, have slowed down population increase in Sweden and

TABLE 2
APPROXIMATE POPULATION OF SELECTED COUNTRIES, 1700–1800
(In Thousands)

Country	1700	1750	% increase
France[1]	19,250	21,750 (1755)	13.0
Russia[4]	13,000 (1722)	19,000 (1762)	—
Italy[2] (area of 1910)	11,500	13,150	14.3
Poland[3]	—	11,000/11,500 (1764)	—
Spain[2]	7,250	8,600	18.6
England and Wales[5]	5,826	6,140	5.4
Ireland[5]	2,540	3,125	23.0
Scotland[5]	1,040	1,250	20.2
United Kingdom[5]	9,406	10,515	11.8
Prussia[2]	1,790	2,260	26.3
Prussia[2]	5,100	6,420	25.9
Non-Prussian states of First German Empire[2]	5,800	7,050	21.6

1800	% increase	Comments
27,500	26.4	
29,000 (1796)	52.6	The 1796 figure excludes population of areas annexed to Russia under Catherine II.
16,900	28.5	Habakkuk[3] gives the figure for Italy as a whole as 15,484 (1750), 18,091 (1800) from K. J. Bellöch, *Bevölkerungsgeschichte Italiens*, Vol. 3 (Berlin, 1961), p. 354
—	—	
10,480	21.9	Habakkuk[3] gives the following figures for Spain: 9.308 (1768); 10,410 (1787). Vicens Vives gives a figure of 12 million for 1808, more representative of Spanish population at the beginning of the nineteenth century than that derived from the inadequate census of 1797.
9,156	49.1	
5,126	66.9	
1,599	27.9	
15,972	51.9	
3,180	40.7	Provinces of 1688
8,800	37.1	1846 boundaries. Habakkuk[3] gives the figures of 3,617 (1763), 5,015 (1780), and 5,844 (1793) for Prussia, including accessions of territory in 1722.
9,320	32.2	

TABLE 2 (continued)
APPROXIMATE POPULATION OF SELECTED COUNTRIES, 1700–1800
(Per Thousand)

Country	1700	1750	% increase
Belgium[2]	1,610	2,150	33.5
Holland[2]	1,100	1,460	32.7
Portugal[2]	1,739	2,662	53.1
Sweden[2]	1,640	1,790	9.1
Denmark	665[2]	806[3]	21.2
Norway	587[2]	591[3]	—
Finland	—	422[3]	—
Hungary (Inner)[6]	1,718 (1720)[3]	—	—
United States[7]	250	1,260	404.0
China[8]	150,000 (1700)	225,000	50.0
Japan[9]	25,000	26,922 (1732)	7.7
		25,918 (1750)	3.7
India	—	130,000[10]	—

1. SOURCE: J.-C. Toutain, "La Population de la France de 1700 à 1959," *Cahiers de l'Institut de Science Economique Appliquée*, suppl. no. 133 (Paris: January 1963), pp. 16, 22. Habakkuk (see note 3) gives the following figures for France from indicated sources: 22,000 (1752–63); 24,000 (ca. 1770); 26,900 (1801).

2. SOURCE: W. Bowden, M. Karpovich, and A. P. Usher, *An Economic History of Europe Since 1750* (New York: American Book Co., 1937), p. 20, derived, with some modifications, from K. F. W. Dieterici, "Über die Vermehrung der Bevölkerung in Europa seit dem Ende oder der Mitte des siebenzehnten Jahrhunderts" (paper delivered before the Academy of Sciences, Berlin, May 16, 1850, published in *Abhandlugen der k. Akademie der Wissenschaften*, Berlin, 1850), pp. 73–115.

3. SOURCE: H. J. Habakkuk, "Appendix: Estimated Growth of Population in Europe and North America in the Eighteenth Century," in *The American and French Revolutions* (Cambridge: At the University Press, 1965), vol. 8, *The New Cambridge Modern History*, pp. 714–15.

1800	% increase	Comments
2,960	37.7	
1,795	22.9	
3,420	28.5	Habakkuk[3] gives a quite consistent figure for 1732 (2,100), but a much lower figure for 1800 (2,900).
2,340	30.1	Habakkuk[3] gives a quite consistent figure for 1775 (2,021).
926[3]	14.9	
883[3]	49.4	
833[3]	97.4	
6,468 (1787)[3]	—	
5,297	320.3	
313,000 (1794)	39.0	
25,471 (1798)	−1.7	
—	—	

4. Source: (Official census [revision] data) Peter I. Lyaschenko, *History of the National Economy of Russia: To the 1917 Revolution*, L. M. Herman, trans. (New York: Macmillan, 1949), p. 273.
5. Source: Phyllis Deane and W. A. Cole, *British Economic Growth, 1688–1959*, 2d ed. (Cambridge: At the University Press), p. 6, where sources are indicated.
6. On the Hungarian figures, Habakkuk[3] notes (p. 715): "Hungary from G. Thirring, Magyarország Népessége II Josef Koraban (Budapest, 1938), p. 36; the population of Hungary as a whole, i.e. with inclusion of Transylvania, Croatia and the military frontier, was 9,516,000 in 1787 (ibid., p. 34). The estimate for the whole country in 1720 was 2,582,000 but S. Szabo (*Ungarisches Volk*, Budapest, 1944) considers that from 3 to 3½ millions would be nearer the mark."
7. Source: Evarts B. Greene and Virginia D. Harrington, *American Population Before the Federal Census of 1790* (New York: Columbia University Press, 1932), pp. 4, 5. (1700 and 1750); census of the year 1800 in U.S. Department of Commerce, *Historical Statistics of the United States* (Washington D.C.: Government Printing Office, 1960), p. 7.

8. SOURCE: Ping-ti Ho, *Studies on the Population of China, 1368–1953* (Cambridge, MA: Harvard University Press, 1959), pp. 264, 266, 268–270. The 225,000 estimate for 1750 is in the midrange of Dwight H. Perkins' estimate in *Agricultural Development in China, 1368–1968* (Chicago: Aldine Publishing Co., 1969), p. 216. Perkins' approximations for Chinese population at key dates are (pp. 16 and 216): 1600, 120–200 millions; 1650, 100–150 millions; 1750, 200–250 millions; 1770, 270 ($\pm$ 25) millions; 1850, 410 ($\pm$ 25) millions. He notes (p. 216): "These figures are meant to indicate a range in which there is perhaps an 80 per cent chance of the true figure being included."

9. SOURCE: Irene B. Taeuber, *The Population of Japan* (Princeton: Princeton University Press, 1958), p. 22. These figures are for "commoners" and exclude upper and lowest social classes. See text, pp. 79–80, including revisionist dissent from the Taeuber estimate.

10. SOURCE: R. Mukerjee, *The Economic History of India, 1600–1800* (Allahabad: Kitab Mahal, 1967), p. 19. Moreland's famous estimate of Indian population at the death of Akbar in 1605 is approximately 100 million, as compared with Pran Nath's careful estimate of 100–150 million for 300 B.C. Speculating on precensus Indian population data, Kingsley Davis concludes, in his book, *The Population of India and Pakistan* (Princeton: Princeton University Press, 1951), p. 26: "The best policy seems to be to revise Moreland's figure for 1600 upward to 125 million, and to assume that population remained at this point for one and a half centuries more, after which a gradual enhancement of growth began, accelerating as 1870 approached." Using the basic analysis developed by J. M. Datta in "A Re-examination of Moreland's Estimate of Population of India at the Death of Akbar," *Indian Population Bulletin*, vol. 1 (1960), J. D. Durand emerges with a somewhat different picture of Indian population before 1870 in "The Modern Expansion of World Population," *Proceedings of the American Philosophical Society*, vol. 3, no. 3 (June 1967), pp. 148–9. Durand estimates a range of 160–214 million for both 1750 and 1800, with population increasing during the seventeenth century and the first quarter of the eighteenth century, then arrested for a half century due to the Afghan invasions of India, the struggles with the British, the Bengal famine of 1771, and other disasters with demographic consequences. Population is, as in Davis' reconstruction, assumed to be increasing before the 1871 census.

Russia in the first quarter of the eighteenth century. At different dates, then, from the end of the Thirty Years' War in the mid-seventeenth century to the easing of strains on France, Sweden, and Russia in the course of the 1720s, population expanded in various parts of Europe by release from abnormal constraints. European population, including that of Russia, was perhaps 170 million in 1750, 210 million in 1800. This release was reflected in both higher birth rates and lower death rates in a manner typical of the dynamics of pre-industrial societies that had passed through demographic crises during which the two rates had also moved inversely, but in the other direction. As the following crude but suggestive regional estimates for England and Wales indicate, the rise in population in the period 1751–80, as compared to the first half of the century, appears to have stemmed from just such a combination of higher birth and lower death rates, whereas the rise in the subsequent twenty years is primarily a consequence of the estimated decline in death rates (Table 3).[30]

In continental Europe, the population increase of the eighteenth century was quite general and, with the minor exceptions of Holland, Denmark, and Portugal, the increase was greater in the second half of the period. These movements appear to have been connected not only with the rebound from earlier demographic constraints but also with the balance between population and opportunity for increasing agricultural production. For example, in Russia, Finland, and certain Prussian provinces the availability of empty lands encouraged early marriages and permitted expanded populations to survive. In Ireland, the introduction of the potato, along with expanded agricultural exports to England, played a similar role.

The point is reinforced by the relatively low rates of population growth in regions where the expansion of agriculture was inhibited; for example, in Spanish Estremadura, Tuscany, and the Po Valley. The same principle operated through birth control in France from the very late eighteenth century as the peasants tried to preserve the size of the family's holdings under a regime in which neither primogeniture nor a significant frontier of arable land were factors, but the reduced birth rate had its impact in the nineteenth, not the eighteenth, century.

A puzzling and still unresolved question is whether the population expansion in Europe of the second half of the

TABLE 3
ENGLAND AND WALES
AVERAGE REGIONAL BIRTH AND DEATH RATES, 1701–1800
(Per Thousand)

	Birth rates			Death rates		
	1701–50	1751–80	1781–1800	1701–50	1751–80	1781–1800
Northwest	33·6	39·6	39·8	28·0	26·7	27·0
North	32·6	35·1	35·1	28·5	26·8	25·3
North and Northwest	33·1	37·3	37·6	28·2	26·7	26·2
London Area	38·0	38·5	37·9	48·8	43·3	35·1
South	32·8	36·6	37·1	30·6	29·0	26·0
London and the South	34·5	37·2	37·4	36·4	33·6	29·1
England and Wales	33·8	37·2	37·5	32·8	30·4	27·7

SOURCE: Phyliss Deane and W. A. Cole, *British Economic Growth*, p. 127.

eighteenth century was wholly the product of the familiar demographic dynamics of traditional societies, responding to release from a previous demographic crisis plus expanded acreage in some areas, or whether it was also affected by the processes of modernization under way. This question, in turn, relates to the question whether it was a decline in death rates or an increase in birth rates that accounts primarily for the well-established fact of population increase. These matters are complicated by such great regional disparities in demographic experience as the abnormally high death rates in large urban areas where infectious disease could easily implant itself and rapidly spread (for example, London as shown in table 3); the ability of mixed farming areas to survive bad harvests better than those producing grains alone; and the vulnerability of seaports and undrained marshlands, where tuberculosis, typhoid, and malaria were more difficult to avoid. Moreover, dogmatism remains inappropriate because reliable overall data on birth and death rates are lacking, and microstudies, based on local records, have begun only recently. All serious analyses of population dynamics in Europe of the eighteenth century conclude with a plea for further research.

The most solid fact about Europe in the second half of the eighteenth century that bears on this matter is the gradual subsidence, leading to virtual elimination in the nineteenth century, of demographic crises caused by chronic harvest failure and epidemic disease. With respect to the former, the improvement of domestic transport routes and the enlarged domestic and international trade in grain certainly played a part. And so, in certain areas, did the coming of the potato—normally less variable in its yield than wheat—and other improvements in agriculture to be considered later in this chapter. There is a possibility, at least, that the spread of soap and easily washed cotton textiles reduced the danger of infection as did some improvement in the purity of the water supplies. There is also a possibility that resistance had gradually built up against certain epidemic diseases. On the other hand, the weight of present evidence, as mobilized by McKeown and Brown, is that, with one exception, the considerable innovations in eighteenth-century medicine and medical practice did not result in a significant reduction in mortality. Without anaesthesia and antiseptics, improved surgical skill did not cut the death rate; infection similarly frustrated changes in midwifery and the expansion of hospitals and dispensaries; the increased use of mercury, digitalis, and cinchona was too slight to reduce death rates significantly. But it is possible that inoculation against smallpox may have had some slight effect on mortality, although the evidence is not strong. It is clear that only with widespread vaccination in the nineteenth century did medicine dramatically contribute to the decline of smallpox as a cause of death.

The impact on population of rapid industrialization itself is primarily an issue for research on the nineteenth century. Urbanization, in general, appeared to generate abnormally high death rates in the eighteenth century. The expansion of London's population, for example, had to be fed by substantial migration, although the death rate there fell from its extremely high level in the early part of the century, which has been induced in part by a grain surplus that permitted the gin mania to take hold. The evidence on the industrial, mainly textile, regions of northwest England suggests that the rapid expansion of population was fed primarily by natural increase, with birth rates higher and death rates lower than the national average. But we are dealing for most of the century with a manufacturing sector that suffused the rural countryside, and the data are not sufficiently precise to trace with accuracy the course of death and birth rates in the last two decades of the century, when urbanization markedly accelerated. The demographic dynamics of the war years in Britain (1793–1815) also remain clouded. It is possible that increased opportunities for industrial employment lowered the age at which women married, extended the period of fertility, and raised birth rates, but this remains to be proven.

We conclude, in general, that Europe in the eighteenth century experienced a classic rebound from a prior period of demographic crisis. This rebound was strengthened and prolonged by public policies (notably in Russia and Prussia) that encouraged the opening up of new lands, by improved transport and enlarged commerce in grain, and by the coming of the potato and other agricultural improvements. Famine and epidemics declined as a feature of European life. In Britain, the agricultural export surplus and low food prices of the early eighteenth century may have generated a later population increase of particular force, equivalent to that in European areas where there were agricultural frontiers to develop,[31] since Britain's export capacity was sufficient to finance grain imports when, starting in the 1750s, bad harvest years began increasingly to require such imports.

The population increase in the colonies that became the United States is, of course, unique in the eighteenth century. It reached and held a level of about 3 percent per annum, a figure close to the maximum in contemporary developing nations. Here the mechanism is clear. Abundant land and the production of commercial as well as subsistence crops made possible early marriages and the survival of large families in an environment where low population density reduced the incidence of infectious disease. The nonwhite (mainly slave) population increased over the century from about 1/7 to 1/5 of the total.

The situation in China paralleled to some degree that in Europe. In both cases population expansion in the eighteenth century reflected respite from prior bloody conflict. In China, an upward population trend began with the inauguration of the Ming dynasty in 1368, but it was broken in the first half of the seventeenth century by struggles between the Ming and the Manchu who succeeded to them. In the course of the battle, Chang Hsien-chung with his army ". . . set out to murder virtually everyone in Szechwan and neighboring areas and may have come close to success."[32] There is little doubt that Chinese population declined significantly as a direct and indirect result of the struggle. The first Manchu emperor was enthroned in 1644, but the mainland was not fully consolidated until 1659, and there were further rebellions to be dealt with until the conquest of Formosa in 1683. Population expansion in the latter part of the century was probably slow. It may have brought the figure for 1700 (say, 150 million) near to the level of a century earlier.[33]

The eighteenth century was a time of "almost unprecedented peace and prosperity,"[34] a fact that is faithfully reflected in the population estimates. The local histories provide much evidence of rural prosperity in eighteenth-century China, and many contemporaries deplored "wasteful and extravagant living"[35] in the cities. Food output increased in part because maize and sweet potatoes brought from America permitted dry hills and mountains to be tilled. Population moved into north and southeast China, and decimated Szechwan was resettled.

It is Ping-ti Ho's judgment that China's population between 1750 and 1775 achieved an optimum level, given the amount and quality of land available and the existing technology.[36] In any case there is—as in Britain—evidence of rising food prices in the latter part of the eighteenth century and growing concern for the pressure of population growth on living standards. Hung Liang-chi (1746–1809) published his essays on the disproportion between the increase in the means of subsistence and the increase in population in 1793, five years before the first edition of Malthus' *Essay on Population.*

The evolution of Japanese population in this period—indeed, the whole course of economic development in the late Tokugawa era—is undergoing lively revisionist study.[37] The older view would assert that the kind of strains beginning to be felt in late eighteenth-century China yielded in Japan not a slowing down of population increase but an absolute decline between 1750 and 1800.[38] The consolidation of Tokugawa rule in the seventeenth century, and the closing off by, say, 1688 of all but limited. contacts with foreigners launched a period of internal tranquility and population expansion. Land under cultivation increased from about 3.7 million acres in the late sixteenth century to 7.5 million acres in the period 1716–36. In parallel, population increased from about 18 million in the last quarter of the sixteenth century to an eighteenth century peak of 26.9 commoners in 1732. The census figures exclude members of the imperial household, nobility, administrators, the military, as well as their employees and dependents. They also exclude beggars, vagrants, prostitutes, etc. There is some difference of opinion about the size of these excluded classes; estimates range from 1.5 to 4.0 million.

On this view, Japanese population varied at an approximately stable level in the century and a quarter before the arrival of Commodore Perry, with a slight net decline until 1804 and a slight (6 percent) increase from 1804 to 1852. This Malthusian equilibrium was maintained by a mixture of pressures (e.g., regional crop failures and other natural disasters) which raised the death rate and family limitation through birth control, abortion, and infanticide. Data on the cities as well as on the agricultural regions of Japan exhibit the sensitivity of this marginal population to disaster; for example, the bad harvests of 1783–7, with their staggering direct effects in certain regions and more dilute widespread consequences (since some food surplus areas were involved), brought the Japanese population down by more than one million between the 1780 and 1792 censuses. Recovery to the 1780 level did not take place until 1828.[39]

The revisionist view would challenge the validity of the official census data and hold that accounts of famine in the late Tokugawa era are exaggerated. Their emerging portrait is not that of a rigid feudal society, constrained by Malthusian limits until released by the Meiji restoration. From *han* censuses drawn up for tax purposes, revisionists suggest a population growth rate of about .5 percent per annum well into the nineteenth century, similar to that for pre-industrial Europe, and they match this portrait with an expansion of commerce, increased urbanization, enlarged handicraft manufactures, and rising real wages. In short, the late Tokugawa era emerges from this portrait as an active period of preconditions for takeoff to which the first phase of the Meiji Restoration (1868–1885) is a vigorous extension rather than an extraordinarily compressed revolutionary transformation.

For our limited purposes, it is not necessary to arbitrate between what might be called the classic and the revisionist view of late Tokugawa Japan. Both portraits are consistent with the dynamics of pre-industrial societies. The revisionists do not claim that a modern industrial revolution occurred in late Tokugawa Japan. They are simply asserting that the kind of lively agricultural, commercial, and handicraft manufacturing expansion, accompanied by population increase, that marked Europe and China for most of the eighteenth century (as well as early Tokugawa Japan) continued into the nineteenth century and did not encounter Malthusian limits.

In general, then, population movements in the world of the eighteenth century were governed by forces which had operated over all of previous recorded history: war and peace, the vagaries of the weather, and the availability of arable land. The extension of domestic and international commerce raised the upper limit, as did the diffusion of a few new crops, notably, the potato in Ireland, the sweet potato and maize in China. But excepting the probably marginal impact of innoculation against smallpox, modern science and technology, on present evidence, played no significant role. On the other hand, the classical forces at work in the Malthusian balance decreed that the eighteenth century would be an age of population increase that would place the various societies under a pressure that would in turn reinforce or damp the process of growth, depending on the manner in which the resources and ingenuity of the population led them to respond to the challenge.

In attempting to summarize the policies applied to European agriculture in the period under examination, I am reminded of one of Stephen Potter's better ploys. He suggested that a useful way to break into a loquacious discourse at a cocktail party was to observe: "But it's different in the South." Down to the present day a good deal of controversy among economic historians on agricultural matters takes the form of this kind of gamesmanship, for the fundamental fact about the European agricultural structure inherited by the statesmen of the mercantilist era was its variety within the nation states as well as among them. These differences were rooted both in geography and centuries of earlier history, and, with a few notable exceptions, they were subject to change by public policy at only modest pace.

In particular, the scope for public policy was affected by the two central questions Herbert Heaton tersely put: "What was the relationship between the peasant and his landlord, and who was the entrepreneur?"[40] Obviously, the answers were closely related.

It is an oft-told story that England emerged by the end of the sixteenth century with its land mainly owned by country gentlemen (and some nobility) with large estates and by yeomen with more modest holdings.[41] The land was tilled by their tenants, who held old rights to grazing on the common land, as well as to the woodlands; some of them, in fact, had copyhold rights tantamount to ownership. The extraordinary growth of London and the expansion of the woolen industry helped gear this system to the market, and in the seventeenth century, a shift in relative prices increased the attraction of cattle raising. The social prestige attached to land owning maintained a flow of new landlords drawn from those successful in urban pursuits, and there were more subtle osmotic family connections between industry and commerce on the one hand, and farming, on the other. The upshot was a more vigorous entrepreneurship in English farming than in most parts of the continent, a greater drive to make money, to innovate on the basis of practices drawn from Holland and France and, later, from their own study, invention, and experiment. Although the most dramatic changes in British agriculture are associated with the second half of the eighteenth century, when prices tended to rise, the innovating impulse can be traced back to the period of lower prices, starting in the latter decades of the seventeenth century, if not even earlier.

There were, of course, absentee landlords who gave little time and attention to their fields, and there were the normal resistances to change among tenants and others who did not wish to risk the possible consequences of new crops or methods, notably when they involved encroachment on their own traditional rights and privileges. But from the seventeenth century forward, British public policy was addressed to marginal management of an agriculture with a considerable dynamic of its own, yielding between 1700 and 1767 a net export of wheat in all but four years, despite the rapid expansion of the urban population.

Government management came to rest, above all, around support for and mitigation of the worst consequences of the drive to enclose the land for more profitable use. Between 1727 and 1760, 74,518 acres of common pasture and wasteland were enclosed by Acts of Parliament, aside from those enclosures that were by mutual agreement; between 1761 and 1792, as wheat prices tended to rise and Britain moved toward a food deficit position, 478,259 acres were enclosed.

In addition, the government acted to ease hard times for both farmers and consumers who depended on the vicissitudes of the harvest and price movements. In the second half of the seventeenth century, when agricultural prices tended to decline, a series of Corn Laws were passed. Exports were encouraged, except in scarce years, and a sliding scale of duties was imposed on wheat imports, high when the domestic price was low and vice versa. This system, in various forms, persisted until the Corn Laws were repealed in 1846.

The setting of French agriculture was somewhat different. There were areas of highly sophisticated commercial agriculture, in the region supplying the Paris market and in the winegrowing areas, for example. As noted, English farmers of the seventeenth century learned from the best French as well as Dutch practices, but overall the landowning and tenure system lent itself less well to vigorous entrepreneurship and innovation. The land itself was owned by the crown, church, nobility, well-to-do townsmen, and by peasants who could bequeath or sell their holdings, although they were still encumbered with certain feudal dues.[42] In addition, the land was worked by tenant farmers, sharecroppers, and landless farm workers.

In this framework, French mercantilist policy focused on the inescapable problems posed for the nation by periods of scarcity and famine. The broad object of policy was, of course, self-sufficiency in food supply, but throughout the seventeenth century bad harvests caused severe human suffering in particular regions. The response of Colbert and his successors was straightforward: shift grain from surplus to deficit areas in France; expand grain imports; deter or act against hoarding; take special measures to feed the poor. The difficulties faced in bad harvest years were one factor in Colbert's policy of trying to eliminate domestic trade barriers and to improve internal communications. During periods of surplus, exports were permitted and, even, encouraged. On the other hand, there is no evidence that seventeenth-century French mercantilism sought to introduce new methods and increase grain output. Its initiatives were confined to discouraging the production of tobacco in France, to protect the West Indies' interests and to ease the operation of the tobacco monopoly, and to encouraging hemp production, for naval as well as commercial purposes; horse-raising, for military and agricultural purposes as well as to save foreign exchange; cheese and wine production, to expand export earnings; and the production of textile raw materials, to enlarge the domestic raw materials base for French industry.

In the eighteenth century there is a new strand. French agriculture began to share the scientific and innovative temper at work in industry, stimulated by the physiocratic challenge to mercantilism, the propaganda of government, and by the British example, symbolized as well as diffused late in the century by the writings of the English agriculturalist, Arthur Young. Government and some of the larger landlords looked to new methods, and from 1750 Paris reversed its policy and began to encourage the abolition of common pastures, permitted the partition of common land, and exempted from taxation for a decade land reclaimed from waste. These efforts yielded an impressive acceleration in agricultural production; in one possibly exaggerated calculation, an annual rate of increase of .32 percent between 1701–10 and 1751–60 moved up to a rate of 1.33

percent in the next twenty years.[43] They also met strong resistance from a peasantry that felt pushed aside and still burdened by residues of feudal obligations as well as a regressive tax system. But the centers of entrepreneurial enterprise in France were fewer than in the gentry-dominated English countryside, the population pressure was less, and the small peasant more deeply dug in.[44] Perhaps, above all, urbanization was at a lower level in France than in England (see page 168). In 1800, London's population was some 900,000, twice that of Paris. In both countries the existence of large, well-organized urban markets exerted a powerful effect on the efficiency of agriculture in the accessible countryside, but the impulse was clearly stronger in England.

Spanish land in the eighteenth century was held in five major forms:

- royal estates, mainly in mountainous and other uncultivated areas, the better lands having been sold off
- church lands directly owned, plus substantial areas under church jurisdiction
- land owned by municipalities, some open for common use, the rest rented to private individuals
- land owned and administered by the nobility
- land owned by small peasant proprietors, of whom there were in 1797 some 364,000, or 22 percent of the working force engaged in agriculture

The municipalities were, apparently, the largest landowners, with the nobility and church next in importance.[45] Most peasants rented their land, but rent systems varied from virtual ownership in Catalonia, like the English copyhold and French *censier* arrangement, to a system of progressive subleasing, which left peasants in Galicia, Asturias, and Andalusia paying impossibly high multiple rents.

Spanish agricultural output rose in the course of the

century. Increasing population and urbanization led to a slow rise in prices, from a low point in the early 1720s, to a rapid increase starting in the 1750s. Against this background, possibilities for increasing agricultural methods became attractive. Following the style of new French doctrines and institutions, societies and academies for improving agricultural productivity were set up. Finally, the government acted in three major directions: to improve transport and irrigation in agricultural areas; to institute a free national market in grain, a measure imperfectly implemented; and to reduce the rights and powers of the Mesta by a series of measures begun in the 1750s, which strengthened the producers of grain and nonmigratory livestock and worked to the disadvantage of the sheepherders who, from the opening of the fourteenth century, had consolidated an important position in international trade, as well as in the economic and political life of Castile. In addition, the government responded to a convergence of rising population, rural poverty and unrest, and the spreading ideas of the Enlightenment by canvassing various proposals for land reform. Royal decrees sought to open up unused land for poorer peasants, but a shortage of capital apparently frustrated their intent.

Eighteenth-century agricultural policy in Prussia was dominated by Frederick the Great's goal of expanding the population of his state by inducing immigration. By 1786 every fifth inhabitant was a colonist. [46] Substantial new acreage was opened up by large-scale drainage schemes. Frederick personally and vigorously introduced new methods in agriculture, driven on by his policy of maintaining food reserves in case of war as well as by the need to feed a rapidly expanding population. He looked, in particular, to English methods. His entrepreneurial task was eased by the fact that the King of Prussia owned and directly administered a large part of the land. At the beginning of the eighteenth century between a quarter and a third of the

Prussian peasants worked fields in the royal domain. Frederick's innovations ranged from the encouragement of potato-growing to horse- and cattlebreeding, and included experiments with tobacco, the expansion of dairy farming, and the increased production of raw materials for textiles. To provide capital for these ventures, Frederick engaged directly his own resources and set up three agricultural credit banks.

The land tenure systems within Prussia varied considerably and included areas where the typical holdings ranged from large estates to marginally self-sufficient peasant plots. Frederick's policy moved in two not wholly consistent directions: to increase the peasant's security of tenure on the land and the consolidation of strips. Fundamentally, he left the problem of land tenure to his successors, as did his contemporaries in France, Spain, and Russia.

The primary feature of Russian agriculture in Peter's time and in the years that followed was the cultivation of unoccupied lands, notably in border areas now more secure in the south-central portion of the country. This extension of acreage was accompanied by a few innovations in the Prussian manner, among them efforts to improve stockbreeding, stimulate the production of silk, flax, and hemp, and substitute the scythe for the sickle. But little of Dutch, English, and French practice—and the fashion of agricultural innovation—made its way effectively to the East. The expansion of Russian acreage, however, was on a scale to permit Russian population to double during the eighteenth century, a proportionate increase exceeded only in the precocious North American colonies.

X

Evidently, the emergence of states asserting increased authority and accepting increased responsibilities within their realms and obsessed with war and the possibility of war, brought with it new forms of administration and new efforts to mobilize funds for public purposes. And the dual requirements were often closely related.

In general, the movement was away from administration in mediaeval style (by individual servants of the sovereign), and toward more specialized and professional government departments which mobilized an expanding proportion of national revenues in the hands of the state and carried forward, with varying degrees of efficiency, the expanding functions of the national governments.

The Swedish case, in this context, was important because of its relation to Sweden's transient major power status and its role as a model for others. Swedish administrative reform took place early in the seventeenth century, and was consolidated in 1634, after the death of Gustavus Adolphus. The traditional offices attached to the crown were converted into five departments dealing with defense, foreign affairs, finance, justice, and the royal correspondence. The heads of each department (who were also senators) sat in the Council of State; reflecting that collegiality, Swedish cabinet members, down to the present day, have their offices together in a central chancellery, and are supported by small staffs, with their departments elsewhere in the capital. Local administration was placed in the hands of appointed provincial governors.

The problem of raising money for the crown was complicated in Sweden by the changing relative powers of the king, the higher nobility, and the lower orders in the Diet. A pattern developed in which the king, working with parts of the Diet, constrained the nobility, but when Gustavus Adolphus came to the throne in 1611 an equilibrium was achieved between the king and the nobility through the talents and statesmanship of Axel Oxenstierna. On that basis, wide-ranging reforms were carried out, including the mobilization of an increased proportion of public revenues in the form of cash. Under heavy financial pressure from military expenditures, the power of the crown was extended in 1655 by the enforced restoration of certain royal estates granted temporarily to the nobility—the so-called Reduction. In the period of regency (1660–75), the nobility successfully asserted its prerogatives against the crown, but Charles XI (1679–97) reimposed royal control over the estates of the higher nobility and established a viable fiscal system (including the creation of a national bank), which permitted the maintenance of a standing army and rendered Sweden independent of French subsidies. The fiscal strains of the Northern War and its outcome yielded a shift toward government of limited royal power, including the emergence of two contending political parties, the Hats and the Caps. Their relative fortunes became tied not merely to their foreign supporters (France and Russia, the Hats; England, the Caps) but to the course of domestic economic policy.[47] In 1772, the movement toward parliamentary and party government was set back when Gustavus III made common cause with the Hats and reestablished a period of strong but not absolutist rule, rooted once again in collaboration between the monarch and the lower orders in the *Riksdag.* Twenty years later this phase ended, once again in a reaction against royal authority linked closely to the financial strains of indecisive military struggle.

The interweaving of administrative, military, financial, and constitutional history in Sweden has its nearest counterpart in the story of England in the seventeenth century which finally yielded the settlement of 1688, although the religious issue was firmly settled in Sweden as early as the 1520s when Lutheranism was adopted by the state.

As elsewhere in Europe, English public finance at the end of the sixteenth century was a mixture of private royal revenues, from land and other sources, and taxes of more modern kind. The last quarter-century of Elizabeth's rule had seen taxes tripled, crown lands sold off, and monopoly privileges granted in ways that provoked increasingly parliamentary resistance.

This straitened background made it peculiarly difficult for James I and Charles I to rule without parliamentary assent. Despite a tightening of central administration during his reign, Charles was forced into money-raising measures that stirred opposition and confronted him with the hostile Parliament he was forced to summon to deal with the rebellion of the Scots. The civil war and Commonwealth ensued. At the Restoration, Parliament was both less and more generous than it knew. It aimed to grant Charles II £1,200,000 per annum to cover both personal and a substantial part of public expenditures. The yields were overestimated from some of the taxes granted, but underestimated from the customs. During the Second Dutch War, Charles progressively went deeper into debt and, in fact, came close to bankruptcy in 1672. Subsidies from his cousin Louis XIV were insufficient to meet his residual needs. But with the war's end in 1674 and a revival in trade, the yield on customs permitted him to operate with financial independence of Parliament.

That was also the position of James II in 1685 when Parliament renewed a life grant of the customs revenues, permitting him almost to quadruple the standing army, an act that helped turn London against him.

In the settlement with William and Mary in 1689, Parliament had in mind all that had transpired since the financial strains at the end of Elizabeth's reign. It exacted tight control over the purse strings as well as some direct leverage over the army, a final break with Catholicism, and adherence to the Declaration of Rights.

What confirmed and consolidated this system, however, was the fact that king and Parliament were together, initially at least, in the long struggle against Louis XIV. The financial strains of the contest to prevent French hegemony required extraordinary financial measures that only a king respectful of Parliament could have inspired. It is with the years 1688–91 that modern British budgetary statistics begin, including the first consolidated figures for civil expenditures.[48] With barely five years of respite, Britain and France were at war from 1689 to 1713. Out of that sustained pressure came the Land Tax, based on older precedents but reassessed in 1692 at 4 shillings to the pound, providing about 40 percent of the revenue during the years of conflict. The Bank of England, founded in 1694, from which the government could not borrow without parliamentary assent, and high protective tariffs whose annual yield increased by two thirds over the war years were also born of that period. A maze of excise taxes provided the bulk of residual revenue. About one third of expenditures during the war years was financed by loans.

The political system that emerged in the eighteenth century out of this convergence of a constitutional revolution and the strains of protracted war had these characteristics:

- The sovereign retained the right to select and dismiss his (or her) ministers (or seek extraministerial advice)[49] and exercised, in general, the executive authority, although the royal power to make war was explicitly limited by parliament in 1701.
- An enlarged group of specialized cabinet ministers emerged, with a small inner cabinet.
- The Treasury as an institution came to exercise surveillance over public expenditures as a whole and attained status of *primus inter pares.*
- Under Walpole in the period 1721–42, the First Lord of the Treasury came to exercise powers which approximated those of later prime ministers, but his role was not institutionalized.
- The exercise of effective executive power required the

mobilization of parliamentary majorities, accomplished more by patronage than through party organization, which was too lax for the purpose.
- The judiciary developed increasing independence, not only of the executive but of the House of Lords.
- Local administration was conducted by the justices of the peace who were subject to no central control.

This loose-jointed system successfully weathered the strains of the eighteenth century, adapting to monarchs of varying talents, fulfilling the essential tasks of government in a setting that granted the individual considerable scope for initiative as well as intellectual and religious freedom.

While Britain was evolving a combination of shared political power and a fiscal system of some rigor, France was tightening the administrative structure of a still absolute monarchy without major fiscal innovation.

The period of protracted war had increased annual expenditures from 130 million livres in 1689 to 264 million livres at the peak in 1711.[50] These figures convert, roughly, into £8.5 million and £14.4 million, when adjusted for the relatively depreciated livre. They suggest a French expenditure rate twice that of England in 1689, with 1711 about 50 percent higher than the English peak year (1710).

Certain major differences between English and French war finance reflect policies and trends that illuminate the striking shift in relative power that occurred during these years. First, English naval expenditures remained high throughout, while French naval outlays diminished relatively with the passage of time. Throughout the war years, 40 percent of total English expenditure was on the army, 35 percent on the navy. In the Nine Years' War, the French proportions were 65 percent and 9 percent, respectively; in the War of Spanish Succession, 57 percent and 7 percent.[51] Second, although war damped the English economy below the levels it would otherwise have attained, the decline was not sufficient to frustrate the increase in excise taxes whose yield roughly doubled over the period 1689–1713. In France, the yield on excise taxes declined absolutely, reflecting the uneven but severe depression of these years. The excise contributed only 5 percent to total French revenue at the end of the war as opposed to about one-third in England. Similarly, the high and relatively sustained level of English foreign trade permitted customs to make a much greater contribution to revenue than in France. Third, the French were thus forced to rely on loans to a substantially higher degree than the English, who raised two-thirds of their requirements by taxation. The public finance of both nations was heavily burdened for some years by debt charges, but the French burden was greater. Fourth, due to the success of public finance measures, including the creation of the Bank of England and some borrowing from the Dutch, English interest rates declined despite the exigencies of the period, while the French had to pay increasing amounts to mobilize resources outside the tax system.

Between 1660 and 1685, tax farming had finally given way in England to Treasury control of a reasonably modern kind. There were no major changes in France except the creation in 1681 of the General Farm of the Taxes (which centralized the collection of the excise) and measures to reduce fraud and the sale of offices and otherwise to render the existing tax system more efficient. The requirements of the war period pushed the capacity of the fiscal system to its limit and beyond. Two new taxes—the poll tax of 1695 and the *dixième* of 1710—were designed to exact contributions from all classes and groups, including those exempt from the basic land tax, the *taille*. They failed in various respects to fulfill their purposes but represented the introduction of the important principle of universal tax liability which was retained beyond 1714 and extended in 1750 by another war tax that became permanent, the *vingtième*. Against this background, exacerbated by the depressed state of the French economy, the government reached out for all manner of long- and short-term loans and the massive sale of public offices, again conducted through private intermediaries.

As peace came, the weaknesses of the French system were palpable, including the lack of a central bank which had served Holland and England so well during the wars. In the period 1716–20, the regent permitted John Law his extraordinary effort to solve the French fiscal problem by converting the public debt into holdings of his Company of the Indies, which was underpinned in its latter stages by a monopoly of foreign trade, tax collection, and the power to issue paper money. But the real long-term possibilities of commercial development did not match the short term speculative hopes, and the scheme fell in. The social and economic impact of Law's failure on the French economy varied; there was some long-run stimulus to French overseas enterprises, but the concept of a central bank was discredited until the time of Napoleon. The fiscal system fell back into its old patterns.

At times of peace and expanding French commerce and production, the tax system was technically viable, and, like Walpole in England, Fleury (in power 1726–43) cultivated for a time a policy of peace. From the 1720s, French production and trade moved up more rapidly than that of Britain, but France of the eighteenth century did not and, perhaps, could not avoid war. The fiscal system broke down after 1783 under the cumulative burden of a debt funded at excessive interest rates and the successful resistance of special interest groups to reform, despite the gallant efforts of a famous sequence of Controller-Generals.

The reasons for this failure have long been argued and

reargued. Three points appear critical from the perspective of this analysis. First, administratively, the French government collected taxes and floated loans at excessive cost. Reliance on city governments rather than a central bank, on capitalist tax collectors rather than public servants, was exceedingly expensive; it amounted to a 6 percent annual interest charge on the debt. Second, politically, a weak, theoretically absolutist monarchy had the worst of both worlds. Its measures lacked the sense of legitimacy imparted to taxes agreed to by an elected parliament. Tax evasion, in fact, acquired a certain legitimacy. On the other hand, the monarchy's power to alter the tax system was diminished by privileges accumulated in the past from the crown, privileges difficult to revoke in both theory and practice, given the actual balance of political power in eighteenth-century France. Third, economically, the lower level in France than in England of per capita foreign and domestic trade and a somewhat lower level of income per capita led to lesser relative (though absolutely rising) yields from customs and excise taxes and greater relative reliance on land taxes.[52]

The French administrative structure that embraced these vulnerable fiscal arrangements reflected, on a wider front, its central dilemma. By the time of Louis XIV, the king had effectively acquired both total formal authority and total responsibility for government, but the society ruled by the monarchs of the *ancien régime* was, in fact, one of diffuse power and increasing complexity. The king required, therefore, either the power fully to enforce his will or institutions that might have permitted a sharing of power and responsibility with the nobility and the towns, the church and the privileged provinces. The latter option was denied by the nature of absolute monarchy. It was natural, therefore, to seek to resolve the dilemma by building a central bureaucracy capable of reaching as far as possible into detailed administration of the realm. This, of course, was the path pursued in the seventeenth century.

The heart of the system lay in the division of the country into some thirty units administered by the *intendants,* except in frontier provinces that were under military administration. The responsibilities of the *intendants* included but went beyond fiscal matters to embrace the whole terrain of public policy. Some developed and sustained a considerable degree of independence from Paris, especially those from noble families with strong, long-established local ties. The *intendants* lived in a world where orders from above had to be carried out (or not) in a setting of strong entrenched local interests, rooted in heritages from the past or the realities of local power, with the support of small staffs at best. Above were the councils of state, under which emerged increasingly recognizable modern government ministries. With these the *intendants* engaged in an endless two-way flow of instructions, reports, and sometimes debates.

The councils of state, as elsewhere in Europe, elaborated from the advisors to the king. Four were of major continuing importance: the *conseil d'état,* in foreign affairs; the *conseil des Depêches,* in internal administration; the *conseil privé,* in legal matters; and the *conseil des Finances,* usually dominated by the Controller-General of Finance, who, like the British Chancellor of the Exchequer, acquired progressively widened powers.

The detailed administrative history of this, like other, governmental systems, is complex, full of ad hoc adjustments and anomalies that persisted out of the past. But with the slackening of royal energy after Louis XIV, policy decisions flowed less from the councils than from the rise and fall of individuals out of the interplay of court politics with the bureaucracies, increasingly manned by professional public servants, taking more to themselves. In an administrative sense, the *ancien régime* was becoming more efficient as it drew to its close, foreshadowing much that was continuous with developments during the revolutionary and Napoleonic period and the post-1815 years.[53]

In Spain, the Bourbons progressively altered the structure inherited from Hapsburg rule, during which a group of royal councils had loosely administered the partially unified kingdom. In 1707, a powerful Council of Castile was set up as the primary instrument for executing royal authority, and after 1714, specialized ministries were created to deal with the major tasks of government. At the time of Charles III they were five: State, War, Finance, Justice, and Marine and the Indies. The Bourbons first moved to bring effective uniformity to local administration by appointing for each of the major regions a captain-general who administered policy in consultation with an *audiencia*, or magistracy. By midcentury these arrangements were strengthened by the appointment of *intendants,* in the French style, whose main functions were economic, including the supervision of tax collection.

At the close of the seventeenth century the Spanish government was near bankruptcy. The royal revenues from Castile and the American colonies were committed to meeting debts to private financiers; the notoriously heavy excises were expensively farmed to Genoese and French bankers; the patrimony of the crown had been reduced by sales of land and offices; the Church commanded a high proportion of the income above minimum levels of consumption; the taxation on foreign trade was, by mercantilist standards, perverse, with raw material imports and manufactured exports taxed, manufactured imports and raw material exports encouraged. Among Spain's few assets was the tradition that neither Church nor nobility was wholly exempt from taxation.

In the course of the eighteenth century a series of

reforming administrators, working with the Bourbons, radically altered the fiscal system. The Frenchman Orry provided the financial basis for the Spanish role in the War of Spanish Succession by retrieving crown leases and other alienated property rights; increasing taxes and the efficiency of their collection including taxes from Aragon, Valencia, and Catalonia, where Madrid had previously exercised dilute control; and extracting funds from the Church. In the postwar years, Alberoni reformed the tariff system to reduce foreign imports, and experimented in Valencia with a reduction in excise taxes, while improving the administration of fiscal policy. A relatively equitable but severe land tax was installed in Catalonia. Patiño extracted enlarged funds from Spanish colonial trade and provided the resources for an expanded navy. Under Charles III, steps were taken further to modernize the tax system, including the institution of greater uniformity and efficiency in a customs system increasingly geared to the encouragement of Spanish industry. In the course of this evolution, tax farming was ended.

As the eighteenth century unfolded, objectives of welfare and growth came to play an enlarged and quasi-independent role in Spanish economic policy, but, from beginning to end, the military power of the state remained the dominant objective of the government. In these mercantilist terms, Spain had recouped remarkably: in 1700, it had commanded an army of 20,000, a fleet of 20 ships, and an empty treasury; in 1800, 100,000 men, 300 ships, and a treasury of 650 million *reals*.

In Spain, this rebound was accomplished on a population base that had expanded in the eighteenth century from, say, 7.25 to perhaps 12 million. In the century after the end of the Thirty Years' War, an even more remarkable feat was accomplished in Prussia. At the end of his reign in 1740, on a population base of a little over 2 million, Frederick

William I bequeathed to his son, in addition to a large war treasury in cash, an efficient field army of 72,000, as compared to a comparable force in France of 160,000 and 130,000 in Russia, whose populations were more than seven times greater. This tour de force was accomplished by a series of tax and administrative measures linked in a straightforward way to the Hohenzollerns' military objectives; 70 percent of public expenditure was for military purposes in the first half of the eighteenth century.

The process was begun when the Great Elector of Brandenburg began to make himself financially and militarily independent of the scattered and quasi-independent areas of Germany over which he had inherited a kind of sovereignty. This was accomplished by three lines of action: the achievement by negotiation and pressure of a direct annual tax ("Contribution") paid by the regional estates to the royal treasury, in support of the standing army, on the understanding that the nobility would be exempt from taxation and that their control over their peasants would not be challenged; the imposition and improved collection of excise taxes; and the systematic exploitation (and reclamation) of the royal domains, which formed a large part of the realm (25–33 percent). The domain lands were farmed out on six-year leases, for a fixed annual rent, to crown bailiffs. As in Russia, the nobility were committed to state service. For a time, French subsidies helped give the Prussian king increased freedom of action.

The role of the domain lands in supporting the Prussian state and army is, technically, the most unusual feature of this fiscal system, although it is paralleled, in degree, by the policy of the Swedish kings. In France, Spain, and England, this source of revenue had been systematically eroded before the eighteenth century as the kings struggled through one war-induced financial crisis after another. In

1740, they yielded in Prussia an income about equal to both the Contribution and the excise taxes.

The Prussian administrative system flowed, in the first instance, directly from the collection of excise taxes and the Contribution.[54] The former was the responsibility of the local commissaries (*Steuerräte*); the latter, the rural commissioners (*Landräte*). They, along with the bailiffs on the royal domains, came to exercise wider administrative functions, like the French and Spanish *intendants,* but in all three cases, the foundation of their position lay in the requirements of royal income.

The administrative system above the Prussian local officials came to center in a General Directory for Finance and Domains from which information and, when requested, advice flowed to the king for decision.

The complexities of life in the rapidly developing Prussia of the eighteenth century altered this simple hierarchy. Four ministers were at the heart of the Directory, with both regional and functional responsibilities. To them were added an expanding number of Privy Financial Counsellors. Under Frederick William, foreign affairs and justice were placed in the hands of separate ministries, outside the Directory. In the time of Frederick the Great, more functional ministries were created to promote trade and industry; to administer Silesia after 1742; for military administration, mining, forestry, etc. This system of diffused and sometimes competing bureaucractic responsibilities served Frederick the Great adequately, providing a sensitive response to his compulsively detailed direction of affairs. It required extensive reorganization early in the nineteenth century when Prussian vicissitudes after 1786, notably its defeat by Napoleon, demonstrated its inadequacies under lesser men.

The rise of the Russian state in the sixteenth and seventeenth centuries faced less deeply entrenched regional, class, and urban vested interests than the Hohenzollerns initially confronted. The tsar was the recognized source of authority, and all social groups—nobility, townsmen, and peasants—were expected to serve his purposes. On this basis, a centralized system of tax collection and administration evolved in the seventeenth century, along with serfdom, designed to assure that the land was worked, and that corvée labor and military manpower were available when wanted.

A national assembly (*zemsky sobor*) had existed, but from the mid-seventeenth century it was seldom convoked by the tsar and it faded away.

In making executive policy, the upper nobility was grouped in the *Boyarskaya Duma*, an advisory council to the sovereign. Some forty administrative departments (*prikazy*) had proliferated, with overlapping regional and functional activities, and local administration was conducted by provincial governors (*voivodes*). As elsewhere, taxes were levied on land (after 1679, on homesteads), and there were extensive excise taxes. When hard pressed, the government debased the currency.

In the course of the seventeenth century, membership in the council of boyars showed some tendency to shift from noble families to men of talent chosen by the tsar for life appointment.

Under the strain of Peter's endeavors, this system proved inadequate. To meet his vastly expanded wartime outlays, Peter and his agents moved in many directions. They debased the coinage in 1700–03, extended excise taxes, confiscated monastic estates, raised custom revenues, and in 1718, imposed a poll tax. In 1724, when corrected for price changes, government revenue was twice that of 1701 and three times the level of 1680. But in the period 1710–20 the tax burden on the peasant may have amounted to 64 percent of the grains harvested.[55]

Peter also radically reformed the administrative structure in several stages. The *Duma* was finally succeeded by an administrative Senate of nine members, which had the power to act (under surveillance of Peter's agents) when the tsar was away from the seat of government. The *prikazy* were superseded by nine administrative colleges, on the Swedish model, constituting, in effect, conventional ministries. The heads of the colleges were members of the Senate, their deputies were initially foreigners. Their jurisdiction covered the whole of Russia and their functions were defined to avoid overlapping. Local administration came more fully under central control of the Senate and colleges, accompanied by a large expansion of supervising bureaucrats and rather elaborate efforts to render local governments more efficient by subdividing their jurisdictions and creating specialized functional bodies within them.

This relatively modern and rational administrative structure did not survive intact and without vicissitudes during the eighteenth century. Three years after Peter's death, the system of local administration was judged excessively expensive and some of its new features abandoned. Politically, the nobility conducted a series of efforts to dilute their commitments to royal service and to strengthen their personal hold on their serfs,[56] although the Bank of the Nobility, which lent on the security of the estates, came in the second half of the century to hold the mortgages on a great deal of the nobles' land.

The central government's grip on the sources of revenue weakened and the state moved toward bankruptcy under Elizabeth at midcentury. It was rescued by Shuvalov, a senator the queen called to her aid. He initiated a series of revenue raising Petrine expedients to which were added two authentic innovations in Russian policy: the abolition of internal customs barriers, compensated for by high mercantilist import duties. But by and large Peter's modifications in the structure of tsarist rule he inherited set the framework for a century and more beyond.

XI

The policies initiated and the economic changes stimulated by governments reviewed in this chapter foreshadowed something of the future and paralleled events out of the past.

With respect to the future, the economic tasks undertaken by governments in early modern Europe approximate those of the least industrialized parts of the post-1945 developing world. In Black Africa of the 1960s, for example, the newly formed nations also concentrated on improving internal communications, seeking and applying simple industrial technology behind protective tariff barriers, expanding exports, increasing food supply for an expanding and urbanizing population, increasing public revenues, and improving public administration. They, too, were concerned with the problems of building effective statehood and generating a sense of nationhood among regions with older local ties and peoples with a narrower sense of identity. It is not wholly an anachronism to assert that the preconditions for takeoff were slowly being built from the fifteenth to the eighteenth centuries, from London to St. Petersburg, from Stockholm to Madrid.

The role of security problems in shaping these broadly similar technical agendas, of course, differs. The preindustrial nations of the contemporary world live in an arena dominated by vastly more advanced and powerful states. They go about their business in an era when economic and social progress for the population as a whole is a major, direct, and virtually inescapable objective of public policy. The impulse to modernize is strongly reinforced now, as in the past, by a desire to be strong in a world of still-contending nation states. But, evidently, the balance of political motivations is different now from what it was in the European arena of contending monarchies. Nevertheless, the protracted struggles of the 1960s and the 1970s in the Middle East and Southeast Asia have managed to reproduce something of that environment, as military imperatives sometimes converge and sometimes clash with the process of economic modernization.

One cannot review the domestic economic policies of the major nations in early modern Europe without sensing the grip on their political life of the unrelenting pattern of struggle within which they were trapped. Of course, a normal round of life went on for men and women high and low in these societies. Rulers spent their time worrying about how to stay in power as well as about war and diplomacy. The well-to-do sought status and pleasure and the means to sustain these amenities for their families, whether at Versailles or in the British countryside or in the growing urban centers where men could grow rich from commerce or manufacture, banking, tax farming, or service to the state. Even Peter the Great could divert scarce resources to try to manufacture in Russia Venetian mirrors and French tapestries. The less advantaged struggled, as always, to feed and clothe themselves and their children and to achieve a little firmer grip on a piece of land. But the major changes in policy of the kind briefly surveyed in this chapter—those that helped set the stage for industrialization—flowed with striking directness from the military needs of the monarchs, as they saw them. In scale, military activity was the largest single form of investment. In all its manifestations, including the burden of public debt, it dominated the national budgets. With the partial exception of the religious issue, it dominated also the other dimensions of politics. The great constitutional issues, from the struggle of the English Parliament for control over the purse-strings to the status of noble and serf in Petrine Russia, are all linked to the imperatives of military conflict.

There is no way to write a counter-factual history of those times. The endemic military conflict was costly; it wasted resources that might have been used for constructive purposes, but without military conflict and the expectation of war, there would have been less impulse to undertake some of the constructive policies that form part of the matrix from which modern economic growth emerged.

In all this, the politics of early modern Europe is consistent with a longer past, with the story of the premodern empires sketched earlier. There is much similarity between the economic policies of the rulers of ancient states, on the upswing of their cycles, and those of the rulers in early modern Europe.

But there are three differences. First, more than in the past, the European rulers perceived and acted on the proposition that their interests in revenue for military purposes required an expansion in production. They used their powers not merely to maximize their revenues from a static production base but to stimulate an increase in output. Second, with the passage of time the idea was formulated and spread gradually into political life and policy that the expanded wealth of a nation was not merely an objective to be pursued as a means to a larger military end, but that increased production and welfare were in themselves legitimate objects of state policy. By the end of the eighteenth century, neither Adam Smith nor Arthur Young had fully triumphed, but the notion that there was virtue in manufacturing and trading and in producing food with greater efficiency for reasons beyond the power of the state had gained force. Third, in one of its essential dimensions, the underlying assumption that had for long governed the relations between states began to change; namely, that the gain of one had to be the loss of another. It was increasingly perceived that the prosperity of one's trading partners was a national interest. Perceptions of this kind brought Britain and France to the negotiation in the Eden Treaty in 1786. Seven years later Europe did enter a full generation of struggle over the balance of power, as it had a century earlier, because geography was not as expansible as the wealth of nations, but, before the end of the eighteenth century, the doctrinal basis was. laid for somewhat less contentious economic relations among nation states.

These three distinctive strands in thought and policy arose not from the dynamics of European politics itself, but from the interplay of political life with what we were all brought up to call the commercial revolution and the scientific revolution, and to which we now successively turn, for without these ingredients—particularly the latter—the policies described here would have been not the preconditions for takeoff but the prelude to yet another cyclical decline.

3

The Commercial
Revolution

I

The old concept of the commercial revolution remains a useful and valid notion. It embraces the remarkable expansion of international trade—to Asia, the Western Hemisphere, and Africa—in the wake of the voyages of discovery at the end of the fifteenth century, with all its consequences, within Europe and beyond, down to the beginning of the British takeoff after 1783. From that time the industrial revolution itself begins to shape the scale and patterns of world trade. The question here is: How did the commercial revolution relate to the onset of the industrial revolution? To get at that question in an orderly way, it may be useful to summarize briefly how the commercial revolution unfolded.

II

The commercial revolution may be said arbitrarily to have begun in 1488 when the Portuguese Bartholomew Díaz rounded Cape Horn and thus pioneered a non-

Mediterranean route for trade to the Far East that soon involved direct European contacts in the whole arc from Japan to the Persian Gulf. Over the next thirty-four years, the coastline and islands of the Western Hemisphere were also probed from Labrador to its southern tip, and one of Magellan's five ships came home, without the expedition's leader, after circling the globe. This sequence was influenced to a degree still under debate by the rise of Turkish power in the Levant and eastern Mediterranean, after two centuries of weakness, which had permitted Europe to dominate trade to the Far East, despite the land bridge to be crossed. European trade with the Orient did not cease, but it was conducted thereafter in a less easy environment.

The old trading world that was enlarged and restructured by the Portuguese and Spanish pioneers had three key elements: the Mediterranean, dominated by the Italian city states, notably Venice and Genoa; the Baltic, dominated by the Hanseatic League; and the *entrepôt* cities of the Low Countries, of which Antwerp had emerged as dominant by the end of the fifteenth century.

Over these routes, Europe traded in the south its metals and manufactures for oriental spices, cotton, silk, drugs and jewels, while in the north, the Hanseatic League dominated the mouths of the European rivers from Novgorod to Bruges, bringing Baltic grain, timber, and some Swedish copper in exchange for western wool, textiles, and fish. Into this system flowed also continental wines and salt from Biscay and Portugal.

The new routes and empires were, of course, initially dominated in the sixteenth century by the Spanish and Portuguese, the empires they built, and the flow of bullion they injected into the world's trading channels. Whereas Charles V opened imperial trade to his non-Spanish subjects, Philip II, after his succession in 1556, tried to limit access to Castilians. Genoa linked itself to these new dynamic developments, associating its financial, naval, and military skills with Iberia.[1] Venice held its own for a time by doing the best it could in dealings with the Turks, and by turning to industry and its agricultural hinterland. The French, mainly occupied with their internal struggles, harassed the Spanish bullion fleet, but, initially, they were only marginally affected by the newly reshaped world trading framework. The English responded more assertively to the widened horizons by piracy and slave trading, and, under Burleigh, by building the naval strength that ultimately permitted them to face down the Spanish fleet in 1588. A decade earlier, the long, frustrating English struggle to break the monopolistic hold over its trade in the Baltic was won, with the expulsion of the Hanse merchants from their extraterritorial base in London's steelyard and the creation in 1579 of the Eastland Company. The founding of the Muscovy Company in 1555, the Spanish Company in 1577, and the Senegal Adventurers in 1588 reflects also the new English spirit of trading enterprise. But the Low Countries underwent a more remarkable transformation. The cities and towns of this strategically located region superseded Venice as Europe's *entrepôt,* building many of their institutions and practices on Italian experience and innovation.

This development was then crosscut by the protracted struggle of the Netherlands against Spain, launched with the rebellion of 1559, brought to a truce in 1609, and finally settled only in 1648. The upshot was the sacking of Antwerp in 1574 and 1583, and of other towns of southern Netherlands; their subsequent failure to reachieve their old commercial status; the division of the Low Countries, with the southern provinces pacified and the seven northern provinces emerging, after an heroic defense, as the Dutch Republic with Amsterdam, hitherto of minor importance, quickly becoming Europe's greatest commercial and banking center.

In the seventeenth century, the hard core of the Dutch *entrepôt* trade followed the late mediaeval pattern: the flow to Amsterdam from the Baltic of grain, timber, naval stores, and metals, the latter reflecting much expanded Swedish copper and iron exports; of wool and cloth from England, and from the Mediterranean, wines, salt, silk, and spices. But to these were added the products of the Western Hemisphere and the Far East. Amsterdam organized the carriage, financing, and redistributing of this trade, processing some of the commodities in transit. The Dutch also moved out promptly in the seventeenth century to build an imperial position of their own in the Far East, the Indian peninsula, the Persian Gulf, Cape Horn and West Africa, the northeast coast of South America, and the east coast of North America. The Dutch East India Company was set up in 1602, the West India Company in 1626, and, by 1652, the last of its major claims was staked out at the Cape.

All this gave Amsterdam access to spices and Indian calicoes, sugar, tobacco, and bullion, as well as whale oil from Spitzbergen, quite aside from the flows of these commodities that found their way to the *entrepôt* from the new trading posts of others.

As the seventeenth century wore on, the extraordinary tour de force of the Dutch Republic became the model and envy of England and France. Charles Wilson catches well the depth and character of the English obsession with the Dutch that eased only when both nations came to face jointly, under Dutch leadership, the threat represented by Louis XIV:

> The Treaty of Breda [1667] brought to an end an era of more than a half century during which hostility to the Dutch had become a habit of thought with Englishmen, cutting across differences of birth, class, occupation, and outlook. Translated into action, this hostility had become a pivot upon which a large section of national policy turned. . . . Behind the loud clamour and often palpable

humbug of the arguments about international law, ancient custom, and the like was the fact that the Dutch Republic had taken a lead in trade, shipping, and technology which not only aroused the jealousy of her neighbours—England and France in particular—but gave them a plausible excuse to argue that they were economically exploited and oppressed. . . . The burden of England's tale of complaint was, in brief, that the Dutch carried away from England and her dependencies little but raw materials and semi-manufactured goods, making large profits in the subsequent stages of manufacture and commerce. The skill of the Dutch in selling back manufactures, necessities and luxuries to their victim was only the second stage of a process plausibly represented as one of double robbery.[2]

Like many nations in the subsequent three centuries, the English and French of the seventeenth century did not accept passively this sense of dependency and relative underdevelopment. The English East India Company was founded as early as 1600, and its first trading base set up at Surat in 1609; the settlement of North America began at Jamestown in 1607; the English staked out a position in the West Indies starting at Barbados in 1605; formally organized trade in Africa began in 1618; and from 1670, the Hudson's Bay Company contested the French position in Canada.[3]

Until 1660, the effect of these developments on the scale and character of English foreign trade was modest.[4] Woolens continued to dominate English exports (80–90 percent), and the major dynamic element in the export trade was the development of the lighter woolen cloths— the "new draperies"—for sale to southern Europe, while the Thirty Years' War and, perhaps, the rigidity of the monopolistic trading companies limited sales of the older cloths in the northern markets. Nevertheless, with the passage of time, the new North American colonies and the footholds in the West Indies and India left their mark on such statistical data as exist: imports and reexports of tobacco, sugar, and products from India rose; tobacco moved from eighth to first in London's imports between 1620 and 1640, with sugar surging forward in the 1650s. Reexports rose from under £100,000 in 1640 to about £900,000 in the early 1660s, amounting to 28 percent of English exports. English exports had moved forward at an annual average rate of 1.5 percent between 1600 and 1640. The acceleration of reexports lifted the rate of increase in total exports between 1640 and 1650. On the basis of, perhaps, a doubling in the tonnage of the merchant fleet from the period 1609–15 to 1660, the English not only linked their new imperial positions to home and foreign markets but also carried cargoes directly between foreign ports. This new sense of direction and strength—a confidence that the English could beat the Dutch at their own game— helped produce the Navigation Acts of 1650 and 1651, consolidated and strengthened after the Restoration in 1660, which restricted colonial trade, including reexports of colonial produce, to English merchants and vessels.

III

The English Restoration virtually coincided with Colbert's succession to Mazarin's office in 1661. Up to that point, France, which had established positions in North America, the West Indies, and India, had not developed them with the vigor of the English. Colbert tried to redress the French commercial and naval position with a passionate zeal. In Charles Cole's phrase, his struggle against the Dutch was one of the "major themes" of his career:

> When he came to power, French commerce had suffered sadly from neglect under Mazarin, and from foreign wars and internal disorder. It was losing ground steadily before the triumphant growth of Dutch trade. In fact in 1664 Colbert declared that by an "exact calculation" which he had made, the Dutch were carrying on so much of the French trade that each year the French paid them 4,000,000 *livres* merely in freight and carriage charges. The French

had only a few hundred merchant ships to the thousands possessed by the Dutch. The French navy was in a state of decay. Even the French coasting trade was in Dutch hands, and the French were being ousted from the ocean fisheries. The French were claiming that it was impossible to compete with the Dutch, since it cost far more to build, man, provision, and operate a French ship than it did a Dutch one. In fact to many of the French, commerce did seem "in some sort contrary to the genius of the nation."[5]

In pursuing what he regarded as "peaceful war" against the Dutch, Colbert carried forward three major lines of policy: the institution of tariffs to encourage French exports; a buildup of the merchant marine and of a navy to protect it; and the founding of the East India, West India, and other trading companies designed to push French interests in the Mediterranean as well as into the Baltic and to Africa. His enterprises did not profit the stockholders and his peaceful war against the Dutch became a military struggle against both England and Holland after 1669, with grave economic consequences for France. But he laid the foundations for French naval as well as mercantile and colonial strength, which made France, rather than Holland, England's greatest adversary of the eighteenth century. And toward the end of the seventeenth century, Frenchmen as well as Englishmen were becoming accustomed to colonial sugar and tobacco and being seduced by Indian calicoes.

While Colbert was pressing the French forward against the Dutch mercantile position, England moved after the Restoration into a phase of overall trade expansion, which may have peaked in 1686–88, just before the beginning of war with Louis XIV.[6] The years at the end of the century (1698–1701) were also peaceful, but this high point, before the beginning of the War of Spanish Succession, probably did not exceed the 1686–88 level. Nevertheless, the best available estimate shows a substantial expansion of foreign trade, with a large percentage increase in reexports. Behind

TABLE 4
ENGLISH FOREIGN TRADE, LATE SEVENTEENTH CENTURY

	1663–69	1699–1701	Percentage Increase
	(£000)	(£000)	
Exports	3,239	4,433	37
Reexports	900	1,986	121
Total exports (say)	4,139	6,419	55
Total imports (say)	4,400	5,849	33

SOURCE: Ralph Davis, "English Foreign Trade, 1660–1700," in W. E. Minchinton, ed., *The Growth of English Overseas Trade in the Seventeenth and Eighteenth Centuries* (London: Methuen & Co., 1969), p. 92, reprinted from *Economic History Review*, 2d ser., vol. 7 no. 2 (1954).

NOTE: The problem with English trade figures in this period is that overall data are lacking until 1699–1701. London data, difficult to correct for tariff changes, are available for 1663–69, but a rough estimate of trade through other ports is required to compare the 1660s with the end of the century.

these figures are the unfolding operational consequences of the widening of the world trading system we call the commercial revolution:

- an explosive expansion in tobacco imports and reexports, accompanied by a sharp fall in price;
- similar but less dramatic trade and price trends in sugar;
- a rise in Indian calico imports from insignificant levels before the Restoration to 240,000 pieces in 1663–69 and 861,000 in 1699–1701, two-thirds of the latter reexported;
- a doubling, in the same period, of miscellaneous manufactured exports, which, although only 8 percent of total exports at the end of the century, reflected the expansion of the colonial market in North America and stimulated production in English metalworking industries of some technological significance.

In addition, the slave trade with Africa was expanding to supply labor to West Indian plantations, as well as the

Newfoundland fisheries, from which ships sent from England delivered their cargoes directly to the West Indies and the Mediterranean, as well as to English ports.

To this new trading pattern the Spanish and Portuguese colonies in America contributed a critical lubricating element—a flow of bullion. Gold and silver financed not only Iberian imports of English and French goods and commodities coming through the Dutch *entrepôt*, but also the imports from the Far East (and, to a lesser extent, the Levant) where an effective balancing demand for European products did not exist but an apparently inexhaustible demand for bullion did.

From the turn of the century, we have reasonably reliable English foreign trade statistics and, from the second decade, less reliable French data. We know that English trade was severely damped until the end of the War of Spanish Succession in 1713 and then rose until war intervened again in 1739.[7] France was even more severely set back in the war years, but a strong revival also began in the 1720s.

The most complete statistical portrait of the evolution of international trade after 1720 is that of Michael Mulhall, presented in Table 5. The major problem with Mulhall's table is that it does not provide statistical sources or the exchange rates used in converting trade figures into British pounds. Moreover, figures for the year 1780, notably the British data, which are abnormally low, are distorted by the War of American Independence whereas the data for 1800 reflect a particular phase of the Napoleonic Wars as well as the British post-1783 takeoff. Nevertheless, if used with caution, Mulhall's calculations are valuable and do not grossly violate what we know from other evidence about the changing scale of international trade over these eighty years.

Certain specific characteristics of the table should be noted:

TABLE 5
Approximate World Trade: 1720, 1750, 1780, 1800
(In Millions £ Sterling)

Country	1720	% World	1750	% World	% Increase from 1720	1780	% World	% Increase from 1750	1800	% World	% Increase from 1780
Great Britain	13	15	21	15	62	23	12	10	67	22	291
France	7	8	13	9	86	22	12	69	31	10	41
Germany	8	9	15	11	88	20	11	33	36	12	80
Russia	8	9	14	10	75	17	9	21	30	10	76
Austria	2	2	4	3	100	6	3	50	8	3	33
Italy	3	3	5	4	67	7	4	40	10	3	43
Spain	10	11	14	10	40	18	10	29	12	4	-33
Portugal	2	2	3	2	50	4	2	33	4	1	0
Scandinavia	2	2	3	2	50	5	3	67	5	2	0
Holland and Belgium	4	5	6	4	50	8	4	33	15	5	88
Switzerland	1	1	2	1	100	3	2	50	5	2	67

Turkey, etc.	2	2	3	2	50	4	2	33	5	2	25
Total: Europe	62		103		66	137			228		66
Europe as Percent of Total World	70		74			74			75		
United States	10	11	15	11	50	3	2	33	17	6	567
Spanish America	2	2	3	2	50	20	11	−67	25	8	25
British Colonies	9	10	9	6	0	1	.5	11	2	1	100
India	5	6	10	7	100	10	5	50	10	3	0
Various						15	8		20	7	33
Total: Outside Europe	26		37		42	49		32	74		51
Total: World	88		140		59	186		33	302		62

Source: Michael Mulhall, *The Dictionary of Statistics* (London: George Routledge and Sons, 1892), p. 128.
Note: Because they have been rounded off, percentage figures do not always add up to 100.

- The increase in British trade is typical rather than extraordinary until the takeoff in the last twenty years of the century when cotton textile and iron exports, as well as raw cotton imports, radically expanded. The statistics catch well the relative recovery of France between 1720 and 1780, although the French value figures used require some deflation for price increases when compared to the British data, calculated in constant prices. The British and German trade data are also exaggerated for 1800 by Britain's quasi-monopoly in reexports from the Western Hemisphere and Hamburg's role as the continent's *entrepôt* at this stage of the Napoleonic Wars.

- The data for northern and central Europe down to 1780 exhibit the economic, as well as military and political, emergence of Prussia and Russia, and a sharing in the general expansion by Austria, Scandinavia, Holland, Belgium, and Switzerland. Here we see in the foreign trade data the widespread economic vitality of the European continent including the continued momentum of post-Petrine Russia as well as that of Prussia under Frederick the Great, and the relatively successful efforts of the Dutch Republic to hold a significant trading position, despite the loss of its seventeenth-century primacy. The 1800 figures reflect the differential impact on this region of the Napoleonic Wars in their first phase.

- Southern Europe was somewhat less dynamic. Italy maintained its modest relative trading position, but Spain, despite its eighteenth-century surge in modernization, lost a little ground relatively. And, we know, Portugal also lost momentum after 1760[8] when Brazilian gold ran down.

- Spanish America, with its large outflow of bullion, held a substantial place in world trade, down to the last twenty years of the century, continuing to lubricate not only northern European commerce with Spain but also European trade with India and even China.

- Although Mulhall isolates the trade of the United States only after 1780, the eighteenth-century expansion of commerce in the colonies was almost as astonishing as their twenty-one-fold population increase. Exports to Great Britain increased 6.6 times from the first to the seventh decade of the century.[9] British trade was about 60 percent of the total for the colonies before the War of Independence.

The commodity composition of this expanded volume of international trade reflects both continuity with the latter years of the seventeenth century and some new elements. Without excessive distortion, the evolving British trade position, on which evidence is most complete, affords a valid way of getting at the major changes in the world trading area as a whole.

Table 6 sets out the commodity composition of English trade for three-year average periods centered on 1700 and 1773, both periods of peace.

The major changes in imports are the following:

- *Linens.* The gentle rise over these years balanced a decline in imports from Northwestern Europe against a large increase in English imports from Ireland, notably after midcentury, and a lesser increase in imports from Russia.
- *Calicoes.* Indian calico imports were, of course, inhibited by legislation, although the limitations eased in the third quarter of the century.
- *Foodstuffs.* The seventeenth-century groceries (notably, tobacco and sugar) continued their remarkable expansion, but to them are added coffee, rice, and tea, the latter subject to large-scale smuggling until 1784. In the

TABLE 6

THE COMPOSITION OF ENGLISH FOREIGN TRADE, 1699–1701, 1772–4

(In £ Thousands)

	1699–1701	1772–4
IMPORTS		
Linens	903	1,274
Calicoes	367	697
Silks and mixed fabrics	208	82
Metalwares	72	7
Thread	79	14
Miscellaneous	215	111
Total manufactures	1,844	2,157
Wine	536	411
Spirits	10	205
Sugar	630	2,364
Tobacco	249	519
Fruit	174	159
Pepper	103	33
Drugs	53	203
Tea	8	848
Coffee	27	436
Rice	5	340
Corn		398
Miscellaneous	174	561
Total foodstuffs	1,969	6,477
Silk, raw and thrown	346	751
Flax and hemp	194	481
Wool	200	102
Cotton	44	137
Textile yarns	232	424
Dyes	226	506
Iron and steel	182	481
Timber	138	319
Oil	141	162
Tallow	85	131

TABLE 6 (continued)

	1699–1701	*1772–4*
Skins and hides	57	164
Miscellaneous	191	443
Total raw materials	2,036	4,101
TOTAL IMPORTS	5,849	12,735
EXPORTS		
Woolens	3,045	4,186
Linens		740
Silks	80	189
Cottons, etc.	20	221
Metalware	114	1,198
Hats	45	110
Miscellaneous	279	1,843
Total Manufactures	3,583	8,487
Grain	147	37
Fish	190	70
Hops	9	136
Miscellaneous	102	329
Total foodstuffs	488	572
Lead	128	182
Tin	97	116
Coal	35	333
Miscellaneous	102	163
Total raw materials	362	794
TOTAL EXPORTS	4,433	9,853
REEXPORTS		
Calicoes	340	701
Silks, etc.	150	501
Linens	182	322
Miscellaneous	74	38

TABLE 6 (continued)

	1699–1701	1772–4
Total manufactures	746	1,562
Tobacco	421	904
Sugar	287	429
Pepper	93	110
Tea	2	295
Coffee	2	873
Rice	4	363
Rum		199
Drugs	48	132
Miscellaneous	84	237
Total foodstuffs	941	3,542
Dyestuffs	85	211
Silk	63	125
Miscellaneous	151	378
Total raw materials	299	714
TOTAL REEXPORTS	1,986	5,818
TOTAL OF EXPORTS AND REEXPORTS	6,419	15,6

SOURCE: After Ralph Davis, "English Foreign Trade, 1700–1774," in W. E. Minchinton, ed., *The Growth of English Overseas Trade in the Seventeenth and Eighteenth Centuries* (London: Methuen & Co., 1969), pp. 119–20.
NOTE: The data are for England and Wales. Despite the Act of Union in 1707, the trade of Scotland was separately recorded in this period.

third quarter of the century, England shifted from a grain export to a grain import position, as population increase and urbanization outstripped the expansion in domestic agriculture.

• *Textile Raw Materials.* Expanded imports of silk (from southern Europe and India), flax and hemp (in part for fustians), yarns, and dyes reflect new directions in textile production, but the increase in raw cotton imports down to 1773 was modest.

- *Iron and Steel.* England became increasingly dependent on iron imports, despite some expansion and technological progress in domestic production, with Russia and, to a modest extent, the North American colonies substituting for Sweden, where total iron exports were strictly limited after 1730 to a total of 40,000 tons. In 1770, Britain was importing from all sources about 50,000 tons a year, approximately equal to domestic production.

The major changes in exports and reexports are the following:

- *Textiles.* A rise in exports to North America, the West Indies, Africa, Ireland, and, to a lesser extent, India permited overall woolen exports to expand in the face of increased protection and self-sufficiency on the European continent, including southern Europe, where the market for English woolens held up until midcentury. The colonial markets also accounted for the bulk of the increased exports in other textiles. English cotton exports remained exceedingly modest, although they were expanding, down to the early 1770s.
- *Metalware and Miscellaneous Manufactures.* Here the rapidly expanding, high-income market in North American colonies stimulated English production of nails, axes, firearms, buckets, coaches, clocks, saddles, etc., thus accelerating a trend that appeared in the latter decades of the seventeenth century.
- *Foodstuffs.* After rising to a peak of almost £1 million in 1750, grain exports fell away as England moved toward chronic deficit status. The rising demand also yielded a decline in fish exports.

- *Raw Materials.* England developed a substantial increase in coal and lead exports, the former to the continent and Ireland, the latter to the continent.
- *Reexports.* Overall, reexports tripled in value over the period, while English exports increased by only 122 percent. In textiles, the expansion of colonial markets compensated for relative sluggishness in continental demand. Northwestern Europe developed as a strong reexport market for coffee and rice, but the rise of sugar production in the French West Indies, and a decline of productivity in the English sugar plantations, virtually eliminated English reexports to that area. The Irish market for reexported groceries expanded strongly as did the colonial market for tea.

The changing direction and composition of French trade in this period can be derived from data available for the two years 1715 and 1787.[10]

French trade also shifted direction toward America and Africa, but the loss of its Indian position to the British reduced the relative role of East Indian trade. The eighteenth-century English expansion of trade with Ireland, which approximately doubled Ireland's proportionate role in imports and exports, was, of course, not shared by France since Ireland was treated by England as a colonial market. The proportion of French trade with the rest of Europe declined, but, as compared to Britain, a much higher proportion of French imports and exports remained oriented to the dynamic continental markets of the eighteenth century. In composition, there was, as in Britain, a revolutionary expansion of trade in the new groceries, including large reexports of the products of the French West Indies.

Crouzet sums up the French position over these years as follows:

... there were several branches of international trade in which the French secured or maintained a dominant position; they continued to be the main suppliers of manufactured goods to Spain, and through Cadiz to Spain's American Empire, while the British had the monopoly of the smaller Portuguese and Brazilian markets; they dominated the markets of Italy and the Levant. Thanks to spectacular progress in sugar and coffee cultivation in San Domingo and to the low prices of these products, which competed successfully with those of the British West Indies where soils were becoming exhausted and production costs were higher, the French snatched most of the entrepôt trade in colonial produce from the English merchants and developed a large and fast-growing re-export trade to Northern Europe. . . . French trade . . . was still more oriented on Europe than the English, and this European trade was growing almost as fast as total trade, certainly faster than that of England with the Continent.[11]

IV

The commercial revolution is a classic example of the widening of the market that Adam Smith believed would encourage specialization in manufacture and an increase in efficiency. It brought to Europe an expanded flow of products to be eaten or smoked, drunk or worn. It generated a new trade with Africa, in which European products were exchanged for human beings dragooned across the South Atlantic to work in the plantations. It implanted in North America a vigorous population of farmers and trappers, fishermen and traders. It yielded a massive flow of bullion that could, as it were, be twice exchanged: once by the Portuguese and Spanish for imports, then again by the English, French, Germans, and Dutch to acquire what Europe wanted from Asian civilizations that had no balancing demand for Europe's products. The question is: How, if at all, did all this relate to the industrial revolution?

Adam Smith published *The Wealth of Nations* in 1776, almost three hundred years after Bartholomew Díaz rounded the Cape of Good Hope and after several centuries of purposeful and intensive European exploitation of the Western Hemisphere and the Far East. Smith perceived the gains to all that had emerged from this exercise in comparative advantage and the even greater gains that might accrue if domestic and international markets were permitted to operate in more open and competitive ways, but he failed to detect the technological revolution that was about to occur.[12] As we shall see, there was a good deal going on in the expanding little world of technology that he might have perceived after 1760; but the fact is that, down to his time, the commercial revolution and the widening of the market did bring about specialization of economic functions, but it did not yield an industrial revolution. *The Wealth of Nations* accurately reflects the state of technology actually at work in the 1770s; it is a tract centered on the expansion of commerce, not the refinement of industrial method, despite Smith's observations on the manufacture of pins and watches. As Ashton notes of the period 1700–1760, "Britain experienced no revolution, either in the technique of production, the structure of industry, or the economic and social life of the people."[13] As of 1760, the machines used in British cotton manufacture were still "nearly as simple as those of India."[14]

And yet we know these changes in the scale and structure of international commerce must, somehow, have related, at least in part, to the industrial revolution that began in Britain in the 1780s.[15] To get at this matter usefully, we must make a distinction between the effects of expanded trade on real income and its effects on the process of invention and technological innovation. The two processes are not identical; income, output, and population can expand without substantial change in technology.

First, with respect to real income, the expansion in trade had a good many positive direct effects. It reduced the cost of sugar, tobacco, tea, and other items of popular consumption, and it provided increased employment in manufactures, at levels of income higher than those that would have been attained in alternative employment, for those producing for export or processing imports.

Second, a whole range of activities connected with trade increased, again expanding real income: commerce itself, banking, insurance, ship and port construction, and the scale of internal trade, notably to distribute the enlarged flow of American and Asian commodities. All this enlarged the middle class and the capital available for manufacturing purposes.[16]

Third, enlarged trade brought with it directly certain kinds of increased manufacturing or processing activity. Crouzet summarizes well this kind of linkage in eighteenth-century France:

> . . . the eighteenth-century European economy was organized around a number of big seaports, most prosperous being those with the largest share in the growing colonial trade, such as Bordeaux or Nantes; each of these had, not only its own industries, but also its industrial hinterland in the river basin of which it was the outlet. For instance, Bordeaux had shipbuilding yards, sugar refineries, distilleries, tobacco factories, and glassworks, while along the Garonne and its tributaries were to be found industries such as sail and rope making, foundaries making guns for West Indiamen and boilers for sugar mills, manufactures of linens for slaves and woolens for planters, as well as cornmills producing fine flour for export to the West Indies. The seaboard provinces of France were undoubtedly the most industralized in the eighteenth century, but the influence of the great seaports penetrated far into the interior; for instance, Pierre Léon has shown how much the industries of a landlocked province such as Dauphiné were also interested in the West India trade.[17]

Similar processes of trade-related industrial expansion can be traced in Holland, Spain, and some of the North German ports, as well as in Britain.

The multiplier effects of these income-expanding consequences of the increase in foreign trade are, of course, hard to measure. In Britain, they contributed to the relative expansion of the population living in concentrations of 5,000 and over from a maximum of thirteen percent at the beginning of the eighteenth century to, say, sixteen percent at midcentury, and twenty-five percent by 1801.[18] Excepting those for Holland, the continental figures were clearly lower, but there was almost certainly a relative as well as absolute rise in their urban populations since, with the exception of Spain during the Napoleonic Wars, foreign trade per capita increased, as roughly measured in Table 7.

There was nothing historically unique about this kind of expansion in trade, increase in urbanization, stimulus to commerce-related institutions, and growth in handicraft processing and manufactures. The widening of the market carried with it many of what we now call modernizing institutions, activities, and attitudes, but it did not set in

TABLE 7
FOREIGN TRADE PER CAPITA, 1720, 1750, 1800
(In £ Sterling)

	1720	1750	1800
Great Britain	1.9	2.8	6.2
United States	—	2.4 (1769)	3.2
Holland and Belgium	1.3	1.7	3.2
Germany	.7	1.1	2.0
Portugal	1.0	1.1	1.2
Spain	1.3	1.6	1.1
France	.3	.5	1.1
Russia	.6	.7	1.0
Italy	.3	.4	.6

SOURCE: The trade figures used in this calculation are from Table 5, above; the population figures, from Table 2, above.

motion a self-reinforcing process of industrial invention and innovation. Production was generally by long-familiar methods. There were, as in the ancient empires in phases of expansion, constant returns to scale rather than increasing returns. There was, again, capital widening but not significant capital deepening.

Our conclusion thus far, then, is that, like the domestic policies of government analyzed earlier, the commercial revolution contributed to an expansion of income and contributed to Europe's ability to support an enlarged population, but it did not, in itself, set in motion a regular flow of new technology that was actually absorbed into the economic process. Without such a flow, the expansion of income and population could have gone on for some time, as new and old regions within the world trading system were further developed within the framework of then existing technology, but, sooner or later, Malthusian limits were bound to be reached and Europe would have experienced a downward cyclical movement—like that in nineteenth-century China and many previous civilizations—as it had in the fourteenth and seventeenth centuries. An expanded trade in groceries, expanded merchant fleets, expanded cities and ports, banks, and processing industries were not enough by themselves to set in motion self-sustained growth.[19]

But this lateral expansion of European and world economy did have several significant links to the industrial revolution.

First, the expansion of income and population created a market environment where demand curves were shifting to the right. This was not a setting that guaranteed inventors and innovators would respond by creating and installing new technology, but, clearly, it made such a response easier and more natural.

Second, there was urbanization. The increase in the

absolute numbers of people, in Europe and in the North American colonies, pulled out of the agricultural sector into urban life expanded the pool of those likely to respond to the incentives offered by rising yields from invention and innovation, in the context created by the scientific revolution.

Third, there was some oblique linkage of foreign trade to the new technologies that were at the heart of the first phase of the industrial revolution. These technologies arose in Britain from three problems: how to produce good pig and wrought iron cheaply with coke as the fuel; how to make a reasonably efficient steam engine; and how to spin cotton with machinery.

British dependence on iron imports (from Sweden, then also from Russia and the American colonies) was an embarrassment in a warlike, mercantilist age, and iron manufacture faced not merely an expanding domestic demand but an extremely rapid expansion in the demand for hardware from the relatively rich and rapidly expanding population in the North American colonies.

The first major use of the steam engine was to make deeper coal seams accessible by pumping out water, at a time when increased demand for coke in ironmaking contributed something to a coal requirement already expanding in response to rising population, increased urbanization, and increased manufacturing activity with old technologies. Some part of this increased demand for coal related to the requirements of foreign trade.

Above all, the introduction to the British market during the seventeenth century of Indian calicoes by the East India Company revealed a latent demand that would not be denied. The import-inhibiting legislation of 1700 and 1720 turned out to have the effect of a high protective tariff behind which British inventors and innovators ultimately solved the problem of matching with machinery the deftness of Indian hands in using cotton as warp. By the time that problem was solved, there already existed a substantial industry skilled in dyeing Indian white calicoes and in manufacturing fustians of cotton weft and linen warp. On this foundation, the cotton textile industry could move rapidly forward to supply overseas as well as British markets, when the technical breakthroughs were achieved.

Foreign trade played its role in the story of these three critical sectors, but, in each case, it was quite a narrow role. The commercial revolution set in motion demands that made it increasingly profitable to solve these problems on the supply side with new technology, but a new mentality was required to yield the corps of inventors and entrepreneurs who actually created the lowered cost curves that define technically the industrial revolution. Thus, more than the commercial revolution is required to explain the industrial revolution, a Smithian widening of the market was not enough. The great innovative breakthroughs were linked also to the scientific revolution. We turn, therefore, to the knotty question of how science, invention, and innovation were related.

4

Science, Invention,
and Innovation

I

It is the central thesis of this book that the scientific revolution, in all its consequences, is the element in the equation of history that distinguishes early modern Europe from all previous periods of economic expansion. The domestic economic policies pursued by the activist rulers of the mercantilist era and the commercial revolution do not, in themselves, account for the coming of the first takeoff and the spreading industrial revolution that dominated the world arena in the two centuries that followed.

In one part of our minds most of us would accept this assertion. There is an almost biblical, or at least sagalike, quality in the tale that begins with Copernicus, the canon of Frauenburg, who set, as it were, the earth in motion around the sun, but held knowledge of his new system to a restricted circle until his death in 1543. The tale moves on to Copernicus' vindication by Galileo and his telescope, and the latter's repression by the Inquisition; it embraces on an increasingly crowded and animated stage the contributions of Brahe and Kepler, Gilbert, Huygens and Descartes; and is climaxed by the brilliant synthesis of young Newton in 1666, who then allowed himself another twenty years of probing, reflection, and the absorption of new observations before publishing formally his unifying equations.

The drama and meaning of the sequence from Copernicus to Newton led Whitehead to observe: "Since a babe was born in a manger, it may be doubted whether so great a thing has happened with so little stir."[1] And, more flatly, Butterfield: ". . . since the rise of Christianity, there is no landmark in history that is worthy to be compared with this."[2]

Looking back from the 1970s, one is not likely to challenge this assessment. It is not merely a question of moon shots, nuclear weapons, satellite communications, wonder drugs, and computers. It is that we know or sense that the scientific revolution irreversibly changed the way man thought and felt about himself and society, about the physical world, and about religion. The scientific revolution also related, somehow, to the coming of the first industrial revolution at the end of the eighteenth century.

Here we face a problem on which there is neither clarity nor consensus. The first phase of the industrial revolution involved the application by private businessmen of new methods on a significant scale for making cotton textiles, the rapid spread to many industries of an increasingly efficient steam engine, and new ways of producing good wrought iron with coal as the fuel. Behind these developments and prior to them, many men in many places had labored to solve practical problems of production in new ways, on a scale and with a purposefulness never before to be observed in history. The results of their efforts were many small changes as well as the famous breakthroughs which figure in the patent records and textbooks of economic history. It is by no means obvious that the cumulative work of astronomers and physicists, mathematicians and chemists during the sixteenth and seventeenth centuries is fundamentally related to the practical achievements and decisions of these innovators, contrivers, and inventors. And, if we accept instinctively that a linkage existed, it is not evident on the face of it what the linkage was.

II

In trying to get at the connections among science, invention, and innovation, it may be useful to begin with some rather formal and abstract propositions.

Science and invention represent forms of investment within a society. Men devote time and current resources to producing new knowledge of new, more efficient ways of doing things. A decision is required to forego some other activity and accept the risk of failing to achieve a result valued by the society or sought by the scientist or inventor in personal fulfillment. Similarly, an act of innovation by an entrepreneur, public or private, involves risk. He must decide to invest his own or borrowed capital in a new form of production or service. He may or may not receive the higher profit for which he hopes.

Viewed in this way, the volume of resources, including human talent, devoted to fundamental science and to invention in a given society at a particular period of time can be symbolized by quite conventional supply and demand curves.[3] A demand curve would exhibit the expected yield to be derived from the application of additional resources to the pursuit of fundamental science, with the existing scientific stock given. Since the results of pure science do not enter directly into the private economy (except in certain contemporary sophisticated industries with great laboratories), the demand for scientific achievement may reflect the premium in prestige and academic status a given society attaches to such achievement, or public subsidy. A supply curve would exhibit the volume of resources actually offered by a given society to the pursuit of fundamental science at a particular period of time in response to such incentives. A particular individual may or may not be responsive to the expected yield from the pursuit of fundamental science. Some men are driven to search for new knowledge by inner compulsions not closely related to external reward, but for substantial numbers of human beings one can expect that talent would be responsive in degree to the rewards, financial and otherwise, a society offers for scientific achievement.

A similar pair of curves would exhibit the demand for inventions and the supply of talent and resources offered in response to the expected yields. Here we are closer to the marketplace. Therefore, for invention, one can probably presume somewhat greater elasticity of supply in relation to expected yields, and this is borne out for our period by the fluctuation of inventions with peace and war, prosperity and depression. But we are also dealing with men with an instinct to express a creative talent, and the shape of the supply curve for inventors may also reflect nonmaterial rewards.[4]

The purpose of viewing science and invention in these static supply-and-demand terms is extremely limited. It is to suggest that the actual volume of talent devoted to these enterprises within a society at any given time is the result, on the side of demand, of the premium, economic and/or otherwise, a society attaches to these activities, and, on the side of supply, of the extent to which the system of education, social opportunity, and values within a society leads men of potential scientific and inventive gift to offer their talents in these directions; for, as we have noted, achievements in science and invention are cumulative and the numbers engaged matter. The simple point here is that the numbers can be increased if the demand curve shifts to the right, since some elasticity in supply is likely, but the numbers can also be increased if the supply curve shifts to the right, under the impact of a change in social circumstances, social values, or the intellectual and philosophical environment. In dealing with the scientific revolution, we confront changes of both kinds.

So much for a simple, static picture. Over a period of time, the demand curves and supply curves lose their independence and begin to interact. A demand curve that shifts steadily to the right can shift the whole supply curve to a new position; it can induce a substantial increase in the numbers of talented men devoting themselves to science and invention; the achievements of such men can, in turn, stimulate an interest in and awareness of their potentialities which increases the effective demand for their efforts; that is, it can shift the position of the demand curve. That dynamic also proved an important element in the story of the seventeenth and eighteenth centuries.

Now another basic question: How do science and invention evolve if, in fact, increased numbers of talented men devote themselves to these activities?

We assume that progress in science is cumulative and is a function of the volume of talent and resources applied to the solution of particular problems. Therefore, the development of a particular branch of science through time might be shown as a curve exhibiting, after an episodic start with low yields, a period of gradually increasing returns; a rather dramatic breakthrough, bringing together in a new and striking way the insights previously accumulated; and then a period of refinement, framed by the new paradigm, ultimately subject to diminishing returns to additional applications of talent and resources, as shown in Chart 2, below.[5]

CHART 2
MARGINAL YIELD IN A BRANCH OF SCIENCE

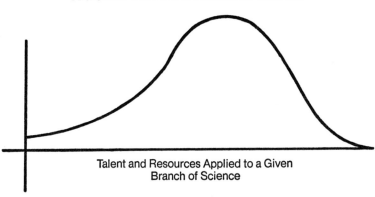

Talent and Resources Applied to a Given
Branch of Science

For fundamental science as a whole, the experience of the past three centuries does not permit us to predict diminishing returns. Its overall course, like that of production in growing economies, would sum up movements in numerous sectors, some in a phase of increasing returns, others in a phase of diminishing returns; some expanding rapidly, others less so or even stagnating or declining. The marginal yield from fundamental science would exhibit a gradual rise (with breakthroughs averaged out), levelling off, at some point, when fundamental science on a world basis became a sufficiently massive effort to exploit economies of scale. In a rough-and-ready way, marginal returns were equated as among science, invention, and other forms of investment of talent and resources. Chart 3 exhibits these characteristics.

Curves of similar general shape to Chart 2, reflecting phases of increasing and diminishing returns, would characterize the yield from the application of talent and resources to particular lines of invention, when dramatic

CHART 3
MARGINAL YIELD FROM SCIENCE AS A WHOLE

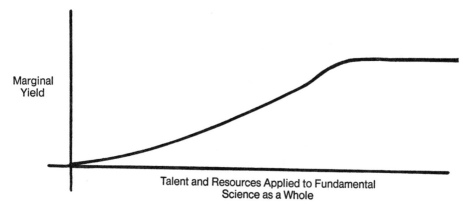

Marginal
Yield

Talent and Resources Applied to Fundamental
Science as a Whole

breakthroughs generally occurred against the background of much cumulative effort by many hands; a curve like that in Chart 3 would show the yield from invention as a whole.

We can regard, then, the pursuit of science and invention as a form of investment by societies or, as knowledge moved more freely across international boundaries, by an international society. Like other forms of investment, they appear to have been subject to certain general patterns that decreed, in the modern era, phases of increasing and diminishing returns in particular sectors and relative overall stability in the profit rate, when the quantum of resources applied had reached a certain point.[6]

Now, how are science and invention related? The simplest assumption would be that invention is the application to practical matters of a particular branch of fundamental science. In that case, the productivity of talent cumulatively applied to invention in a given field would rise, with an appropriate time lag, as the stock of fundamental scientific knowledge was built up in the related field.

Science and invention would then be closely linked in a straightforward way, with each following, with suitable lag, a pattern like that in Chart 2. As we shall see, this close, automatic linkage of science and invention is precisely what cannot be assumed in the sixteenth to the eighteenth centuries. A major puzzlement to be explored later in this work is what linkages did and did not exist between science and invention. For our purposes at this point in the argument, however, we can continue to assume they are closely, positively, and functionally connected, without specifying the nature of the connection.

If we take that view, what determines the areas of science and invention to which talent and resources are applied? The answer, in simple economic terms, would be that men devote their creative scientific and inventive talent to solving the problems whose solutions will yield the greatest profit, as determined in the marketplace or by public authorities. In short, we can assume, formally, that necessity is the mother of science and of invention. It determines the areas of science and the kinds of inventions developed at particular periods of time, with suitable lags required for the creative processes to work their way to solutions.

There is an important element of truth in this proposition, with respect to invention, that has long been recognized,[7] although necessity, or profit, is, in itself, no guarantee that human knowledge and ingenuity will always provide a fruitful response. The link of necessity to fundamental science is less clear. The sequence in which modern science (mathematics, astronomy, physics, botany, chemistry, etc.) developed is related to ease of observation and tools for experiment and measurement.[8] Moreover, fields of science have an inner life of their own, in which the participants carry forward their work, debating and probing contrapuntally, relatively insulated from the demands of the active world. At different times and places, these external demands have played their part in shaping the lives and activities of scientists and have, to a degree, affected their work. But we are dealing with a linkage less powerful and more remote than that which shapes the pattern of invention.

Despite the quasi-independence of science and the limitations on the proposition that necessity is the mother of invention, the pool of scientific knowledge and the pool of inventions can be regarded as a productive stock on which a society can draw. But until the innovating entrepreneur acts, science and invention represent potential, not actual, increases in the productivity of the economy.

The number of existing inventions actually incorporated in the current volume of investment at any period of time can be presented in various ways. Perhaps the most useful is to modify the familiar Keynesian marginal efficiency of capital curve by drawing above it a theoretical optimum curve in which the current demand for investment would contain within it all existing profitable inventions. The gap between the actual and optimum curves would exhibit for any society, at a particular period of time, the propensity to innovate. The level of investment (and the degree to which inventions were incorporated in the capital stock) would be determined, in the Keynesian world, by the intersection of the rate of interest (as set by the intersection of a liquidity preference curve and the supply of money) and the actual marginal efficiency of capital curve.[9] The point to be made here is, simply, that, with a given stock of inventions available, the quality of entrepreneurship—the number of entrepreneurs willing to take the risks of innovation—will help determine the productivity of actual investment outlays and the progress of the economy. And this factor, like the numbers engaged in science and invention, can be influenced by noneconomic as well as economic factors at work in a given society at a particular period of time.

Now, what happens if an innovation in a particular sector is pursued over a period of time? How does the notion of rising and then declining yields from a particular inventive breakthrough (Chart 2) translate itself into economics? Here there are two familiar and closely related formulations: the case of increasing returns and the concept of a leading sector in the growth process.

The case of increasing returns has recently been re-opened for discussion among economists.[10] A major innovative breakthrough does not yield the familiar upward sloping supply curve that gives us, with a downward sloping demand curve, a point of price and output equilibrium. Using the diagram in Chart 4, I. D. Burnet describes the outcome as follows: "Contrary to one's first impression, [Chart] 4 is representative of an explosion rather than an equilibrium. Starting, for example, from P_1Q_1 in period T_1, industry decides to expand production in period T_2 to Q_2, which reduces costs to P_2, which inspires industry to expand production to Q_3 . . . and so on. The only constraints to the explosion are the time lags involved in accumulating capital, refining technology, acquiring tastes, training the work force and so on."

After citing some famous cases of explosive growth in particular sectors (from the Model-T Ford to ball-point pens), he asserts: "The entrepreneur lucky enough to discover a virgin field of consumer demand can look forward to a golden age of self-generating growth."

In fact, Burnet's falling supply curve must level off for any given breakthrough that lowers costs with an increase in output. Ultimately, constant or diminishing returns will set in, for trees do not grow to the sky and deceleration is

CHART 4
THE CASE OF INCREASING RETURNS

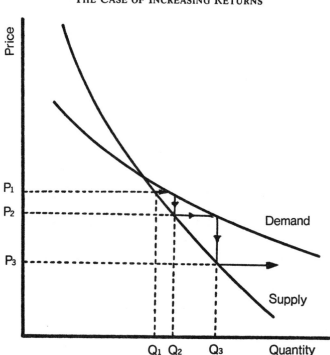

inevitable, as his reference to a succession of innovations implies.

Translated from Burnet's world of the lucky entrepreneur to the path of an industry that has seized on a major technological innovation, we find that, after a possible phase of acceleration, deceleration becomes the normal path of increases in output and decreases in price. This was the powerful insight of Simon Kuznets in his *Secular Movements in Production and Prices*. He concluded:

As we observe the various industries within a given national system, we see that the lead in development shifts from one branch to another. The main reason for this shift seems to be that a rapidly developing industry does not continue its vigorous growth indefinitely, but slackens its pace after a time, and is overtaken by industries whose period of rapid development comes later. Within any country we observe a succession of different branches of activity leading the process of development, and in each mature industry we notice a conspicuous slackening in the rate of increase.[11]

At any period of time, a growing economy is characterized by a few accelerating sectors and many decelerating sectors moving forward, or declining, at different trend rates, when cleared of short-period fluctuations. In a rough-and-ready way, these rates tend to be related to the time of the last major technological breakthrough which granted them a phase of increasing returns. The pace of deceleration for a national industry can be affected by a wide range of factors, among them, the likelihood that technological change, after an initial breakthrough, will yield diminishing marginal reductions in cost; the possibilities that the quality of entrepreneurship will decline after an industry's heroic generation of innovation; that the diffusion of technology abroad may reduce a given national industry's share of the world market; that price and income elasticity of demand may diminish with expanded consumption and incomes.

The sectors enjoying high rates of growth and increasing returns link backwards to those that supply them with machinery and raw materials; laterally, they stimulate the growth of cities and regions where they take hold; and they link forward through externalities and the creation of bottlenecks which it becomes profitable to widen with new inventions and innovations. The multiple impact of a new leading sector thus requires one to think in terms of a leading sector complex, rather than a single sector.

In the end, then, the economic result of the convergence of sustained scientific, inventive, and entrepreneurial effort is the emergence of a powerful case, or cases, of increasing returns and of a leading sector complex capable of lifting the economy into a new stage of growth. Self-sustained growth consists of a continued flow of creative effort in these three domains—science, invention, and innovation—yielding new cases of increasing returns and new leading sector complexes as the older impulses inevitably lose their power to lower costs and expand total production.

As we turn from these stylized observations back to history as it unfolded in the sixteenth, seventeenth, and eighteenth centuries, we shall find that forces operating on demand and on supply are hard to distinguish sharply, that the link between science and invention is complex and difficult to trace with precision, that the discrete branches of science took time to become clearly differentiated, and, of course, that precise measurement of the marginal and average productivity of the pool of science and the pool of invention is impossible at any period of time. Nevertheless, we can see a buildup of scientific activity and a deepening of the pool of basic science; we can trace a buildup, after a lag, of inventive activity clearly linked to pressures arising in the marketplace and obliquely linked to the world of science; and then, after another shorter lag, we can observe entrepreneurs successfully seizing on the potentialities thus created and launching an economic expansion unique in history based on increasing returns, and yielding the first leading sector complex.

III

Modern science began with no apparent effective demand for it, either from the marketplace or from public authorities. On the contrary, in shifting the center of the universe from the earth to the sun, Copernicus knew he would face ridicule. He circulated his manuscript to the few who would appreciate his achievement, including high officials of the Church, but he agreed to publish his great work only on his deathbed in 1543. He was driven on by an inner impulse to make sense of the universe. On the other hand, he was already part of a living and accepted world of science. The Church permitted him to spend a good part of his round of life as a mathematician contemplating what was known of astronomy, and he lived in a time when the accumulation of observations with the naked eye already had posed a challenge to the Ptolemaic system, a challenge he felt free to try to meet:

> It was the extreme complexity into which the system had grown by the end of the fifteenth century that offended the mathematical mind of Copernicus. By that time more than eighty spheres were found necessary "to save appearances," as the phrase went—i.e. to account for the observed movements—and, even so, the movements were not completely explained. It seemed to Copernicus unlikely that God, who could do all things perfectly, would make such an ugly universe, and he accordingly turned back to the long dis-credited idea that the Earth moved, to see if, by thus relieving the spheres of some movements, he could account for the rest by a simpler system. He soon saw that this was possible, and for some thirty years, in season and out, he worked unceasingly to devise a new universe, pencilling his ideas on scraps of paper, the margins of books, and even on walls, until he had completed a scheme which not only explained all that Ptolemy's scheme had done, but did so more exactly and with only thirty-four spheres.[12]

In the century that followed, a series of remarkable men simultaneously added to the body of observation and struggled to design hypotheses that were consistent with them. They were driven by the logic of their quest to find the laws that governed motion both on earth and in the heavens. With the publication of Newton's *Principia* in 1687, a synthesis was achieved that embraced their ob-servations and partial insights. With elegance, Newton had brought together into a coherent system inertial motion, centrifugal force, universal gravitation, and the mathemati-cal formulae governing its behavior.

Like other grand intellectual breakthroughs, Newton's

synthesis both reflected a phase of prior effort by many minds and had large further consequences of its own. That prior effort had five characteristics. First, the small circle of men seeking to discover the laws of heavenly and terrestrial motion in the sixteenth and seventeenth centuries knew they were involved in a great adventure. They knew the received image of how things worked was wrong, and they were out to establish new fundamental truths. This was a conscious revolution, and it generated among those engaged an authentic excitement and dedication. They knew they were up to big business, indeed.

Second, the effort was truly international, engaging men from Cracow to London, from Scandinavia to France, Holland, and Italy. They knew each other's work, moved about, and benefitted greatly from the printing of books.

Third, the effort was carried forward by a counterpoint between mathematics, which drove them back to the lucid statement of basic principles and relationships, and observation. They needed telescopes and other instruments, and they worked closely with lens-grinders and instrument-makers. Newton's final calculations were drawn from a French field expedition of 1672, which provided more accurate measurements of the earth's distance from the sun and of the dimensions of the earth itself. But the power of his impact lay in finding mathematical uniformity in a large universe of observations.

Fourth, the new experimental approach to science spread beyond astronomy and physics and stirred men to generalize its meaning. William Harvey, product of Cambridge and Padua, returned to London to establish by painstaking observation the *Movement of the Heart and the Blood*, but in Holland, too, the study of anatomy was intensively pursued by the new methods from early in the seventeenth century. In England, the new experimental method—or philosophy—found in Francis Bacon a nonscientist expositor who glimpsed the full possibilities of uniting theory, observation and experiment, and practical application. And Bacon was not alone; the new modes of thought and observation touched every field of human endeavor.

Fifth, in the course of the seventeenth century this new method and philosophy, this new vision of the possibilities, became institutionalized and achieved the active support of public authorities who saw in its practical implications a means of increasing the power of the state. The first scientific institutions were founded in sixteenth-century Italy and Spain. In Germany, academies were set up at Rostock in 1622, Leipzig in 1651, Schweinfurt in 1652, Berlin in 1700. The first secretary of the English Royal Society was Henry Oldenburg, of Bremen, and one of its first enterprises was to engage in systematic correspondence with the continental scientists.

The origins of the Royal Society lay in gatherings of men of philosophical and scientific bent in London, from about 1645, and at Oxford, from about 1648. The two groups kept in touch and came to hold their meetings regularly at Gresham College in London. On November 28, 1660, they discussed the founding of a college to promote "Physico-Mathematicall Experimentall Learning." A year later, Charles II offered to join the society, and the name Royal Society first appears in a publication of 1661. The first charter of incorporation was formalized in 1662. The council of the Royal Society first met in May 13, 1663.

Like the Royal Society, the French Academy of Sciences began with private, informal meetings. In the early 1660s, the group of some fifteen scientists included Pascal and Huygens. In 1666, they were invited by Colbert to meet in his home and, then, in the Royal Library. In 1699, the society was transferred to the Louvre under the name of Académie des Sciences. Its initial efforts were devoted to experimental work and the encouragement of geometry, astronomy, physics, chemistry, mechanics, and anatomy. It also became the instrument for granting official approval to French inventions, and, year by year, a brief account of inventions sanctioned can be found in its *Mémoires,* sandwiched in among the learned papers of scientific substance.

Some fifteen citizens of the North American colonies became members of the Royal Society, among them Cotton Mather and Benjamin Franklin. Increase Mather led a group that set up in 1683 the short-lived Boston Philosophical Society. But Franklin's Junto, formed in 1727, directly led on to the setting up in Philadelphia of the American Philosophical Society sixteen years later, "for Promoting Useful Knowledge among the British Plantations in America." Partly reacting to its success, Boston responded in 1780 with the American Academy of Arts and Sciences. These and a good many other societies reflect the prompt transfer across the Atlantic of the scientific revolution in all its dimensions.[13]

Before turning to the linkage of science, invention, and technology in the post-*Principia* period, let us draw back and ask the question: Where did the scientific revolution itself come from? Was it an autonomous response of men of scientific bent to the reabsorption of science from the ancient world and its slow fracturing by cumulative further observations, or did it arise as a response to the practical needs of the active world of the sixteenth and seventeenth centuries?

The problem is illustrated in a relevant way by G. N. Clark's reply to the argument of the Soviet scholar B. Hessen on how the scientific revolution of the seventeenth century came about.[14] Hessen, an explicit Marxist, argues that "Newton was the typical representative of the rising bourgeoisie and in his philosophy he embodies the characteristic features of his class"[15]; that "the scheme of physics was mainly determined by the economic and technical tasks which the rising bourgeoisie raised to the forefront"[16]; and that "the main contents of the *Principia* . . . is a survey and systematic resolution of all the main group of physical problems."[17] The key physical problems related to transport, mining, and war, and they embraced the fields of hydrostatistics, hydrodynamics, aerostatics, dynamics, mechanics, and ballistics. Newton, in Hessen's analysis, emerges not as a scientist, but as a purposeful problem-solver for his social class, an association that Hessen uses also to explain Newton's clinging to religion and his failure to move on from his own constructs to a general doctrine of materialism.[18] To all this Clark responds that:

- Newton, born to the declining yeomanry (his heir-at-law a laborer), was not linked to a rising commercial bourgeoisie; he was as nearly a pure scientist as one is likely to find until he went to the Royal Mint in 1696, after his creative days were past.
- The study of optics, which engaged Newton, was motivated not by the prospect of profit but by an interest in improving eyesight and relates also to the problem of perspective in art.
- Much work during the scientific revolution related to medicine, art, and architecture, fields that transcend the moneygrubbing interests of the bourgeoisie.
- Music and its formal structure contributed significantly to the scientific thought of the sixteenth and seventeenth centuries.
- Problems of war, which sometimes related to but were not identical with commercial interests, engaged some scientific thought and effort, of which Newton disapproved.
- Science is "not merely the study of certain subjects: it is

study by certain methods," and the scientists of this era were caught up in the excitement of elaborating the experimental method.

- Religion palpably motivated, in part, Newton's search to understand the universe, as it did Boyle and others.
- Finally: "The disinterested desire to know, the impulse of the mind to exercise itself methodically and without any practical purpose, is an independent and unique motive."[19]

Clark's response to Hessen effectively casts doubts on the adequacy of a rigid Marxist framework, but, in so doing, it underlines the many links of the scientists to the society of which they were a part. It illustrates well the complexity of explaining how, in the sixteenth and seventeenth centuries, so much of the best human talent of Western Europe was drawn to science. As Sir James Jeans points out, we are dealing with the same kind of puzzlement we face in explaining the greatness of Greece in the fourth century B.C. and of Elizabethan England.[20] He could have cited the artists of Renaissance Italy, the painters of seventeenth-century Holland,[21] and other times and places where human creativity flowered in extraordinary ways in one direction or another. Charles Wilson, speaking of these phenomena, says: ". . . nothing eludes explanation so frustratingly as these explosions of collective and individual genius. . . ."[22] Without pretending to a final explanation, I would suggest that, in each case, there were three elements present: some kind of demand or patronage, even if only just sufficient to permit men of talent and ardor to subsist while they pursued their natural bent; a large, fresh concept that related to currents of thought or feeling, problems or aspirations in the society as a whole; and a method that could be taught to lesser as well as greater men and built up incrementally until its possibilities found a limit. Changes in the mood and requirements of the society and the exhaustion of a method and line of approach converge to set a time limit on these golden ages. They leave their residue for all time, but talent and genius turn in other, often more diffuse, directions.

In any case, these three elements were present in the scientific revolution of the sixteenth and seventeenth centuries. The work of science did not cease with the publication of the *Principia.* On the contrary, it may be said to have only begun in its modern form. More men accepted the philosophy and method of purposeful, experimental science. But the eighteenth century was a period of refinement and elaboration in mathematics, physics, and astronomy. Only with Lavoisier, toward the end of the century, does a new great synthesizer emerge to launch the era of modern chemistry.

What concerns us here, however, is not the history of science and its inner rhythms, but the links between pre- and post-Newtonian science and the sequence of inventions and innovations that detonated the British takeoff after 1783. They were related, but how?

IV

The task of analysis would be greatly simplified if we could demonstrate clear, direct links between new propositions derived from basic science and inventions. But the central fact is that the critical inventions of the eighteenth century did not flow directly from such propositions or even from the scientists themselves. The Royal Society persisted to a degree in the Baconian spirit which had partially led to its creation. In June 1699, Savery exhibited his model of a "fire-engine" before the Society, which also played its part in improving the Royal Observatory at Greenwich, in the change of the calendar in 1751, in improving the ventilation of prisons, and in the protection of ships and buildings from lightning. But, in general, the interest and energy devoted to practical matters fell away rather quickly after the founding, diverted perhaps by the protracted period of war from 1689 to 1713. Even less than the French Academy can the Royal Society be said to have sponsored or developed the major inventions of the eighteenth century.

As for the link to scientific propositions, there is only the much debated possibility that Professor Joseph Black's theory of latent heat stirred James Watt to conceive of a separation of the condenser to yield a more efficient steam engine. The weight of the evidence now is that this direct connection did not exist, despite Watt's fruitful contacts at Glasgow with Black.[23] There is also the intriguing case of Leblanc's method for manufacturing soda, which evolved late in the eighteenth century under the supervision of scientists of the French Academy. But, Gillispie notes:

> Leblanc seems to have found his process, not through some flashing theoretical insight, but by means of a fallacious analogy with the smelting of iron ore. Not only so, but after he had worked it out, neither he nor any of the other artisans interested in alkali production made any attempt to investigate or explain the nature of the reactions involved. They concentrated their efforts—though for a long time with no success—on trying to make money by one method or another—in Leblanc's case by first persuading the Government to subsidize him.[24]

It is clear, then, that the inventions of the eighteenth century were not the product of scientists or derived simply from scientific propositions. From direct evidence we know they were the work of a special breed who, in increasing numbers, strove during the eighteenth century to do things more efficiently, making large improvements and small, in workshops as well as laboratories, only a few getting to the

British patent office or receiving the blessing of the French Academy.

Nevertheless, the scientific revolution, by indirection, supplied the three elements that were missing from the ancient world and converted a setting of slow-moving economic expansion into an industrial revolution.

1. *The Philosophic Impact.* First, and perhaps most important of all, was the character of Newton's synthesis. By embracing a wide range of observed phenomena in a few axiomatic propositions, man was put in a position to understand, to predict, and to manipulate nature. One could find in Newton's world an elegant reaffirmation of the Deity as did Newton and Edmund Halley. Or one could fudge the theology of the matter as did Pope:

> Nature and Nature's laws lay hid in night;
> God said, Let Newton be! and all was light.

Or one could find in the order of nature a phenomenon that required no Christian deity who gave to man on earth a special place. And Newton's God, who had once set the magnificent clockwork into motion, left man lonelier. But, paradoxically, the scientific revolution also gave man a new sense of power and of confidence that an order of nature was there to be found, and that such knowledge was the key to solving problems and, therefore, shaping to a degree his own destiny. This new sense of power—the Faustian outlook, to use David Landes' designation—suffused the literate Western world. Few read Newton's *Principia*, but its triumphant message, popularized by many hands during the eighteenth century, had the kind of impact that the work of Marx and Freud, Einstein and Keynes were later to enjoy. By changing the way man looked at the world around him, the Newtonian perception increased, in ways impossible to measure, the supply of inventors and the willingness of entrepreneurs to introduce innovations. And it broke in the minds of rulers and bureaucrats the age-old sense that the cycle within fixed technology was man's natural destiny. To return to R. V. Jones' *bon mot*, they could now conceive of progress and try to legislate for it.

2. *Scientists and Tool-makers.* More narrowly, the experimental method, built into the scientific revolution, directly increased the supply of inventions, through the two-way linkage of scientists and tool-makers. The discipline of the experimental method forced men, in the phrase of William James, ". . . to forge every sentence in the teeth of irreducible and stubborn facts."[25] The commitment to humility in the face of fact required ". . . an active interest in the simple occurrences of life for their own sake."[26] The scientists needed pumps and telescopes, the microscope, the thermometer, the barometer, and accurate clocks. Inventors and others could also use them. As Lilley concludes: ". . . scientists like Gilbert, Galileo, Guericke, and Boyle became willing to learn what they could from the craftsmen and to take over craftsmen's apparatus to make scientific instruments."[27] The separation of the man of learning from the craftsman—to be observed from ancient Greece to mediaeval Europe—began to disappear. We would have to take this linkage seriously even if we had only the case of the gifted instrument-maker at Glasgow University, but there is more to it than the story of James Watt.

3. *Scientists, Inventors, and Innovators.* Stemming from the Faustian outlook, the pursuit of principles of maximum generality by the experimental method was understood, from an early stage, to open the way to practical and profitable inventions and innovations. This was, of course, a central theme of Francis Bacon before Newton emerged on the scene; and, from Galileo's interest in shipbuilding, mine pumps, and artillery to Newton's fruitless alchemy,

some of the scientists interested themselves directly in practical matters. The Baconian linkage of science to material progress was greatly strengthened by the web of osmotic ties that grew up between scientists, inventors, and entrepreneurs. Ashton, for example, observes:

> The sciences were not . . . as yet so specialized as to be out of contact with the language, thought, and practice of ordinary men. It was as a result of a visit to Norfolk, where he had gone to study the new methods of farming, that the Scottish landowner, James Hutton, became interested in the constitution of soils; and the discoveries that made him the most famous geologist of his day owed something to the navvies who were cutting the clays and blasting the rock to provide England with canals. Physicists and chemists, such as Franklin, Black, Priestley, Dalton, and Davy, were in intimate contact with the leading figures in British industry: there was much coming and going between the laboratory and the workshop, and men like James Watt, Josiah Wedgwood, William Reynolds, and James Keir were at home in the one as in the other. The names of engineers, iron masters, industrial chemists, and instrument-makers on the list of Fellows of the Royal Society show how close were the relations between science and practice at this time.[28]

There were other significant meeting places as well. Robert Schofield has documented the vital nexus provided by the Lunar Society of Birmingham, which did not lose momentum until the 1790s.[29] There were similar provincial societies in Manchester, Derby, Liverpool, Bristol, and Leeds, among others.[30] These linkages were probably stronger in eighteenth-century Britain than elsewhere, but they existed to a degree in France and other parts of the West.

Thus, the lack of simple, demonstrable linkages between emerging propositions of science and particular inventions of the eighteenth century by no means reduces the importance of the scientific revolution in the equation that finally yielded the industrial revolution. The three indirect linkages set out here between the world of science and those of invention and innovation were powerful. They withdrew, as it were, the graphite rods from the atomic pile and permitted an ultimately explosive set of interactions to occur. James Watt, for example, put his oblique debt to Professor Black extremely well, in setting aside his alleged dependence on the theory of latent heat: "Although Dr. Black's theory of latent heat did not *suggest* my improvements on the steam-engine, yet the knowledge upon various subjects which he was pleased to communicate to me, and the correct modes of reasoning, and of making experiments of which he set me the example, certainly conduced very much to facilitate the progress of my inventions. . . ."[31] Gillispie on the seventeenth and eighteenth centuries and Schmookler on the United States in the twentieth have generalized Watt's gracious acknowledgment that science could introduce the inventor to the properties of the physical world and to methods and perceptions he might not otherwise command. Schmookler sums up as follows:

> The negligible effect of individual scientific discoveries on individual inventions is doubtless due to the orientation of the typical inventor, even those well trained in science and engineering, to the affairs of daily life in the home and industry rather than to the life of the intellect. The result, however, does not mean that science is unimportant to invention, particularly in recent times. Rather it suggests that, in the analysis of the effect of science on invention, the conceptual framework of the Gestalt school of psychology is perhaps more appropriate than is that of the mechanistic, stimulus-response school. The growth of the *body* of science conditions the course of invention more than does each separate increment. It does this by making inventors see things differently and by enabling them to imagine different solutions than would otherwise be the case. The effect of the growth of science is thus normally felt more from generation to generation than from one issue of a scientific journal to the next.[32]

In the end, then, the growth of the stock of scientific knowledge does relate to the productivity of inventive activity when the old separation of the domains is broken down, as it was from the sixteenth to the eighteenth centuries, although the connection is not the simple one postulated earlier for purposes of stylized exposition.

V

It was almost a century and a half between the death of Copernicus and the publication of the *Principia;* it was three quarters of a century from that date to the acceleration of British inventions at the end of the Seven Years' War, it was another twenty years before the application of certain of these inventions to production on a substantial scale led to the British takeoff. It took time for the body of science to build up, for its philosophy and methods to diffuse, for increasing numbers of inventive men to focus their efforts on breaking the key bottlenecks that limited the productive process, and for them to find solutions.

We know that, so far as invention was concerned, the British scene altered strikingly, starting in the 1760's. Although patents granted are an imperfect index of inventive activity, they are, on the whole, useful, and their movement conforms broadly to what we know from non-statistical evidence on British technology (Table 8).

Regular English patent records begin in 1617, although their grant reaches back to Elizabethan times. The numbers vary a good deal by years and even decades. It would require substantial detailed research to explain their year-by-year movement before the eighteenth century, when they exhibit a more or less regular sensitivity to times of war and economic fluctuations. In that century, their level lifts after the War of Spanish Succession, but does not exhibit a sharply rising trend until the 1760s. A second

TABLE 8
NUMBERS OF ENGLISH PATENTS GRANTED IN EACH DECADE,
1630–1809

1630/39	75	1720/29	89
1640/49		1730/39	56
	4		
1650/59		1740/49	82
1660/69	31	1750/59	92
1670/79	50	1760/69	205
1680/89	53	1770/79	294
1690/99	102	1780/89	477
1700/09	22	1790/99	647
1710/19	38	1800/09	924

SOURCE: B. R. Mitchell, with Phyllis Deane, *Abstract of British Historical Statistics* (Cambridge: At the University Press, 1962), p. 268.

sharp lift comes at 1783, with the end of the American War of Independence and the beginning of the British takeoff.

What is clear is that, as the century wore on, increasing numbers of Britons were devoting their attention to invention, asking for and being granted patents. Their activities ranged over a wide front. From these data we can deduce nothing significant about how the demand for inventions and their supply interacted. We have only the net result.

Turning from patent data to the key sectors where significant technological change occurred, we can say something more. In textiles, ironmaking, and the creation of an efficient steam engine we can observe a concentration of inventive talent in response to clear-cut economic incentives. Whatever other human motives may have been at work—creative striving, search for prestige, fame, etc.—a straightforward interest in financial gain was clearly present and important.

Under the Acts of 1700 and 1720, the demand for fustians was rising, notably in the years of peace between the Wars of the Spanish and Austrian Succession (1713–40). Responding to a challenge from the woolen industry and the vigorous response of the growing fustian industry, Parliament, in 1735, affirmed the legitimacy of producing printed goods of linen yarn and cotton wool in the so-called Manchester Act, reflecting the location of the new rapidly expanding textile center. After 1745, the quality of certain Indian cottons began to deteriorate, increasing the demand for British products abroad. The pressure to find ways to expand output and to produce a pure cotton cloth became intense.

In this environment came the sequence of famous inventions: Kay's flying shuttle, first introduced in the 1730s and widely adopted in the 1750s and 1760s by weavers, furthered the incentive to increase productivity in spinning; Paul's carding machine, patented in 1748, moved into operation in Lancashire about 1760; Hargreave's spinning jenny, radically increasing the amount of yarn that could be spun by a single operator, was introduced in the 1760s, but not patented until 1770; Arkwright's water frame, patented in 1769, permitted at last the production in Britain of a yarn strong enough to serve as warp as well as weft, yielding cotton cloth that could match the Indian product; and Crompton's mule, in which the jenny and the water frame were combined. In 1785, Arkwright's patents were cancelled and the new technology was available to all. As a manufacturer of the period reflected: "From the year 1770 to 1788 a complete change had gradually been effected in the spinning of yarns. That of wool had disappeared altogether and that of linen was also nearly gone: cotton, cotton, cotton was become the almost universal material for employment."[33]

The pressure transmitted itself across the Atlantic to

America. In 1793, a young graduate of Yale, Eli Whitney, went to South Carolina to serve as tutor to the children in a wealthy cotton planter's family. There, by his own account, he heard endless talk "that if a machine could be invented which would clean the cotton with expedition, it would be a great thing both to the Country and to the inventor." He promptly conceived of the cotton gin and produced a model in ten days after discussing it with his employer. He received his patent in 1794; the British industrial revolution was accelerated; the Cotton Kingdom—and slavery—were consolidated in the American South. In 1793, the United States exported less than a half million pounds of cotton; by 1800, 18 million pounds; by 1815, 83 million pounds.

Here is how British imports of raw cotton from all sources increased over the whole sweep of the century.

TABLE 9
RETAINED BRITISH IMPORTS OF RAW COTTON, 1695–1804:
OVERLAPPING TEN-YEAR AVERAGES
(In Millions of Pounds)

1695–1704	1.14	1730–1739	1.72	1765–1774	4.03
1700–1709	1.15	1735–1744	1.79	1770–1779	4.80
1705–1714	1.00	1740–1749	2.06	1775–1784	7.36
1710–1719	1.35	1745–1754	2.83	1780–1789	15.51
1715–1724	1.68	1750–1759	2.81	1785–1794	24.45
1720–1729	1.55	1755–1764	2.57	1790–1799	28.64
1725–1734	1.44	1760–1769	3.53	1795–1804	42.92

SOURCE: Phyllis Deane and W. A. Cole, *British Economic Growth, 1688–1959*, 2d ed. (Cambridge: At the University Press, 1967), Table 15, p. 51.

The slowly rising curve moves explosively from the 1780s, rising by almost nine times between 1770–79 and 1795–1804. This is what a case of increasing returns (and a leading sector) on the production side looks like in real life. On the side of prices, we lack equally conclusive data, which, ideally, should cover various kinds and qualities of yarn and cloth. But we do have the price of a widely used cotton yarn, supplied in Baines' classic history of the industry, which he believed exhibited strikingly "the reduction made in the price of cotton clothing by the effect of machinery:"[34]

TABLE 10

PRICE OF BRITISH COTTON YARN, No. 100, 1786–1832

In the year 1786, yarn No. 100, sold for	38s.
1787	38s.
1788	35s.
1789	34s.
1790	30s.
1791	29s. 9d.
1792	16s. 1d.
1793	15s. 1d.
1794	15s. 1d.
1795 spun from Bourbon cotton	19s.
1796 Ditto	19s.
1797	19s.
1798 from Sea Island cotton	9s. 10d.
1799	10s. 11d.
1800	9s. 5d.
1801	8s. 9d.
1802	8s. 4d.
1803	8s. 4d.
1804	7s. 10d.
1805	7s. 10d.
1806	7s. 2d.
1807	6s. 9d.
After many fluctuations, in	
1829 it sold for	3s. 2d.
1832	2s. 11d.

SOURCE: Edward Baines, *History of the Cotton Manufacture* (London, 1835), p. 357.

The decline, even during the years of wartime inflation down to 1815, is striking, for money wages and fuel costs were rising. On the other hand the cotton gin was so effective that, almost alone, raw cotton did not rise in price during the inflation of the Revolutionary and Napoleonic Wars (see Table 11), and the increased availability of Sea Island cotton produced the sharp drop from 1798 shown in Table 10.

The exceptions to the general pattern are important: bar iron actually declined in price; the rise in the pig iron price is relatively modest as compared to most other commodities. The behavior of the iron price reflects a second, concurrent case of increasing returns, Henry Cort's process of puddling and rolling wrought iron, which took hold in the 1780s, after a long prior history of inventive experiment and incremental improvement in the pig iron branch of the trade.

In iron, Britain had two problems to solve: how to substitute coal for increasingly expensive charcoal in making pig iron, and how to find a process for making wrought iron (and steel) that would permit the exploitation of inferior English ores and free the processing branch of the industry from dependence on Sweden, Russia, and, after 1776, the United States.

In the manufacture of pig iron, the first patent for the use of coal was granted as early as 1589, but with no apparent commercial application. Abraham Darby, whose patent was taken out in 1707, experimented for some time before producing in the 1720s a thin-walled casting which found a commercial market, despite the lower price of pig iron produced with charcoal.[35] In the early 1750s, a rise in the relative cost of producing charcoal pig iron (due mainly to fuel costs) resulted in a rapid shift to coke as fuel. Around 1750, 5 percent of pig iron was produced with coke; in 1780, about 70 percent. But, due to the high silicon content, the

TABLE 11
SELECTED BRITISH PRICES, 1792 AND 1814

	Raw Cotton (excluding duty) (d. per lb.)	South Down Wool (d. per lb.)	British-manufactured Copper (d. per lb.)	British Leather Butts (d. per lb.)	Wheat (s. per quarter)	British Bar Iron (£s per ton)	British Pig Iron (£s per ton)
1792	27.1	14.4	105.0	19.0	41.2	16.1	64.0
1814	27.5	24.8	155.0	26.3	73.9	14.9	80.0

SOURCE: A. D. Gayer et al., *Growth and Fluctuation of the British Economy, 1790–1850* (Oxford: Clarendon Press, 1953), supplement, *British Basic Statistical Data*, part 3, III (unpublished but available on microfilm at University Microfilms, Ann Arbor, Michigan).

cost of purifying coke-produced pig iron in the manufacture of wrought iron remained high. This meant that more pig iron and more coke had to be used to produce a unit of bar iron, the cost differential being perhaps thirty percent.

Cort's puddling and rolling technique not only solved this cost problem, but permitted coal to be used throughout the production process and unified the operations of puddling, hammering, and rolling the metal. This was done by reheating the pig iron with coke until it formed a paste, stirring it with iron rods until the impurities were burnt away, and passing it between iron rollers which pressed out the remaining dross. Cort's process led to a rapid concentration of a hitherto scattered industry as well as to an enlargement of the units of production.

The effect of this breakthrough on British iron output was almost as dramatic as that in cotton textiles.

Arkwright's and Crompton's inventions lent themselves to steam power; and, as Edward Baines observed, progress in cotton "would soon have found a check upon its further extension, if a power more efficient than water had not been discovered to move the machinery. The building of mills in Lancashire must have ceased, when all the available fall of the streams had been appropriated."[36] Cort's invention virtually required steam power, which was already in use in the iron industry. Watt's engine—which reduced fuel expenditures to perhaps half their previous level—is thus an integral part of the first phase of the industrial revolution, quite aside from its long-term implications.

The concept of a steam engine has a long history, but in the course of the seventeenth century its possibilities were increasingly explored in England and on the Continent, including, especially, by Denis Papin, a French Huguenot, who worked with both Christian Huygens and Robert Boyle, taught at Marburg, and was a member of the Royal Society of London. But it was Thomas Savery who first

TABLE 12

APPROXIMATE BRITISH PIG IRON OUTPUT, SELECTED YEARS,
1700–1818

(In Thousands of Tons)

1625–35	26
1700	15
1720s	20–25
1750	28
1760	35
1775	44
1780	54
1785	62
1788	70
1790	87
1791	90
1796	125
1802	170
1806	250
1818	325

SOURCES: For 1625–35 and the 1720s, Phyllis Deane, *The First Industrial Revolution* (Cambridge: At the University Press, 1965), pp. 103–4; for the years between 1750 and 1791, Charles K. Hyde, "The Adoption of Coke Smelting by the British Iron Industry, 1709–1790" (Mimeographed paper delivered at the Conference on the "New" Economic History of Britain, Cambridge, 1972); for the years between 1796 and 1818, Arthur D. Gayer et al., "The Growth and Fluctuation of the British Economy, 1790–1850," Supplement, *British Basic Statistical Data*, Part One, Table 16 (unpublished but available on microfilm at University Microfilms, Ann Arbor, Michigan).

built a more or less workable engine to lift water from the deep galleries of the copper mines in his native Cornwall. He patented his engine in 1698 and presented a model to William III at Hampton Court, described it to the Royal Society in 1699, and explained it in a pamphlet published in 1707, engagingly entitled *The Miner's Friend*. His engine was inefficient and somewhat given to explosion. Initially in collaboration with Savery, Newcomen patented a more serviceable engine in 1705 which, with various modifications (including a safety valve), served in the mines and a good many other functions until Watt's more efficient engine emerged in the 1760s. (It was first patented in 1769.) While repairing a working model of a Newcomen engine in 1763, Watt defined the two key weaknesses that yielded an excessive expenditure of fuel: after each piston stroke, the temperature had to be raised within its cylinder; and the condensation of steam was incomplete, since the cylinder was insufficiently cooled by the water poured on it. Here is how Watt described the principle of the separate condenser at which he arrived in 1765: "To avoid useless condensation, the vessel in which the steam acted on the piston ought always to be as hot as the steam itself. . . . To obtain a proper degree of exhaustion, the steam must be condensed in a separate vessel, which might be cooled to as low a degree as was necessary without affecting the cylinder."[37] In building his engine, Watt was supported through much travail by two major entrepreneurial figures, John Roebuck and later Mathew Boulton. Parliament extended his patent in 1775 for twenty-five years, despite Burke's eloquent protest. With this private and public innovative support, and further refinements of the machine, it was carefully nursed into a wide variety of applications, starting in about 1775 from Watt and Boulton's base in the latter's Soho works in Birmingham. It was used first in pumping water, then in blast furnaces and other metal works, and, finally, in textile, flour and malt mills, the pottery industry, and sugar refineries. One of its early applications was to pump water from the Seine to supply the Chaillot district in Paris. Some 500 of Watt's engines were at work by 1800, when his patent ended, and, after many financial vicissitudes, Boulton's faith was vindicated, Watt was a rich man, and modern industry had acquired its most essential long-term foundation. The short-run effects of this radical reduction in the cost of power and its almost complete locational mobility had revolutionary consequences over a wide range of industrial processes.

What we see, then, in eighteenth-century Britain, in cotton textiles, iron, and steam engine—and in agriculture, chemistry, and transport as well—is both a sustained inventive response to profit possibilities and a corps of entrepreneurs willing to take the risks of innovation. In the case of Boulton and Watt, we observe the inherent ambiguity in a dynamic setting of too rigid a separation of demand and supply. Without Boulton's capital, patience, tact and imagination, Watt's invention might well have been aborted. The entrepreneur's demand is critical to the inventor's supply. All in all, the scale of the response and the size of the corps of innovating entrepreneurs, interacting in complex ways, proved sufficient, after protracted effort, to set in motion the leading sectors of the British takeoff.

VI

The scientific revolution, as we have seen, was a European and not a uniquely British phenomenon, and so was its popularization, in which Voltaire and other continental figures played an active part. The commercial revolution profoundly affected all of Western Europe and its effects penetrated beyond to the East. Vigorous mercantilist governments throughout Europe moved to build national markets and implant and protect the best technologies available. Habakkuk can conclude: "There were a number of industrial areas in Europe which, around the middle of the eighteenth century, did not differ very widely in the state of their techniques or in the nature of their organization: Saxony, Silesia, the mining areas of Germany, the metallurgical and metal-processing centres of the Urals, the silk industry at Lyons, textile production in Barcelona."[38]

Why did the pace of British invention accelerate around

1760 and the scale of innovation in the 1780s in a way not matched on the Continent? The question can be asked of a number of European nations, but it is most relevant to France, both at the time and in retrospect judged to be the most likely industrial competitor to Britain.

Table 13 sets out some basic economic data on the two countries in the eighteenth century.

TABLE 13

FRANCE AND GREAT BRITAIN IN THE EIGHTEENTH CENTURY: BASIC ECONOMIC DATA

	France			Britain		
	1700	1780	1800	1700	1780	1800
Population[a] (in millions)	19.25	25.6	27.4	6.9	9.0	10.8
Urban Population[b] (in millions)	3.3	5.7	6.4	1.2	2.2	3.2
Foreign Trade[c] (in £ millions)	9	22	31	13	23	67
Iron Production[d] (in 000 tons)	22	135	—[g]	15	60	190
Cotton Consumption[e] (in million lbs),	.5	11	—[g]	1.1	7.4	42.9
Agriculture Production[f] (1700 = 100)	100	155	177	100	126	143
Industrial Production[f] (1700 = 100)	100	454	700	100	197	387
Total Production[f] (1700 = 100)	100	169	202	100	167	251
Income Per Capita[f] (1700 = 100)	100	127	142	100	129	160

NOTES AND SOURCES:
a. French population figures are from J.-C. Toutain, "La Population de la France de 1700 à 1959," *Cahiers de l'Institut de Science Économique Appliquée*, suppl. no.

133 (Paris: January 1963), p. 16. The 1780 figure is the estimate for 1776; the 1800 figure, for 1801. The British figures, covering England, Wales and Scotland, are from Phyllis Deane and W. A. Cole, *British Economic Growth, 1688–1959*, 2d. ed. (Cambridge: At the University Press, 1967), p. 6, for the years 1701, 1781, and 1801, respectively; the figure for Scotland's population in 1781 taken, by extrapolation, as 1.44 million.

b. French urban population (in concentrations over 2,000) is from Toutain, "La population," p. 54, with the 1780 figure roughly extrapolated backward from the rate of increase between 1791 and 1796. The British data are from percentages for population in concentrations over 5,000, estimated by Deane and Cole, *British Economic Growth*, p. 7, but corrected to include those in concentrations between 2,000 and 5,000. The problem of correction, however, is not easy. The Deane and Cole estimate of, say, 25 percent in concentrations above 5,000 in Great Britain in 1801 compares with Williams' estimate of 40 percent in concentrations above 2,000 for England and Wales in that year. If the figures for Scotland were comparable in structure to those for England and Wales, this suggests 15 percent of the population of Great Britain living in units between 2,000 and 5,000. On the other hand, Williams estimates 15 percent living in units between 2,000 and 20,000 in 1801. This seems more nearly correct. French data, from Le Duc de Boulainvilliers, *État de France*, (London, 1752), quoted in W. Bowden et al., *An Economic History of Europe Since 1750* (New York: American Book, 1937), p. 6, suggest that, in the late seventeenth century, the figure over the range of 2–5,000 was about 5 percent, and it did not change much during the eighteenth century. Therefore, I have added 5 percent (rather than 15 percent) to the Deane and Cole proportions, to arrive at the total urban population figures.

c. The French figure for 1700 is Arnould's average for 1716–20, from E. Levasseur, *Histoire du Commerce de la France, Première Partie: Avant 1789* (Paris: Librairie Nouvelle de Droit et de Jurisprudence, 1911), p. 512, converted at 25 livres tournois per English pound. It is somewhat higher than Mulhall's estimate for 1720 (£7 billion). Mulhall's figures, *The Dictionary of Statistics* (London: George Routledge and Sons, 1892), p. 128, are used for 1780 and 1800. British data are from Elizabeth B. Schumpeter, *English Overseas Trade Statistics, 1679–1808* (Oxford: Clarendon Press, 1960), pp. 15–16, and are consistent with Mulhall's figures.

d. The British figure for 1700 is extrapolated backward from the 1720 estimate of 17,350 tons (Deane and Cole, *Economic Growth*, p. 22, including note 3), although there are estimates as high as 25,000 tons for 1720. Mulhall's figure for British iron production in 1700 is as low as 12,000 tons (*Dictionary*, p. 332). The French figure for 1700 and the British figure for 1800 are from Mulhall, the latter being roughly consistent with the reasonably firm estimate for 1806 of 250,000 tons, given the extraordinarily high rate of expansion in the iron industry at this time. The French and British iron production figures for 1780 are the estimates for the 1780s ("on the eve of the Revolution") of François Crouzet, "England and France in the Eighteenth Century: A Comparative Analysis of Two Economic Growths," J. Sondheimer, trans., in R. M. Hartwell, ed., *The Causes of the Industrial Revolution in England* (London: Methuen, 1967), pp. 151–2. Pierre Léon in "L'industrialisation en France en tant que facteur de croissance économique, du début du XVIIIe siècle à nos jours," in *Congress et Colloques I* (Contributions to the First International Conference of Economic History, Stockholm, August 1960) (Paris and the Hague, 1960), pp. 177–8 and 198. His estimates suggest a figure of about 60,000 tons in 1789, rising sharply over 100,000 tons by 1800, under the impact of wartime requirements. Mulhall's figure for 1800 (60,000 tons) is much lower than Léon's and, by implication, Crouzet's. Mulhall's figure for Britain in 1790 (68,000 tons) is comparable to Crouzet's.

e. The British figures for retained cotton imports are averages for the years 1700–09, 1775–84, and 1795–1804, from Deane and Cole, *Economic Growth*, p. 51. The French figure for 1780 is for the year 1786, from Crouzet, "England and France," p. 151. The British figure for that year is 19.1 million pounds, the cotton industry being already in a rapid stage of acceleration not shared by France. The French estimate for 1700 is Mulhall's figure for 1688, *Dictionary*, p. 160, assuming no expansion in this troubled period in French economic history.

f. For France, Jan Marczewski's calculations, in "Some Aspects of the Economic Growth of France, 1660–1958," *Economic Development and Cultural Change* 9 (April 1961), 375–76, are converted to index numbers, with 1700 = 100, so as to be roughly comparable with the calculations of Deane and Cole, *Economic Growth*, p. 78. Marczewski (p. 376) uses two methods for calculating gross physical product: one assumes the 1905–13 price relation of agricultural and industrial goods; the other assumes a moving relationship weighted by the average values added at current prices of the two sectors for each pair of decades. The former data are used in Table 13. The latter method yields higher growth rates as follows: for total production, 100, 260, 341; for per capita production, 100, 196, 239. I would not attempt to arbitrate this large discrepancy except to note that the severe depression around the turn of the century in the French economy makes the increase down to the 1780s more credible than may at first appear, but my overall impression is that Marczewski's first method somewhat damps, his second method somewhat exaggerates overall French growth in the eighteenth century. French growth is, however, in any case slightly exaggerated, since 1780 is the index number for 1781–90 and 1800 is the index number for 1803–12. As noted earlier (43, ch. 2), Marczewski's calculations of the increase in agricultural production (derived from Toutain) are controversial and widely judged to show an excessive increase.

g. The French economy deteriorated during the 1790s and did not revive until the first decade of the new century. The 1800 figures are almost certainly below the peak levels attained before 1793.

These data suggest the following:

- France had the larger population, but both populations were rising, the British at a faster rate, particularly after midcentury.
- Both nations were becoming more urban, the British more rapidly, but the French urban population remained twice as large, or more.
- French foreign trade rose more rapidly than Britain's

until 1780, achieving a similar overall level, although its initial level was abnormally depressed and the proportion of trade to the population (and national income) was markedly less.

- Until 1780, French iron production was greater than Britain's.
- Until the post-1783 British surge, the increased consumption of cotton in France roughly kept pace with that in Britain. It should be noted that although the strictly comparable figure to the French "1780" level (11 million pounds in 1786) is 19.1 million, this was after Britain's takeoff had begun.
- The overall production indexes, which should be used with caution, underline the general import of the table and confirm the story so well elucidated by François Crouzet.[39] Despite England's civil war in the seventeenth century, and despite the exertions of Colbert, his predecessors and successors, Britain gained on larger France, which suffered a severe economic setback starting in the 1690's. From the 1720s until 1783, France, from a depressed base, gained relatively on Britain. Both moved forward thereafter, Britain with greater momentum, but the period of revolution and war set back France severely.

As for income per capita, Britain, by all accounts, impressions, and computations, was somewhat richer than France, an outcome to be expected given its larger proportionate urban population. Still more urban Holland led the pack when Gregory King made his computations of income per capita for 1688 at £8 1s. 4d.; England, £7 18s.; France £6 3s.[40] On this estimate, the English-French differential is about 28 percent. Nearly a century later, Adam Smith's ranking was the same.

Starting from this point, explanations of the fact that the

first takeoff occurred in Britain rather than France often emphasize the higher level of demand, notably for cotton textiles, an item of mass consumption. To this argument is sometimes added an impression, since adequate data do not exist, that income distribution in Britain was more even, less polarized between rich landowners and an urban middle class on the one hand, poor peasants and an urban proletariat on the other. Agnosticism is justified here, for there was an ample number of very rich folk indeed in eighteenth-century Britain. Occasionally, the argument is reinforced by reference to population movements: English real wages rose in the early decades of the eighteenth century, when grain was in surplus and population growing slowly, but this relative prosperity led to the population increase in the second half of the century, which is counted a positive factor in demand despite the pressure of rising prices on real wages.

A more sophisticated version of the demand argument is presented in Deane and Cole's *British Economic Growth*.[41] They argue that the relative rise in British agricultural prices in the second half of the eighteenth century (caused in part by population increase) yielded an increase in agricultural incomes that stimulated domestic industrial growth, despite pressure on urban real wages; the consequent rise in British imports yielded also an increase of incomes in certain key British markets that stimulated British exports, an acceleration strengthened by an unfavorable shift in the British net barter as well as gross barter terms of trade. As *British Economic Growth* concludes: "There appears . . . to be a strong prima-facie case for the view that the growth of the home market for industrial goods was closely bound up with the fortunes of the agricultural community, in much the same way as the growth of the export trade depended on the prosperity of the primary producers overseas."[42]

There is reason to question this hypothesis, even in its own terms. While certain long period forces are assumed to have been at work raising the level of British domestic demand (notably, population increase), the parts of the world economy judged most relevant to British imports are treated in terms of short period income effects stemming from the rise in British outlays for imports, related, in turn, to the internal British terms of trade. In fact, we know that life in the North American colonies, the West Indies, and Ireland, as well as in most of the European continent, had a dynamic of its own, including forces making for long-term increase in population and income. When postwar recoveries are examined year by year, it becomes clear that the expansion in British exports did not await, as the Deane and Cole hypothesis would suggest, a prior rise in British imports to supply the overseas incomes required to purchase British goods. Exports promptly rebounded to new high levels, reflecting underlying forces for expansion steadily at work, released by the coming of peace.

The argument in terms of the overall level of demand, then, is an unpersuasive explanation for the technological breakthroughs that define the industrial revolution because, as we have seen, the eighteenth century was, by and large, a period of endemic economic expansion from the North American colonies east through Europe to China. Certainly it was a remarkable period of expansion in France from the 1720s to the 1780s. If one wishes to sharpen the argument with a marginal case, how does one explain the disproportionate role of Scotsmen as inventors and innovators in a country where, as Arthur Young noted, the level of income per capita was less than in France?

We turn, therefore, to the supply side of the equation—the interplay between science, invention, and innovation leading to the radically shifted, downward sloping supply curves of the case of increasing returns. It is somewhere in this interlocked network that British superiority over the French is mainly to be found, but it certainly does not lie in the superiority of British science. Both at the time and in retrospect, French science in the eighteenth century was judged at least equal, and probably superior, to that evolving in Britain, and, in its quality (not quantity), the French equalled or surpassed the British in invention as well. As Peter Mathias concludes:

> The French record of scientific growth and invention in the eighteenth century was a formidable one. Berthollet first revealed to the world the bleaching possibilities of chlorine, first isolated as a gas in 1774 by a Swedish chemist Scheele, which was followed by energetic efforts to promote its manufacture in France. A similar sequence followed with Leblanc making soda from salt and sulphuric acid. Very sophisticated work was done in the production of dyestuffs in France; with varnishes, enamels, and many other techniques and materials. Yet the difference in the rate of industrial growth based on these advances in chemistry between France and Britain in the period 1780 to 1850 was remarkable. Almost all the theoretical work on structures, stresses, and the mechanics of design in civil engineering was French. This did not appear to have much relationship to the speed of development, or even innovations in these fields, as far as economic progress was concerned. The same was true of power engineering and hydrodynamics.[43]

But, as we have seen, the key to successful invention is a sustained process, involving many minds and hands, gradually translating a creative insight into a workable and economically profitable instrument. In commenting on the typical vicissitudes of the inventor, a seventeenth century English writer captured well the painful, stubborn effort required:

> Now not one [invention] of a hundred outlives this torture, and those that do are at length so changed by the various contrivances of others, that not any one man can pretend to the invention of the whole, nor well agree about their respective shares in the parts. And

moreover this commonly is so long a-doing, that the poor inventor is either dead, or disabled by the debts contracted to pursue his design; and withal railed upon as a projector, or worse, by those who joyned their money in partnership with his wit; so as the said inventor and his pretences are wholly lost and vanisht.[44]

Here was one major advantage of the British over the French: out of a smaller population (and a smaller urban population), Britain raised in the eighteenth century larger battalions to undertake the slow, protracted task of refining inventions and bringing them to fruition. Echoing Defoe's dictum on French superiority as inventors, a Swiss calico printer wrote in 1766: "Everyone knows this nation [Britain] whose industry and stubborn patience in overcoming every kind of obstacle are beyond all imagination. They cannot boast of many inventions, but only of having perfected the inventions of others; whence comes the proverb that for a thing to be perfect it must be invented in France and worked out in England."[45]

Although patent data reflect only a limited part of the invention process, this difference in the scale of inventive effort in the two countries during the eighteenth century emerges from the data in Table 14.

These data justify only the most obvious and large conclusions. In both countries, the average annual rate of patents granted and inventions approved rose in the second half of the eighteenth century, but the French increase is more modest than the British. The average annual rate for France increased from about six to twenty-two between the first decade and the years 1788–92; the equivalent British increase in annual rate was from two to sixty-three. Even before the British takeoff began after 1783, there is a fifteen-fold increase between the first decade of the century and the 1770s. Put another way, Britain, starting the century with an invention rate a third that of France, emerged in the latter part of the century with a rate about three times

TABLE 14
ANNUAL AVERAGE PATENTS GRANTED AND INVENTIONS APPROVED:
GREAT BRITAIN AND FRANCE IN THE EIGHTEENTH CENTURY

	Great Britain	France	Great Britain for Comparable Years
1702–11	2	6	—
1712–21	5	7	—
1722–31	10	10	—
1732–41	5	6	—
1742–51	9	4	—
1752–61	10	—	—
1762–71	23	(1760–69 7	21)
1772–81	31	(1770–71 10	25)
1782–91	54	(1789–92 22	63)
1792–1801	72	(1796–98 8	69)

SOURCE: British data, B. R. Mitchell, *Dictionary*, p. 268; French data, Shelby T. McCloy, *French Inventions of the Eighteenth Century* (Lexington, Ky: University of Kentucky Press, 1952), pp. 192–3.
NOTE: McCloy drew his figures (unfortunately incomplete for the second half of the century) from the account of inventions approved by the Academy of Sciences, down to 1754, edited by Gallon; down to 1773, from the *Mémoires* of the Academy of Sciences and from the records of the Institute of France, after its organization in 1794. He notes that there are discrepancies between Gallon's figures and the later *Mémoires*, but the discrepancies are not great. The figures for 1796–8 are obviously damped by the effects of war and political instability. Those for 1789–92 better represent the lift in French inventiveness (and industrial activity) in the prewar years; and they represent inventions from Paris alone (McCloy, p. 193 n.). McCloy concludes (p. 194): "Not only did the second half of the century see a larger number of inventions than the first half, but in this latter period there were many more inventions of real significance." McCloy demonstrates well the effect of wars in the first half of the eighteenth century in damping the number of inventions approved, a phenomenon to be noted also in the British patent data.

higher, and, under the compulsions of its takeoff, it then further widened the gap.

We turn now to the question of entrepreneurship and innovation. Was the operational demand for inventions weaker in France than in Britain? Was the failure of inventions to come forward as rapidly in France, roughly measured in Table 14, the result of lesser entrepreneurial initiative?

So far as the public authorities are concerned, the French were, almost certainly, more active than the British.[46] The French inventor was generally granted monopolistic rights of exploitation for fifteen years and often a pension or grant ranging from a few hundred livres to the 15,000 livres given Réamur, the great entomologist, who developed important insights for the manufacture of paper, steel, and porcelain, in addition to inventing a thermometer. The *intendants* as well as the authorities in Paris were sometimes active in encouraging inventions. The intensity of government interest—and the pace of invention—picked up in the second half of the century as the ferment in Britain was sensed. The French authorities actively sought British inventions and experts, particularly in textiles, from about 1760, and a large number of men and machines crossed the channel, in part due to the work of the Jacobite refugee turned French agent, John Holker. In his brief period of national authority, Turgot (1774–76) was particularly active in offering prizes and subsidies to encourage invention, and his successors maintained his policy over the next quarter-century. In these years, private societies also emerged in many parts of France, the title of the first, in 1776, catching well, if at some length, their general intent: "The Free Society of Emulation for the Encouragement of Inventions which Tend to Perfect the Application of the Arts and Trades in Imitation of that of London." But it is on the side of private entrepreneurship that the French weakness vis-à-vis Britain was critical. As McCloy concludes: "Private business of eighteenth-century France thus was more to blame than the government for failure to pursue invention."[47] French entrepreneurs could mobilize capital for large and profitable ventures, but they did not exhibit an innovating zeal on the British scale.

Turning to particular key sectors, it can be—and has been[48]—argued that the economic pressure to innovate was less in France than in Britain. On this view, French and British entrepreneurs were equally efficient profit maximizers, but the British businessman faced problems and opportunities that more urgently required the introduction of new technologies.

With respect to iron, the French certainly had more ample supplies of timber for charcoal and were less well endowed with coal. The impulse to conserve the one and exploit the other was certainly less. With respect to the steam engine, of which the Frenchman Denis Papin can claim to be the inventor, France faced no urgent problem in pumping water out of the mines equivalent to that which drove on Savery and Newcomen, and those who put the latter's machine promptly to work. What Papin had in mind was a steamboat, which, indeed, the French successfully pioneered in 1783. But in Britain the demand for a pumping engine was more compelling and less visionary. Even in agriculture it can be argued the French pressure for technological change was less urgent. Its population increase and pace of urbanization was at a slower rate than Britain's. Moreover, the substantial increase in agricultural output achieved made France more self-sufficient in the second half of the century than Britain, and gave her a distribution system that largely lifted from the country the risk of famine that had haunted the government in the late seventeenth and early eighteenth centuries. As Arthur Young repeatedly noted, the roads of eighteenth-century France, product of public entrepreneurship, were far superior to those of Britain.

It is in Britain's precocious use of coal as an industrial

fuel that this hypothesis acquires its greatest weight. This strand in the story was first developed, of course, by John Nef, who argued that between 1540 and 1640 Britain experienced an expansion in manufactures, based on industrial uses of coal, that provided the basis for its eighteenth-century technological lead over France. Subsequent analysis had deflated considerably Nef's image of this prior industrial revolution, but, in a thoughtful inaugural lecture, J. R. Harris has returned to Nef's theme, with a somewhat different emphasis and timing.[49] First, Harris holds that there was no distinctive break in the continuity of coal-related industrial development around 1640. Second, he defines the critical process as the emergence of a coal-fuel technology in industry with many distinctive facets, involving furnaces and boilers, crucibles, and a subtle knowledge of types of coal. Moreover, the introduction of coal as a fuel in other industries required creative adaptations, often small but significant. It is this whole complex of changes, slowly and cumulatively evolved, that lifted Britain from a position of dependence on superior continental technology to a position of relative leadership by the beginning of the eighteenth century. Despite their more ample supply of charcoal, French industrialists, often encouraged by the government, sought to acquire British coal-fuel technology during the eighteenth century. But these efforts were unsuccessful or only slowly acquired efficiency, because French manufacturers, foremen, and workers lacked the whole package of skills required to absorb efficiently this technology. They could not be transmitted quickly on a piecemeal basis.

The argument gains force when to it is added the development of a lively and resourceful English hardware industry oriented, in part, to the rapidly expanding demands of the North American colonies. This experience in metalworking clearly helped prepare the way for the surge in machine building required to support the rapid British industrial expansion, late in the eighteenth century.

We are confronted, in the case of British coal and all its implications vis-à-vis France, with a classic dilemma in economic history. Should the relative vitality of German versus French industry in the second half of the nineteenth century be attributed to the location of the Ruhr or to relative deficiencies in French entrepreneurship? Should the late coming of the Russian takeoff be attributed to the dead hand of serfdom and autocratic government or to the fact that no adequate resource basis for Russian industrialization existed until the railroads linked the coal of the Donets basin to the iron of Krivoi Rog? The choice of an answer is complicated because the variables are not wholly independent. If a Ruhr existed on French territory, French entrepreneurship and the industrial structure would have evolved in different ways. If Russian coal and iron lay side by side, it is likely that the government's economic policy would have differed from what it was in, say, the second and third quarters of the nineteenth century, and it is even possible that serfdom would have been liquidated at a more rapid pace.

While accepting the legitimacy of the Nef-Harris strand in the story, I am inclined to give heavy weight to the factors that determined the relative scale of the British inventive and entrepreneurial effort. After all, the emergence of British coal-fuel technology was a creative response to relatively high charcoal prices. It is the responsiveness of British society to the economic challenges and opportunities that emerged in the eighteenth century that, I believe, made the difference.

The point is most clear in the story of cotton textiles. Its ultimate emergence as a rapidly growing leading sector involved elements outside the industry itself, including machine building capacity and the steam engine. But, still, the evolution of the new industry on both sides of the Channel is a critical and identifiable part of the story, and is quite illuminating.

Whatever the differences in income per capita may have been between Britain and France, it is evident that there was a potential mass market in France for cottons, from the latter decades of the seventeenth century forward. That market was absolutely larger than that of Britain and was expanding from the 1720s with the rise of population and incomes. Early in the eighteenth century, Indian calicoes were described as "Fruit défendu, les toiles deviennent la passion de toutes les filles d'Eve françaises."[50] About half the people of France were said to have worn cottons at this time, and the evidence is that the passion did not abate until 1757, when the government finally abandoned its smuggling-ridden inhibitions.

Crouzet argues, however, that despite the rise in British population in the second half of the century, there was a relative shortage of labor in the north of England which constituted an incentive to invent and install laborsaving machinery. His argument is worth full presentation:

> ... up to mid-century the population grew only very slowly. Although it then started growing fast, a number of years had to pass before a large supply of hands was available for the labour market, and by this time demand was again increasing. There was therefore a relative shortage of labour in industrial districts, as is proved by the quite sharp rise in money wages there (not found in the south of England) during the first half of the eighteenth century.
>
> Manufacturers were therefore faced with high and rising labour costs, which was particularly embarrassing in a young industry like cotton, which in practice had to build up its labour force at the expense of the older industries. There must therefore have been great difficulty during the 1750s in meeting the fast-growing demand for cottons, particularly for export to the colonies. But in the 1760s and 1770s, when there was some slackening in demand, the rise in

manufacturing costs was really dangerous. It was now imperative to reduce labour costs and therefore to invent and take up labour-saving machinery. The relative shortage of labour which affected English industry seems therefore to have been one of the most powerful incentives to innovation, not only in the cotton industry but in several others as well.[51]

Aside from the fact that British cotton consumption rose faster in the 1760s and 1770s than in the 1750s (see Table 9), I am skeptical of this explanation for three reasons. First, the most critical problem to be solved in producing cottons in Europe was not economic but technical: how to spin with machines cotton of sufficient quality to serve as weft and supplant linen or other fibers used in the mixed cloths. This was the problem Arkwright finally solved by the method of spinning with rollers on the basis of inventions and experiments reaching back to the 1730s. Second, the record of French inventors in textile machinery and the quite massive encouragement by the French government of both French textile inventions and the introduction of British technology does not suggest a judgment that abundant labor in France made such innovations unprofitable. It must be borne in mind that the eighteenth-century history of the French cotton industry is also dynamic. As Wadsworth and Mann conclude: "By 1760 France thus had the beginnings, at least, of a far more complete 'factory' system than anything which had appeared in the English cotton manufacture. She could also command a better and slightly cheaper supply of raw materials [from the French West Indies] and had access to markets of the same kind as those open to English manufactures."[52] And after 1760 intensive but not wholly effective efforts were underway to acquire and apply the rapidly emerging new British technology. Third, the experience of eighteenth-century Britain, as it unfolded, tended to confirm John Wyatt's calculations of 1736 that the introduction of machinery would increase

rather than decrease employment in the cotton industry.[53]
As the extraordinary growth of Manchester and other
textile centers suggests, the labor supply was found. The
impression one gains is that the inventors and entrepreneurs in Britain were striving for a way to solve
technical problems that would permit an increase in output
of cotton cloth vastly greater than was conceivable with
even an expanded labor supply using current technology.

As Baines said: "The cotton manufacture, though rapidly
increasing, could never have received such an extension as
to become of great national importance, without the discovery of some method for producing a greater quantity
and better quality of yarn with the same labour."[54] The
spinning of yarn was the critical bottleneck, heightened by
the application to cotton weaving of John Kay's flying
shuttle in about 1760. This asymmetry, in the face of a
rapidly expanding demand, did pose the danger that the
price of yarn would rise extravagantly and make "the goods
too costly in comparison with other manufactures."[55] The
objective of inventors and cotton innovators, however, was
not to drive down wages within the existing system but to
change the system. The popular pressure the manufacturers
felt when machines were introduced—or in times of business depression—did not derive from fear of lower wages
but from fear of or from the fact of unemployment.

But Crouzet's argument and that developed here would
agree that the critical difference between Britain and
France in the eighteenth century did not lie on the side of
income levels or demand. We agree that what distinguished
Britain from France, as the eighteenth century wore on,
was the greater scale of the inventive effort that went into
the breaking of crucial technical bottlenecks, and the
greater scale of the entrepreneurial corps that introduced
them as the century moved towards its close. And given the
role of vigorous eighteenth-century entrepreneurs in stimu-

lating inventions, large and small, the two processes were not wholly independent. This difference in scale appears greater than can be accounted for by differences in income per capita, the size of urban populations, or the quality of scientific or inventive achievement. Crouzet is inclined to explain the difference in terms of the sharper challenges confronted by the British, challenges which more urgently required technical innovation than in France. I am inclined to seek the answer in another direction.

VII

Invention and innovation at any period of time are marginal activities in a society. They engage small numbers of human beings relative to the population as a whole. Life goes on in familiar ways, with familiar technologies, while the creative few dream their dreams and struggle with their frustrations in odd workshops and the occasional experimental plant. Only looking backward, after innovation has led on to large new sectors in the economy, are the achievements of the inventors and innovators generally understood, appreciated, and accorded a grand place in history. For example, until the 1780s, and even somewhat beyond, wool manufacture—not cotton or iron—was the giant among British industries.

Students of British invention and innovation in the eighteenth century have long noted the disproportionate role in the germinal inventive and innovational activities of the English Nonconformists and Scottish Presbyterians. In a famous passage, Ashton puts the case as follows:

> Inventors, contrivers, industrialists, and entrepreneurs—it is not easy to distinguish one from another at a period of rapid change—came from every social class and from all parts of the country ... [But] it has often been observed that the growth of industry was connected historically with the rise of groups which dissented from

the Church by law established in England. In the seventeenth century the congregation of Puritans gathered about Richard Baxter at Kidderminster included the Foleys, the Crowleys, and the Hanburys, who were to set up great establishments in places as far afield as Staffordshire, Durham, and South Wales. In the following century members of the Society of Friends played a prominent part in the development of corn-milling, brewing, pharmacy, and banking; and the Quaker families of the Darbys, Reynolds, Lloyds, and Huntsmans came to direct the destinies of the iron and steel industries at a period of rapid change. There were Baptists, like Thomas Newcomen, and Presbyterians, like James Watt, in engineering; Independents, like John Roebuck and Joseph Dawson, alongside the Quakers, in iron-smelting; and Unitarians, including the M'Connels and the Gregs, in cotton spinning. In cotton, moreover, the greatest inventor, Samuel Crompton, was a disciple of Emmanuel Swedenborg—who himself, it may be recalled, was an authority on metals and the technique of mines. Other industrialists, among whom were the Guests of South Wales, drew strength from the teaching of John Wesley. . . . The greatest inventor of the age, James Watt, came from Scotland, as also did seven of his eight assistants in the business of erecting engines. Sir John Sinclair, Thomas Telford, John Macadam, David Mushet and James Beaumont Neilson brought their Scottish vigour of mind and character to English agriculture, transport, and iron-making. Highlanders and Lowlanders, alike, tramped to the Lancashire cotton area, many of them pausing at the little village of Chowbent, where a fellow-countryman named Cannan directed them to centres which offered scope for their several abilities. Among those who took the southern road to fortune in textiles were James McGuffog, James M'Connel, John Kennedy, George and Adam Murray and—bearers of names that are honoured today, not only in Lancashire—John Gladstone and Henry Bannerman. These and other immigrants were not illiterate peasants. Some were sons of the manse, and even those of humbler station had been given at least the rudiments of a sound education in the village or burgh school of their native place.[56]

With respect to innovation, an interesting effort has been made to give Ashton's judgment rough statistical measurement.[57] Everett Hagen tracked down the religious affiliation or inclination of seventy-one of the ninety-two men listed by Ashton as entrepreneurs in manufacturing and transport. The Scots constituted 24 percent of the entrepreneurs, a number more than one half greater than their proportion to the total population, whereas English Nonconformists, who constituted 7 percent of the population of England and Wales, contributed 41 percent of the English and Welsh entrepreneurs mentioned by Ashton. This is a formidable disproportion. Hagen also notes that certain of the Anglican entrepreneurs (notably Boulton) were religious deviants, drawn by Nonconformist doctrines.

It is altogether likely that an analysis of the inventors would yield a similar disproportionate result.

Here we confront a part of the story that transcends mercantilism, and the commercial and scientific revolutions. Behind the emergence of the Nonconformists in the British economy is the whole tale of Europe's offshore island making its way to self-conscious nationhood in the face of the successive challenges of Rome and Spain, Netherlands and France, undergoing its critical and bloody domestic confrontation—and reconciliation—by 1688, a process that affected the fundamentals of political, social, and religious life. In the late seventeenth century one can observe on both sides of the Atlantic the Puritan ardor shifting from theology to the marketplace, and "the mediatorial spirit" (to use H. A. L. Fisher's phrase), built into the Glorious Revolution, makes possible the union with Scotland in 1707.

There is a considerable literature that sought to find in the somewhat paradoxical theology of the Protestant Reformation the clue to the Nonconformists' ardent pursuit of economic ends. But William Petty early perceived what subsequent economic history would confirm about the role of creative minorities in traditional societies—from English Nonconformists to Japanese samurai. Blocked in routes to the top, but not denied access to education and money, they found modernizing activities congenial. In a passage entitled "The Trade of any Country is chiefly managed by the Heterodox party," he said this:

> . . . it is to be observed . . . that Trade is most vigorously carried on, in every State and Government, by the Heterodox part of the same, and such as profess Opinions different from what are publickly established: (that is to say) in *India* where the *Mahometan* Religion is Authorized, there the *Banians* are the most considerable Merchants. In the *Turkish* Empire the *Jews*, and Christians. At *Venice, Naples, Legorn, Genoua*, and *Lisbone, Jews*, and Non-Papist Merchant-Strangers . . . even in *France* it self, the *Hugonots* are proportionably far the greatest Traders; Nor is it to be denied but that in *Ireland*, where the said *Roman* Religion is not Authorized, there the Professors thereof have a great part of the Trade. From whence it follows that Trade is not fixt to any Species of Religion as such; but rather as before hath been said to the Heterodox part of the whole, the truth whereof appears also in all the particular Towns of Greatest Trade in *England*.[58]

Ashton gives great weight in his analysis of the disproportionate role of the Nonconformists in the eighteenth century to the quality of education in Scotland and in the Nonconformist academies. But surely, the kind and quality of education these groups designed for their young related to their view of education as a path to status denied by more conventional routes, and to the possibility of imparting an education geared more closely than, say, Oxford or Cambridge, to the emerging problems of the active world, outside Church and State, where they expected their children to make their way.

Thus the problem of religion in early modern history and all that lay behind Britain's Revolution of 1688 (and the French revocation of the Edict of Nantes in 1685) become directly relevant to the locus of the first industrial revolution. In the creative processes of invention and innovation—where the numbers of men engaged was inherently small, but where numbers mattered greatly—Britain had,

188 HOW IT ALL BEGAN

for noneconomic reasons, stumbled upon a solution to its religious problem and to the problem of Scotland that substantially strengthened its hand in the race to the takeoff barrier. Colbert had been conscious of the economic importance of the heterodox groups in French society, and he protected them. Louis XIV decided for uniformity. It was a double loss for France in an inherently competitive age, the Huguenots strengthened the creative capacity of Britain, Holland, and Germany, and their departure weakened France at a critical period in what proved to be the critical dimension of its race with Britain.

French society did not wholly frustrate its potential inventors and innovators. Despite the image of royal absolutism and Versailles, eighteenth-century France was also a society on the move, with considerable opportunities for vertical mobility. The largest group of French inventors, for example, had been trained through apprenticeship, received some instruction in the sciences, were drawn to the large cities from towns, villages and rural districts, and were from the middle class.[59] And without a cadre of vigorous entrepreneurs, French production would not have risen as it did from the 1720s. But the British Nonconformists contributed a scale and a thrust to the generation and application of new technology that larger France could not match. They were, in my view, the critical margin France denied herself in 1685.

We are left with two interesting puzzles. Neither Holland nor the American colonies suffered the political and social inhibitions of France vis-à-vis Britain. For most of the eighteenth century, income per capita was probably higher in Holland than Britain, while the American colonies expanded their population at an astonishing rate, with high and probably rising per capita incomes, quite possibly above the British level, if Adam Smith was right. Why did the industrial breakthrough not occur in one or the other area?

On the side of demand, obviously both domestic markets were smaller than those of Britain and France, although the Dutch knew how to export. The Dutch also bore an extraordinary tax burden, for defense purposes. But there were also problems on the side of the supply of inventors and industrial innovators. The answer here may lie in the fact that entrepreneurship in Holland was concentrated on trying to hold its ground in international commerce, in all its aspects, shifting, in fact, toward finance rather than industry when the rise of Britain and France constrained its commercial possibilities;[60] whereas the yields from agriculture and international commerce in the North American colonies were so attractive as to prevent a buildup of industrial inventiveness and entrepreneurship. British colonial regulations, of course, were designed to deter manufacturing development in North America in most sectors, but, as American economic history from 1783 to 1806 suggests, (see pages 200–203), it was probably a marginal factor. As compared to Britain, the yields related to industrial entrepreneurship were deficient in Holland and North America, whereas, in France an attenuated supply of entrepreneurial talent, notably in cotton textiles, failed to exploit fully the inventions and the market environment that were, by and large, ready at hand.

5

The World Economy, 1783–1820: An Epilogue

I

This analysis thus far has had two objectives: first, to examine how the interplay of mercantilist domestic policies, the commercial revolution, and the scientific revolution induced in Europe and the North American colonies a process of economic modernization akin to the preconditions for takeoff; and second, how that interacting process, operating erratically but cumulatively, over a long period of time and in many places, reached a critical point in Britain, around the 1760s, yielding a series of inventive breakthroughs and their rapid introduction into manufacturing, starting in the 1780s. In cotton textiles and iron manufacture we can observe two classic examples of the case of increasing returns; in Watt's steam engine, a cost-reducing technological breakthrough with wide application and powerful effects on the location of industry and the optimum scale of industrial plants; and, in all its ramifications, we observe in the explosive expansion of the cotton textile industry the first leading sector complex, with strong backward, lateral, and forward linkages to the economy. Between 1785 and 1802 the first takeoff happened; modern growth began.

As the British made their demonstration in the last two decades of the eighteenth century, the job of industrialization changed its character. Gillispie notes: "In textile manufacturing—and even in metallurgy—French entrepreneurs were shown the way, not by scientific research, but by Englishmen and Scotsmen."[1] And this proved true from Russia to the United States. Despite some inhibitions on the export of technology and despite the closeness with which particular firms tried to guard special tricks in the production process, knowledgeable men and new machines crossed borders. It was possible for followers to learn from leaders. Invention, as well as fundamental science, became an international enterprise, enlarging the potential for all capable of absorbing them.

The challenge represented by the British achievement was promptly appreciated. In France and Catalonia, Switzerland and Saxony, the cotton industry moved forward rapidly in the 1780s on the basis of the British example in spinning cotton with machines. In the United States, the challenge was felt, in even more fundamental terms, as the new nation struggled to find its feet under the Articles of Confederation. Lord Sheffield's pamphlet, *Observations on the Commerce of the American States With Europe and the West Indies,* was read with morbid fascination in the United States. It comforted the British in 1783, as American independence was accepted at Paris, by asserting that the prospects for the new nation were dim outside the British Navigation system, and it concluded that America could not establish extensive manufactures. At Yale in Eli Whitney's time (1789–92), the following question was debated: "Does the National Security depend on fostering Domestic Industries?" And in his *Report on Manufactures* of 1791, Alexander Hamilton enunciated the abiding doctrine of aspiring, relatively underdeveloped nations feeling the weight of the more advanced: ". . . not only the wealth but the independence and security of a country appear to be materially connected with the prosperity of manufactures." The uncertain performance of American diplomacy in these early years, danger on the frontiers, and a sense of continued neocolonial economic dependence gave substance to the Hamiltonian position, although it also evoked Jefferson's initial contrary image of an America to be built by sturdy landowners on an agricultural base, avoiding the human and social costs of industrialization, some of which could already be discerned.

If peace had reigned in the next generation, the British would certainly have maintained, for some time, their initial lead, but, on the basis of the progress achieved in the eighteenth century, yielding palpable momentum in the 1780s, the European continent and the United States would have moved promptly to narrow the gap in the new technologies, and the factory system they spawned, probably behind protective tariffs. War broke out, however, in 1793 and, with brief respite in 1802, continued until 1815.

In one way or another, the French Revolutionary and Napoleonic Wars affected the economic as well as the political life of virtually the whole world trading area—not merely Europe but North America, Latin America, Africa and the Far East. Within Europe their impact varied greatly, but their general effect was to grant Britain a sustained period of virtual monopoly in extra-European trade and to reduce the rate of diffusion of the new technologies below the level it probably would have attained if these had been years of peace. As we shall see, the United States may be an exception to this proposition, but when peace came in 1815, the relative economic power of Britain as a trading nation and its technical virtuosity vis-à-vis the continental states was much greater than it was in 1793.

There was a large gap to be closed, and, as David Landes has demonstrated, a good deal of European economic history in the nineteenth century can be told as the story of how it was closed, in the face of *le défi Britannique.*

In that perspective, the purpose of this chapter is to discuss briefly what the world economy was like around 1820, when the initial period of postwar adjustment had been transited and the more advanced nations faced up to their central economic task: the absorption, from an initially inferior position, of the technologies generated in the late eighteenth century as well as the new technologies which now ceaselessly unfolded; for the minds of men and the institutions within their societies were irreversibly changed by the British takeoff. Invention and innovation had become for the first time in history a more or less regular flow.

II

Table 15 indicates the order of magnitude of the British increase in production and trade from the 1780s to the postwar years, and the principal phases of that expansion, which continued but decelerated from 1802 to the end of the war.

The momentum of the revolution in cotton and iron production emerges clearly, although difficulties and then conflict with the United States slowed the rate of expansion from 1806 to 1815. The movement of the brick index and timber imports correctly reflects the extent to which wartime demands on resources and high interest rates damped housing construction and most domestic infrastructure until the post war years. The foreign trade figures reflect the role of reexports, as well as cotton exports, in sustaining the British trade position, although Napoleon's Continental

TABLE 15
Indicators of British Economic Expansion, 1783–1820

	1783–85	1790–92	1800–02	1814–16	1818–20
Production Indicators					
Hoffmann Industrial Production (total), excluding building, 1913 = 100[1]	2.9	4.2	5.6	7.1	8.1
Raw Cotton Imports (official value, in £ millions)[2]	.4	.9	1.9	2.8	5.2
Pig Iron Production (in thousands of tons)[3]	62 (1785)	90 (1791)	170 (1802)	—	325 (1818)
Timber Imports (official value, in £ millions)[2]	.3	.4	.6	.5	.6
Bricks charged with duty (in millions)[2]	359 (1785)	756	639	737	1001
Trade					
Imports (official value, in £ millions)[2]	14.9	19.5	31.6	31.1	33.4

Domestic Exports (official value, in £ millions)[2]	11.0	16.7	28.3	37.6	38.2
Reexports (official value, in £ millions)[2]	4.1	5.9	18.2	16.2	10.5
Cotton Exports (official value, in £ millions)[2]	.8	1.7	6.8	19.3	21.1
Iron and Steel Exports (official value, in £ millions)[2]	.6	1.2	1.6	1.7	1.5

SOURCES:
1. Walther G. Hoffmann, *British Industry, 1700–1950*, W. H. Chaloner and W. O. Henderson, trans. (Oxford: Basil Blackwell, 1955).
2. B. R. Mitchell, with Phyllis Deane, *Abstract of British Historical Statistics* (Cambridge: At the University Press, 1962). (Reprinted as a Department of Applied Economics Monograph, 1971.)
3. For the years between 1783 and 1791, Charles K. Hyde, "The Adoption of Coke Smelting by the British Iron Industry, 1709–1790" (Mimeographed paper delivered at the Conference on the "New" Economic History of Britain, Cambridge, England, 1972); for the years between 1796 and 1818, Arthur D. Gayer et al., "The Growth and Fluctuation of the British Economy, 1790–1850," Supplement, *British Basic Statistical Data*, Part One, Table 16 (Unpublished but available on microfilm at University Microfilms, Ann Arbor, Michigan).

System had a significant effect on the commercial efficacy of British control of the seas from the Berlin Decree of 1806 until the disintegration of the continental blockade in 1813.

British industrial growth continued in spite of the war, not because of it. Capital was diverted over the war years in several directions that did not converge with the industrial revolution: toward a massive expansion of agricultural output to feed a rapidly growing population at a time of chronically bad harvests and import difficulties; enormous outlays for ships to fight, convoy, and carry the reexports Britain almost monopolized, and for the docks and warehouses needed to support this valuable but distorted commerce; and for war outlays themselves, to support Britain's allies as well as its own forces. British total net public expenditures were running at a rate of almost a third of national income around the turn of the century.

The peacetime performance of the British economy between 1783 and 1792 and the lift in its growth rate in the three decades after 1815 suggest that the war damped the expansion of British industry below the rate it would otherwise have attained.[2] This is certainly the case for the troubled years from 1803 to 1815. Nevertheless, it is a remarkable fact that, building on the momentum of the decade after 1783 and exploiting the trading advantages its naval dominance provided, the British economy expanded substantially over the two decades of war, continuing to diffuse the germinal new technologies in textiles, metallurgy, and steam power.

III

The course of economic events, as it unfolded from year to year, was obviously affected by military operations; by Britain's struggles with Napoleon, the Americans, and others over trade; and by such political events as the

Spanish Revolution of 1808, which opened a new phase in the economic as well as political history of Latin America. On the Continent, too, economic history was affected by the shaping and reshaping of the political map of Europe.

Despite these traumatic, exogenous events, two patterns that were to recur over the next century and beyond took shape in these years. They were the business cycle and the phenomenon of distinctive trend periods.

The phase of economic expansion in Britain that began in 1783 and reached its peak in 1792 contained the first modern business cycle. There was a cycle of mild amplitude running from a trough in 1784 to a peak in 1787, followed by a brief setback in 1788, and then four years of remarkable expansion of much greater amplitude. The eighteenth century (and perhaps earlier periods) had seen relatively short inventory cycles in foreign trade, a pattern that persisted well into the nineteenth century, but the predominant factors shaping business fluctuations during the eighteenth century were the luck of the harvests and war.[3] During the 1780s, however, a major expansion in long-term capital investment occurred, notably in the years 1788–92. As we know, this was a period of rapid expansion in the cotton and iron industries. Industrial expansion is often a major stimulus to investment in urban housing and infrastructure, but industrial investment itself is almost always a relatively modest component of total investment. In the 1780s, the building of canals, turnpikes, and houses and the enclosure and improvement of land were, in scale, the main avenues of investment. Brick production, a good index of investment at this time, almost doubled between 1785 and 1792. All this converged with an export boom focused on the markets in the United States, the British West Indies, and Asia. In 1792, one can observe all the signs of an expansion close to its peak: prices, wages, and interest rates moved up; central bank reserves came under pressure; doubts appeared that credit had been granted wisely, in this case centered on the greatly expanded, fragile country banks.[4] This was the inherently vulnerable setting which was struck in February 1793 by the outbreak of war between Britain and France.

The pattern of fluctuations that emerged, when the crisis of 1793 was surmounted, reflected an interweaving of two cyclical rhythms: an inventory cycle in foreign trade, averaging about four years in length, and a cycle in long-term investment, averaging about nine years. Taken together, they produced a sequence of major and minor cycles that runs quite consistently through the war and postwar period, as shown in chart 5.

The markets closely linked to Britain—notably, the United States—experienced synchronous fluctuations, although not necessarily of the same amplitude.

CHART 5
BUSINESS-CYCLE PATTERN, BRITAIN
1784–1850 (ABSTRACT SCALE).

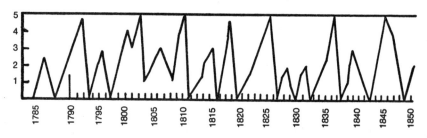

NOTE: For the construction of the chart and the data and analysis that lie behind it, see A. D. Gayer, et al., *Growth and Fluctuation of the British Economy, 1790–1850*, Vol. 1 (Oxford: Clarendon Press, 1953), pp. 342–56. The cyclical pattern from 1784 to 1790 has been added. The dating of major and minor cycles is the following:
    Major cycles: 1788–1793, 1797–1803, 1808–1811, 1816–1819, 1819–1826, 1832–1837, 1842–1848; Minor cycles: 1784–1788, 1793–1797, 1803–1808, 1811–1816, 1826–1829, 1829–1832, 1837–1842.

There were also forces operating on the British economy and the international trading network that transcended business cycles. The price of a quartern loaf of bread in London was 6 1/4 d. in 1792, 17 1/2 d. in 1800, a particularly bad harvest year. But the three-year average, at the turn of the century, was more than 13 d. per loaf.

The coming of war coincided with a period when Britain, in a marginal position since the late 1760s, had become a regular importer of grain. Its rate of population increase was moving up to its historical peak of 1.7 percent per annum in the decade 1811–21, outstripping its considerable capacity to expand domestic agricultural production. This international demand for grain was heightened, in its effect on food prices, by irregularity in the supplies available and by high shipping and insurance costs. The result was a sustained period of relatively high agricultural prices throughout the world trading area and pressure on the real wages of the urban worker. It was also a period of relative prosperity for the farmer and for others whose incomes were geared to agricultural prices and rents. This shift in relative prices and the distribution of income gave way, after 1815, to some thirty years when the trend ran, albeit erratically, in the other direction; that is, food was relatively cheap, real wages tended to rise and the farmers to complain. This long cycle was then repeated with an upswing from the late 1840s to 1873, a downswing to the mid-1890s; and repeated again from the upward turn in the 1890s to the sharp break in the relative prices of agricultural products in 1920, continuing well into the next decade. A somewhat less clear version of an upswing affected the contours of the world economy from the mid-1930s to the break in relative prices toward the end of the Korean War in 1951, and, after twenty years of complaint about unfavorable terms of trade, the farmers of the world may have entered yet another favorable trend period in the early 1970s, with urban real wages again under chronic pressure, and, this time, the possibility of irremediable famine in parts of the world where the rise in population is creating pressures beyond the capacity of the global agricultural system to manage.

The purpose of evoking this long sequence in the present limited context is to underline the complexity of the forces at work on the British and other economies in this critical period. It was a time not merely of the first industrial revolution, but of war and commercial struggle, of cyclical fluctuations suffused with the new deeper rhythm of long-term investment, and a time of strain for urban man, as the increase in population pressed against the limits of acreage and technology in agriculture.

IV

The American economy was, for a time, both beneficiary and victim of this new trading environment.

After an uneven period of recovery that lasted from the end of the war until 1788, the United States, under its new constitution, enjoyed a period of commercial expansion until 1792. Reflecting that prosperity, British exports to the United States more than doubled from 1788 to 1792, moving from £1.7 to £4.1 million. As in Britain, the setback in 1793 was brief. The coming of war, and the impact of the cotton gin, then produced a remarkable expansion in American exports, accompanied by a disproportionate rise in export prices. Exports included grain and naval stores as well as the rapidly enlarging flow of ginned Sea Island cotton. As a neutral country, the United States generated also a major reexport trade, since the French West Indies were opened to American shipping, whose tonnage expanded by more than eight times during the prosperous phase of the war years. Again roughly following the British cyclical pattern, there was a brief recession in 1797, and a boom, set back in 1802–3 by the Peace of Amiens. David Macpherson, a British contemporary, observed: "Thus has the war in Europe turned out a mine of gold and silver to the United States of America. . . . This sudden inundation of nominal wealth must introduce a style of living, and a turn of thought, utterly inconsistent with agricultural and mercantile prosperity, and destructive of the simplicity of manners and frugal habits, which, heretofore, rendered America so respectable in the eyes of the discerning part of Europe."[5]

The trade figures for this remarkable decade are the following:

TABLE 16
U.S. FOREIGN TRADE, 1792–1803
(In $ Millions)

	Exports U.S. Merchandise	Reexports	Imports
1792	19	2	32
1796	32	26	81
1797	24	27	75
1801	46	47	111
1803	42	14	65

SOURCE: U.S., Department of Commerce, *Historical Statistics of the United States* (Washington, D.C.: Government Printing Office, 1960), p. 538.

There was a more limited phase of commercial expansion, until 1806–7, before the United States was whipsawed by the British Orders in Council, Napoleon's response, and Jefferson's embargo. Up to that point, the United States had enjoyed what might be called a Jeffersonian boom based on its agriculture but carrying in its train a vast expansion in ships, banking, and mercantile activity. With profits ready to hand in these directions, it was not a good time to bring into production the new British industrial technologies. In 1790, Samuel Slater, drawing directly on British practice, successfully set up the first American mill to spin yarn, but progress was relatively slow until after 1807, when imports from Britain sharply declined. The textile factory experiment fostered by Hamilton in New Jersey in the 1790s failed. American textiles remained predominantly a domestic industry on the old pattern during the years of commercial prosperity, while America exported its agricultural bounty and imported British manufactures on an expanding scale.

On the other hand, the military insecurity of the United States led Presidents Adams and Jefferson to end its dependence on imported foreign arms and to back Eli Whitney, as well as talented men in the arsenals, in mass-producing guns with interchangeable parts, using power-driven machine tools of some sophistication for the time. Whitney's first contract was granted in 1798, and within a decade he had more or less made good his vision: ". . . the tools themselves shall fashion the work and give every part its just proportion—which, when once accomplished, will give expedition, uniformity, and exactness to the whole." The elaboration of this vision and the mass-produced engineering products it foreshadowed lies mainly with the period beyond 1815, but the episode of the new guns underlined the American capacity to build machinery.

Jefferson's embargo launched a period of Hamiltonian development in the United States. Although there was a limited revival of American trade in 1809–12, the period 1807–15 as a whole was one of commercial inhibition and war, fostering substantial industrial expansion. Slater's example in cotton spinning spread, and, in 1814, Francis Cabot Lowell, again working with British technology, brought weaving too within the factory system with his power looms at Waltham. Between 1790 and 1808, only fifteen cotton mills were built in the United States. In 1809, eighty-seven additional mills were constructed, increasing capacity from 8,000 to 31,000 spindles, eighty thousand spindles were working by 1811. American manufactures in many other fields similarly took up the slack left by the constriction of trade with Britain. Their firms came under great strain with the return of peace, and many collapsed, but the latter stages of the period of war provided the industrial foundations on which New England was able to move into a regional takeoff in the 1820s, centered on the mass production, with American-built machinery, of cotton textiles. There were 795 cotton factories in the United States by 1831, with 1.2 million spindles. Industrialization was well on its way.

But out of the European conflict the United States had also acquired the Louisiana Purchase in 1803, and the way to the West was opened. American development after 1815 reflects a counterpoint, and then, from the 1850s, a convergence of agricultural expansion and industrial development.

V

The years of the French wars left an even more enduring impact on the European continent than on the United States. Although British forces briefly got to Washington, Napoleon's armies and the battlefields on which they fought, from one end of Europe to the other, left a more permanent mark on national memories, attitudes, and policies. The diffusion of French revolutionary ideas; the gradual buildup of a nationalist reaction against Napoleon in Prussia, Spain, Italy, and Russia; the grouping and regrouping of the multiple German states had profound long run modernizing effects on the European societies and their economies. Similarly, Napoleon's consolidation of the law, his tax and education policies, the creation of a national bank, and his revamped administration, with its straightforward control of the departments from Paris, left, despite the restoration of the monarchy, a more modern France in 1815 than had existed in 1789 or, even, in 1799.

In a narrower sense, too, the economic effects of the war were more profound in Europe than in the United States. Despite the creative industrial hiatus of 1807–14, the United States ended where it began, a vital part of the Atlantic economy, with a thickening bond of cotton linking the South to the British mills. The rupture of the Atlantic ties of western Europe was more permanent.

We have noted that for western Europe as for Britain, the widening of trade to embrace the Western Hemisphere and the Far East was a central feature of the eighteenth century.[6] In the first stage of the war, the flow of extra-European supplies to the Continent continued. The British shipped an enormous volume of reexports through Hamburg, while the United States was permitted as a neutral to operate more directly. But the American ships generally returned with British, rather than continental, manufactures, and the whole shipping, processing, and manufacturing substructure, in the arc from Amsterdam to Barcelona and Marseilles, was weakened. In the second stage of the war, the flow to the Continent from overseas was attenuated. From 1803 to 1807, Hamburg was virtually closed as an *entrepôt*. The British tried to deal with the problem by shipping through Lübeck and Danzig on the Baltic, Trieste and Venice (until 1805) in the Mediterranean, with Gibraltar, Malta, and the Greek islands as intermediate bases, but their success was only partial. After

1807, the commercial, shipping, and manufacturing life of the great continental coastal cities virtually collapsed. Grass grew, in fact as well as symbolically, in the streets of Bordeaux. For Spain and Portugal the progressive loss of their American empires, begun in 1808, was a permanent setback. The British export boom of 1808–10, centered on Latin American markets, symbolized the transfer of economic power.

The period of the Continental System, however, provided some compensatory industrial expansion, parallel to that which occurred over the same years in the United States, for in both cases British exports were not normally available, and industry enjoyed, in effect, a very high protective tariff. As we have noted, the continental nations were moving quite briskly to absorb British cotton manufacturing technology before 1793. On the foundations already established, there was rapid expansion in France, Alsace, Switzerland, Saxony, Austria, Belgium, Holland, and Austria. In 1811, Britain had 4.9 million spindles; by 1815, continental Europe had about 1.5 million, of which two-thirds were in France.[7] The application of new technology extended beyond spinning and included a capacity to build textile machinery. The continental industry labored during the war under severe handicaps, including a chronic shortage of cotton and high capital costs. But Crouzet can conclude:

> It is most likely that if there had been no war, if relations with England had been maintained, if a moderate protection had been established, economic and technical progress on the Continent would have been faster. But after all, there was a war. . . . As a matter of fact, the cotton industry was the strategic sector at that stage. It was the only one likely to expand fast, the best suited to machine production, and it required little capital; its development and technical improvement were the best way to introduce the new technology and to train workers and managers in the skills of

machine production and the factory system; also they were the only possible basis for a machine-building industry. . . . On the whole, the cotton industry and especially machine spinning had struck rather strong roots in Continental soil during the Napoleonic wars, and so the foundations for further industrialization had been laid. As a matter of fact, the beginnings of the Industrial Revolution on the Continent could be dated from the simultaneous establishment of machine spinning in various countries, around 1800. . . ."[8]

There was less, but still considerable technological progress in the continental woolen industry; some progress in chemicals; a severe decline in the old linen industry; relative stagnation in pig iron; but some advance in the metal-using industries.

All in all, French industrial production recovered from its setbacks of the 1790s and in Napoleon's time may have achieved by 1810 a level 50 percent higher than in the 1780s,[9] but the last years of the Empire were stagnant, and, as in the United States, many of the war-born firms did not survive the coming of peace. Nevertheless, it is the cotton industry that led the way in French industrial growth until the period 1830–60, when the rise of the heavy industries and railroad building brought France into takeoff.[10] The initial British technological lead of the 1780s, translated during the war into a virtual monopoly in sale of cottons to overseas markets, made the British industry a more massive phenomenon in the economy, with more powerful spreading effects, than were the continental cotton industries. Their national markets, even when protected, did not supply a sufficient base for cotton textiles to serve as the leading sector for takeoff. Quite aside from the effect of the war on the great continental port cities—and the symmetrical expansion of British commercial, processing, and reexporting activity—it was the British dominance of the international trade in cottons, more than any other single factor, that put the Continent in a protracted period of inferiority in the postwar years, a period that did not end until the age of railroads and steel, chemicals and electricity put the continental states on a more even technical and economic base.

Although the French story illustrates well the general character of continental development during the war years, there are significant variations. Belgium, for example, prospered under its linkage to France and the large market it represented. The expansion of its textile and machine-building industries (the latter centered around William Cockerill's plant in Verviers) helped prepare the way for its rapid movement into takeoff (on the basis of coal, railroads, and heavy industry), after it had achieved independence of the Netherlands in 1830.[11] The Rhineland enjoyed similar advantages from its link to Napoleonic France that left a permanent industrial heritage.

The Spanish experience was much less fortunate. The momentum of the hopeful developments of the latter part of the eighteenth century was broken when Spain joined in the war against Britain in 1796, and its profitable and rapidly expanding direct trade with its American colonies was interrupted. Spanish shipping was confined to the Mediterranean until the Peace of Amiens in 1802. As a Spanish historian notes, the Americans as well as the British moved in: ". . . no [Spanish American] port was overlooked by the enterprising Yankee traders."[12] In the six years after 1795, United States trade with Spanish America multiplied more than six times. After brief respite came the Spanish Revolution of 1808 and six years of bloody and disruptive struggle against the French, in which some 300,000 Spaniards died in combat, aside from those lost due to epidemic and famine. From the events of these years flowed the progressive detachment of the Spanish colonies, over the period 1808–25, leaving Spain with only Cuba and the Philippines. It is not until the 1830s that Spain began to move forward again, on the basis of domestic development, after the double trauma of the Peninsular Campaign and the drastic reduction in its overseas position.

For Holland, cut off from its ties to extra-European trade and its financial links to London, this period also yielded a permanent reorientation. British industrial growth and its capacity to mobilize and transfer great sums in loans and subsidies to its allies left London in 1815 the financial capital of the world for the first time, much as New York emerged after the First World War: ". . . the war put an end to Britain's financial tutelage to Holland."[13] In the brief postwar boom of 1816–18, London had already turned the capacity it had developed to finance loans and subsidies to wartime allies to the flotation of foreign loans. Belgium, with its coal and engineering capacity, emerged before Holland as the first major industrial center in the Low Countries.

French, Dutch, and Spanish colonial interests were not wholly destroyed by the processes and outcome of the war and the French were to exert themselves to reachieve a substantial colonial position in the nineteenth century. Moreover, after 1815, the world's trade routes were progressively more open; the environment had become less mercantilist than that which framed most of the eighteenth century. But the great new developments that lay ahead— notably, the railroad—combined with the structural changes in trade and finance from 1793 to 1815 to make the European continent more inward-looking than it had been during the eighteenth century.

Russia, too, was caught up in the possibilities and vicissitudes of the world trading framework during the French and Napoleonic Wars. Like the United States, Russia benefitted at the beginning. Britain needed Russian iron, grain, and timber. British imports from Russia rose in volume (official values) from £1.4 to £1.9 million between the average for 1786–90 and the period 1796–1800, while exports to Russia (including reexports) more than doubled, from £.3 to £.7 million. Throughout the 1790s, Russia sought to extract better terms for its quasi-monopolistic position as an exporter; export duties were imposed, a credit bank for Russian exporters was set up, and the government required a fixed quantity of timber to be purchased for every hundred tons of iron leaving the country.[14] To the rising cost of importing Russian iron was added friction over the British right to search at sea for contraband. In 1800, Russia united with the other northern powers (Sweden, Prussia, and Denmark) to challenge British practice. The assassination of Paul I in March 1801 may have averted a British-Russian war.

All this heightened the British incentive to free itself from its continued import requirement. In 1803, domestic iron was, for the first time, substituted for imports by the navy and other government services. Iron imports declined from their peak of about 46,000 tons in 1801 to about 7,000 tons in 1814, and became again a significant British import only a half century later.

Meanwhile, Russia came to an understanding with Napoleon in 1807. But at just that time the application of the Continental System further restricted its foreign trade, stimulating a certain amount of import substitution in manufactures but producing a period of low agricultural prices.

Napoleon's invasion of Russia in 1812 damaged or forced the evacuation of a good deal of Russian manufacturing capacity around Moscow, but wartime requirements provided a certain amount of stimulus to the metal and metalworking industries, as well as to the textile industries supplying uniforms.[15]

With respect to the industrial technologies, the war years saw a damped continuity with the process underway before

1793 and after 1815; that is, the slow absorption on an essentially experimental or small-scale production basis of the new machinery. In 1805, the first steam engine to be applied in cotton manufacture was set up in St. Petersburg; English linen-spinning machines were installed in 1809 in Alexandrovsk; a simple thresher introduced farm machinery to Russia in 1802. But the large Russian iron industry did not begin to introduce Cort's puddling process until well after the war, in 1836. In wool, the requirements for uniforms were met by the old methods, with 90 percent of the working force serf labor, and the silk industry went into a long decline because of the shortage of raw material during the Continental blockade.

There was more vitality, as everywhere, in cotton, in which industry relatively modern private entrepreneurs operated with hired rather than serf labor. In 1793, the first spinning machine was erected, and the first privately-owned cotton-spinning mill, using machinery from the model plant set up by the government in Alexandrovsk, was opened in 1808. There were eleven cotton-spinning mills in Moscow in 1812, but the full technical modernization of the industry awaited the 1840s, and it was not until the 1850s that the industry began to free itself from a reliance on imported yarn. The extent and limits of Russian industrial progress, the momentum of the last decades of the eighteenth and the opening of the nineteenth centuries, the setback from 1807 to the end of the war, and the declining proportion of serf factory workers are suggested in Table 17, which excludes factories and workers in distilling, brewing, flour-milling, and mining.

In short, the war years saw Russia continue to move forward along late eighteenth-century lines, while falling even further behind Britain than had western Europe with respect to the new technologies, and losing along the way its iron export market to a now essentially self-sufficient

TABLE 17
RUSSIAN INDUSTRY, 1770–1820

	Number of Factories	*Number of Workers*	*Hired Workers*
1770	260	55.3	32%
1804	2,402	95.2	47
1812	2,322	119.0	50
1820	4,578	179.6	58

SOURCE: Peter I. Lyaschenko, *History of the National Economy of Russia*, L. M. Herman, trans. (New York: Macmillan Co., 1949), p. 337.

Britain. Except for a brief period, its industrial modernization did not cease, but Russia was in 1820 still more than a half-century from takeoff.

VI

In the course of the period 1783–1815, events occurred beyond the European and North Atlantic worlds that cast long shadows and deserve brief reference here.

First, Africa. As the eighteenth century moved toward its close, economic and moral impulses began slowly to converge to bring the European trade in African slaves to an end, after three centuries and a half. The moral case against slavery and the slave trade had been articulated in seventeenth-century England, and the Quakers, in particular, carried forward an effective public campaign against the slave trade in both England and the North American colonies. In France, the leaders of the Enlightenment argued the repugnance of slavery to civil as well as natural law. The British loss of the North American colonies added, however, a new strand to the argument. Some British interests began to look to Africa as an alternative market for manufactures and as a potential source of tropical products—a prospect with which the slave trade interfered.

The first effective action against the slave trade, however, was taken by Denmark in 1792. The decision was made to build up the slave population for ten years in the Danish West Indies and to rely subsequently on natural increase for the labor supply.

In 1794, the revolutionary French Assembly decreed an end to slavery in all the French colonies, but not until 1848 was slavery in fact abolished. The American Constitution envisaged that Congress might act to end the slave trade after twenty years, which indeed it did as of January 1, 1808. A series of parliamentary acts between 1806 and 1811 ended the British role in the slave trade, the last making traffic in slaves a criminal offense. The new government of Buenos Aires declared all children born of slaves after January 13, 1813, to be free, thus starting the movement toward freedom in Latin America. At the Congress of Vienna, the slave trade was denounced, but an effort to achieve a common commitment to act against it failed.

The story of slavery had clearly not come to an end. Slaves continued to cross the Atlantic until the mid-nineteenth century, but a turn in the road had been achieved.

There was a less dramatic but still profound turn in the road for India. In 1784, the India Bill had for the first time placed the affairs of the East India Company under a board that came gradually to exercise effective control over its policy. Within that framework, the main events of the period were the establishment by Cornwallis of the Indian civil service on a professional basis, with adequate salaries and a prohibition against engaging in private trade, and the military consolidation of all but the northwest frontier by Wellesley and Hastings, a task not completed until 1823. Of at least equal significance, however, was the ending of the

East India Company's trading monopoly in 1813. It had been eroded by the Act of 1793, which provided shipping for trade outside that conducted by the East India Company. The pressure arose in the first instance from merchants operating in India, under the protection of the Company, who were anxious to transfer their accumulated profits to Europe in the form of Indian exports.[16] Meanwhile, foreign traders (notably, American and Portuguese) had been expanding their trade with India, including delivery of goods into Europe, to the chagrin of British shipping and trading interests. At precisely the time when these interests had succeeded in widening commercial access to India, the balance in the textile trade was shifting heavily toward Britain. The first sample of English manufactured muslin had arrived in India as early as 1783, and the export of yarn from Bengal had stopped by 1786. The rise of the British cotton industry narrowed but did not initially eliminate the market for Indian exports. It was some time before machines could match Indian muslins of high quality, but around 1812 British cotton exports began to move into India on a substantial scale. The ending of the East India Company's monopoly strengthened a trend already underway. British exports to Asia expanded in volume from £1.7 million in 1811 to £4.4 million in 1821. At last, Britain had something substantial to sell in India (and China) beyond bullion; although, of course, the arrival of machine-manufactured cottons set in motion a long disruptive as well as, in the end, modernizing process. An Indian historian concluded: "The year 1800 saw a revolution in India's economy. India was now well started on the road to transformation from being the industrial workshop of the world to one of its richest raw material-producing regions. . . . India entered on a period of de-industrialization . . . ."[17]

The basis for the shift can be seen in Baines' table comparing English and Indian costs in producing various

TABLE 18

COMPARATIVE STATEMENT OF THE COST OF ENGLISH AND
INDIAN YARN IN 1812 AND 1830.

Description of Yarn	English Cotton Yarn Cost per lb.		Indian Cotton Yarn Cost per lb.
	1812	1830	1812 & 1830
No.	s.d.	s.d.	s.d.
40	2 6	1 2¹/₂	3 7
60	3 6	1 10¹/₂	6 0
80	4 4	2 6³/₄	9 3
100	5 2	3 4¹/₄	12 4
120	6 0	4 0	16 5
150	9 4	6 7	25 6
200	20 0	14 6	45 1
250	35 0	28 2	84 0

SOURCE: Edward Baines, *History of Cotton Manufacture* (London, 1835), p. 353.
NOTE: Baines notes that the British relative advantage in weaving was even greater than in spinning.

grades of yarn in 1812 and 1830. Indian costs were static, but the cost advantage already enjoyed by British manufactures in 1812 widened sharply over the subsequent eighteen years, notably in the lower grades of yarn. By the latter period, India and other Far Eastern markets were outranked only by Germany as a purchaser of British cotton manufactures.[18]

The crisis of China comes mainly after the end of our period, starting in the 1830s out of the interplay of its interior dynamics and the callous thrust of the external world for its trade. But both elements are foreshadowed before 1815. In the second half of the eighteenth century, the Manchu dynasty exhibited both brilliance and evidence of decline. The military and political power of the empire was pushed to Korea and Annam, Tibet, Nepal, and Burma. In 1781, the accumulated reserve in the emperor's treasury was over 70 million *taels*. But starting in the 1770s, some classic symptoms of the decline of a dynasty emerged. There were a series of regional rebellions, signs of discontent among the intellectuals, and corruption. With the death of the Emperor Ch'ien-lung in 1796, a time of troubles began.

Interweaving this process was the growing pressure of expanded population on arable land. Per capita acreage, measured in *mou,* is estimated by one scholar as having declined as follows:[19]

1685	5.43
1724	4.83
1753	4.43
1766	4.07
1812	2.85
1872	2.49

If this calculation is roughly correct, it was in the late eighteenth and nineteenth centuries that an acute stage of China's Malthusian crisis began.

Against this background, Britain, the United States, and others began to intensify their trade contacts with China and to press for better terms on which to conduct this commerce. In 1793 and 1816, British missions failed to alter the rather strict rules under which trade was conducted with a designated group of Chinese merchants, the Cohong. But this was the beginning, not the end, of intensified foreign pressure, for the China trade was becoming more interesting, particularly to the British but to others as well, among them the Americans, who had begun coming to Canton to sell furs and to buy tea as early as 1784.

In 1784, the British duty on tea had been sharply reduced. The level of recorded British imports rose, partially because of a reduction in smuggling, but there is an impression that between that time and the turn of the century tea "descended from the palace to the cottage."[20] This process may have been aided by the pressure on real wages of the war years, when ale became relatively too expensive for poor families, directly affected as it was by the high price of grain. In any case, despite the reimposition of high duties after 1800, the tea habit appears to have become well established. The official value of British tea imports moved as follows (in £ millions):

1782–3	.4
1791–2	1.8
1801–2	2.9
1815–6	3.1

Correcting for population, smuggling, and changes in rates of duty, Cole[21] estimates that tea consumption per capita nearly tripled between the early 1780s and the end of the war. More than half the sales of Indian and Chinese goods by the East India Company was tea in the period 1793–1810. In return for this new import from China, the company exported woolen goods, lead and tin (from Cornwall), Indian and then English cotton goods, while it turned a blind eye to the growing illicit traffic in Indian opium, in which the Americans soon joined. With the passage of time, the British demand for tea and other products of China was to increase the pressure to sell both British manufactures and opium in China while the Chinese domestic crisis became increasingly acute. Thus the stage was set for the protracted confrontation in China's relations with the West, which runs from, say, 1834 (when the East India Company's monopoly of the China trade was ended) to the close of the nineteenth century and beyond.

Meanwhile, in Australia a lonely innovator emerged who deserves to be ranked with Eli Whitney. John Macarthur perceived that if this initial "Receptacle for Offenders" was to flourish it required an export that would exploit the abundance of land with little labor and yield a raw material in considerable demand that could bear the expense of a long sea voyage. He decided wool fulfilled these requirements, and by 1797 he was launched on his first experiments in wool-growing with imported merino sheep. A decade later, the first commercial shipment of wool arrived in London. From about 1813, the industry began a phase of rapid expansion; the opening up of Australia was underway; and a major new source of raw materials flowed into the world economy.

We have already referred to the changed status of Latin America set in motion by events of the war years and the reorientation of its trade. As the Latin Americans turned to the long, slow task of building viable modern nation states out of their ancient cultures, and the colonial heritage, they began also the long slow task of economic modernization from a base of foodstuff and raw material exports. By the mid-1820s, Latin America was the major focus of a British capital export boom centered on the modernization and expansion of mines.

VII

The scale and character of changes in the world trading framework are suggested by Mulhall's comparison of world trade figures for 1820 with those of 1780 and 1800 (Table 19).

The great change came during the two decades of the British takeoff before the turn of the century: the sharp relative improvement in the position of Britain and the United States at the expense of France, Spain, and Portugal. Thereafter, the pattern persists, with Russia joining Spain and Portugal in relative decline; Belgium, Holland,

TABLE 19
APPROXIMATE WORLD TRADE: 1780, 1800, 1820
(In Millions £ Sterling)

Country	1780	% World	% Increase from 1750	1800	% World	% Increase from 1780	1820	% World	% Increase from 1800
Great Britain	23	12	10	67	22	291	74	22	10
France	22	12	69	31	10	41	33	10	6
Germany	20	11	33	36	12	80	40	12	11
Russia	17	9	21	30	10	76	22	6	-27
Austria	6	3	50	8	3	33	10	3	25
Italy	7	4	40	10	3	43	15	4	50
Spain	18	10	29	12	4	-33	10	3	-17
Portugal	4	2	33	4	1	0	3	1	-25
Scandinavia	5	3	67	5	2	0	6	2	20
Holland and Belgium	8	4	33	15	5	88	24	7	60
Switzerland	3	2	50	5	2	67	6	2	20
Turkey, etc.	4	2	33	5	2	25	6	2	20

Total: Europe	137			228		66	249		9
Europe as Percentage of Total World	74			75			73		
United States	3	2		17	6	567	23	7	35
Spanish America	20	11	33	25	8	25	30	9	20
British Colonies	1	.5	−67	2	1	100	3	1	50
India	10	5	11	10	3	0	11	3	10
Various	15	8	50	20	7	33	25	7	25
Total: Outside Europe	49		32	74		51	92		24
Total: World	186		33	302		62	341		13

SOURCE: Michael Mulhall, *The Dictionary of Statistics* (London: George Routledge and Sons, 1892), p. 128.
NOTE: Because they have been rounded off, percentage figures do not always add up to 100.

and central Europe holding their own; and the world outside beginning to gain a little on Europe.

By 1820, the first round in the industrial revolution was more or less over. Britain had won by installing the revolutionary technologies in cotton textiles and building a great world trading position on that basis. Others were absorbing those technologies, but except for the regional takeoff in New England of the 1820s and the Japanese textile-based takeoff that began in the mid-1880s, no other area found a sufficient market base to use textiles as the foundation for takeoff. Modernization proceeded slowly until Watt's prime mover, geared to high pressure after his patent expired in 1800, was linked to new developments in iron technology and engineering and the railroad age was born. The beginning of that transition belongs, however, within our period. The first Act of Parliament for the construction of a railroad—the Surrey line, running between Wandsworth and Croydon—was passed in 1801.[22] These early lines were either extensions to canals or connected mining pits to ports close by. The cars were, of course, horse drawn, but ran on iron rails. Meanwhile, the first steamboats and the first locomotives came into operation.

On the basis of earlier experiments and a contemplation of Watt's pump at Chaillot, the Marquis de Jouffroy d'Abbans joined with others to form a company to build and operate steamboats. Jouffroy's first public exhibition of his 141-foot side-wheeler came near Lyon in 1783. The Academy of Sciences insisted that he demonstrate his craft on the Seine, and the venture floundered because Jouffroy could not bear the costs of taking his contraption to Paris.[23] John Fitch and James Rumsey in America, Desblancs and Robert Fulton in France persisted, the latter acknowledging his inspiration from Jouffroy. Having successfully conducted his experiments in France, Fulton returned to New

York in 1806, launching the *Clermont* the next year. Meanwhile, in Scotland, experimental steamboats had been developed and launched in 1788–9, but were left to rot at their moorings.

Even earlier, in 1770, Nicolas Cugnot, a military engineer, built a steam-driven truck to transport artillery. He was backed by the Duc de Choiseul, minister of war. The tests were promising, but with Choiseul's fall from power in 1770 the effort languished and the machine remained in a shed at an arsenal. Napoleon exhibited a brief interest in the vehicle between his Italian and Egyptian campaigns of 1798, but nothing came of it. Once again the Anglo-Saxons saw the invention through to innovation. William Murdock, Watt's assistant, constructed a model steam cart in 1784; Richard Trevithick experimented in 1801 with the first steam-propelled vehicle to carry passengers, and by 1804 he had a reasonably viable locomotive. A few locomotives began to be used on the coal lines, but not until 1829, with Stephenson's *Rocket* on the Manchester-Liverpool line, and the American engines on lines in South Carolina and the Baltimore and Ohio, did the railway age properly begin. It was the railroad and all its works that was to lift a good many nations in the northern half of the world into takeoff between 1830 and 1914, on the basis of the preliminary process of modernization this book has sought to describe.

What can be observed, then, in the century or so before 1783, was an endemic process, from St. Petersburg to the American colonies, leading to the preconditions for takeoff. Agricultural output was expanding; domestic markets were being linked with new roads and canals as mediaeval barriers were reduced; international commerce was increasing, with all it carried in its train; handicraft manufactures were rising; the cities were growing disproportionately; and the scientific revolution set many men in many places to contriving mechanical solutions to economic and technical problems. What varied among the states of Europe was the degree and extent of movement in these directions. Without indulging in counter-factual history, we can reasonably assume that sooner or later the forces at work would have yielded a takeoff elsewhere in Europe (or in the United States), if Britain had not led the way. It probably would not have been long delayed, and cotton textiles would have been the leading sector, for the economic advantages of matching Indian virtuosity with machines was palpable.

Then came the British takeoff and protracted war, accompanied by complex distorting effects on trade and industry, but also by the possibility of copying British methods. More was required for takeoff, however, than learning from the British example or from itinerant British engineers and managers. It was the widespread, diffuse modernization of the Continent from the fifteenth to the eighteenth century (as well as the changes wrought during the Revolutionary and Napoleonic wars) that made the relatively rapid absorption of the British example feasible after 1815. In fact, the sequence of the nineteenth century takeoffs in Europe and the Atlantic relates not rigidly but quite closely to the extent to which preconditioning had proceeded by the close of the eighteenth century: first New England, then (in order) Belgium, France, Germany, Spain, Sweden, Italy, and Russia.

In 1820, there were in various parts of the world traditional societies whose interior life was substantially untouched by Europe's ferment from the fifteenth century forward; for example, Japan, China, and parts of Africa. There were also colonial and other societies that had felt the weight of this new dynamic Europe, but had not yet begun—or, like Turkey, only just begun—to make the painful changes required to survive with dignity in the emerging world of modern technology. For both groups of societies, the road ahead was long. Except for Japan, the takeoffs in Latin America, the Middle East, Asia, and Africa belong with the twentieth century.

VIII

Once the British takeoff happened it is not difficult to account for its diffusion. Of course, for each society that built the preconditions for takeoff and then moved into sustained growth, the experience was unique, requiring creativity, causing pain, bringing frustration as well as profound social and political change. But the brute power represented by sustained industrialization and its potentialities for profit and human welfare proved ultimately irresistible, for two centuries at least. The great intellectual challenge remains to account for how it all began.

Efforts to disentangle Herbert Butterfield's great bundle have been going on now for a long time—at least since Marx and Engel's *Communist Manifesto* in 1848. The academic treatment of the industrial revolution began in the 1880s, with William Cunningham's third volume on British economic history ("laissez-faire") and Arnold Toynbee's lectures. The problem has continued to challenge each generation of economic historians, down through Clapham, Mantoux, Ashton, and Heaton to Landes and Deane, Crouzet, Hartwell, North, and the rest of us. And it should, for if we take the problem head on, it forces us to try to relate the economy to the whole matrix of culture and society, institutions and politics. It concerns one of the great turning points in human civilization, and it should teach us some abiding lessons about the inner mechanics of economic growth.

There are many ways to go about the job. Each takes its shape from hypotheses about the two great questions involved: What dynamic was at work in Europe as it moved forward in its early modern phase from the fifteenth to the eighteenth century? Why, in this setting, was Britain the first nation to translate this endemic process into a revolutionary acceleration in industrial production?

The hypotheses used to get at these questions constitute or reflect implicit or explicit theories about man, about society, and about economic growth. And a historian's theory determines what facts he selects as relevant, which forces at work he brings to the center of the stage.

Every theory about man and his history involves simplification. If one surveys the rich literature on the industrial revolution, it is not difficult to isolate, beneath the welter of detailed description, the hard core of theoretical presupposition that shapes each volume or essay. Occasionally, as in North and Thomas' *Rise of the Western World,* the theory is articulated explicitly, even starkly. More usually, it is embedded in the exposition, but, as R. M. Hartwell demonstrated in *The Causes of the Industrial Revolution in England,* the central theoretical propositions are not difficult to extract.

All serious theories of the industrial revolution view the British industrial breakthrough at the end of the eighteenth century as the climax to a long preceding process as well as the opening of a new phase in human history. All recognize that Europe's exit from feudalism is part of that preceding process in three distinct respects: the emergence of national states; the transformation in land tenure; the attenuation of guild control over manufactures. In all there is a place for the widening of international markets and the more efficient linking of domestic markets. All recognize that the coming into efficient use of new technologies is part of the climactic events that took place toward the end of the eighteenth century. Some would add—and legitimately— that geography and natural resource endowments (or deficiencies) significantly shaped the way the whole process unfolded.

Where are the differences? What justifies yet another essay on this famous theme?

Looking back on the dissatisfactions that led to the writing of this book, I would underline three problems I felt impelled to try to solve.

First, the commercial revolution. Adam Smith and Karl Marx implanted in all our minds the notion that, somehow, the industrial revolution flowed in an automatic way from the commercial revolution, via the expansion of the markets in the one case, the enlargement of a middle class in the other. But if one widens one's frame of reference to embrace the history of Greece and Rome, India and China and other ancient empires, one is driven to Dwight Perkins' conclusion: "There is no natural or irresistible movement from commercial development to industrialization." There is no doubt that the study of the industrial revolution in the West has suffered from historical parochialism. Nevertheless, though it was not in itself a sufficient condition, the commercial revolution was a necessary condition for the industrial revolution. And one of the purposes here has been to specify its rather complex, multiple routes of impact on the equation of economic progress as well as to underline its limits. I am confident that this more differentiated view of the commercial revolution is one direction further research should go.

Second, and similarly, the place of the state and its policy in the equation—all we lump together under the rubric of mercantilism. Here, again, Adam Smith misled us, as in the case of the widening of the market. But the fault is with us, his successors, for in his time and place there was a great deal to be said for his strictures on the residual obstructions to domestic and foreign trade. He was not trying to explain the coming of the industrial revolution; indeed, he had no inkling that it was about to happen. He was concerned to define the rules for an optimum economic system, in a world of peace, enjoying the advantages of specialization, with relatively fixed production functions. He did not consider seriously the kinds of problems that had to be faced still in Germany and Russia, Austria and Spain, for these had been largely overcome in the northwest corner of Europe he knew tolerably well. Nevertheless, from him derives the image of mercantilism as the force that had to be defeated before the industrial revolution could happen. This simplistic view requires modification. We must cast up the account country by country and period by period. For the compulsions set in motion by the endemic struggle for power had positive as well as negative effects at different times and places on the process leading up to the industrial revolution. And these require specification. Here, again, there is ample room for further research, for we have only imperfectly brought together the materials generated by the political and economic historians. And, intellectually, we have only begun to create theoretical concepts that would relate the political and economic processes.

Third, the interplay of science, invention, and innovation. For two hundred years now—from Adam Smith, through Marshall and Robertson, to Samuelson and Kaldor—economists have not been able to integrate satisfactorily the generation of major new technologies with the corpus of economic theory. In dynamic income analysis economists have been driven to a variety of devices that would make technological change incremental and a function of demand or the level of investment. Alternatively, they have put it outside the frame of theory, as an exogenous variable. Even the case of increasing returns has been dealt with mainly, since Marshall, in terms of incremental change, representing improvements associated with the scale of output. There has been, quite literally, no place in formal theory for major inventions and innovations. The quality of entrepreneurship—the willingness and ability of entrepreneurs to accept the creative risks of major innovation—has equally been a subject outside the mainstream of formal economic theory.

There is, then, no accepted framework for dealing in an orderly way with science, invention, and innovation and the complex links among them, but in my view, they are, taken together, the central element distinguishing the story of early modern Europe from previous phases of economic expansion as well as from the concurrent experience of eighteenth-century China and Tokugawa Japan. It is, I believe, the difficulty of ordering these linkages and relating them to the economic process that accounts for the fact that economists have leaned so heavily on the commercial revolution or, as in the case of North and Thomas, on the emergence of private property rights. But in dealing with science, invention and innovation, simple profit maximization propositions do not suffice, and there is no satisfactory short-cut to sorting out their irreducible complexities.

In this terrain, however, there is a body of both historical and contemporary analysis on which to build—the kind of work reflected in the volume edited by A. E. Musson as well as in the writings of, say, Jacob Schmookler and Nathan Rosenberg. This was also the approach I took in *The Process of Economic Growth,* and which I have tried to extend in this book. In a post-Keynesian world where our common fate will depend increasingly on the pace of scientific progress, invention, and innovation in population control, agriculture, energy, pollution control, and raw material substitution, I have no doubt these issues will receive increased attention, on Dr. Johnson's principle that when a man knows he is to be hanged in a fortnight it concentrates his mind marvelously.

Having opened up some of the problems in dealing with the commercial revolution, mercantilism, and the scientific revolution, the task became how to put together coherently such insights as emerged. Here I found the concept of the preconditions for takeoff and the takeoff useful. The former defines the functional changes in a traditional society required to permit and support the first sustained phase of industrialization. Some of those changes are seen here to proceed from aspects of mercantilism, others from the commercial revolution, still others from the early impact on agriculture and industry of the scientific revolution, in its widest sense. And these elements in the equation interact: mercantilism is given a special cast by the diffusion of the Baconian perception to monarchs and their bureaucracies; mercantilism plays a major role in the commercial revolution; the commercial revolution expands the urban areas and its institutions as well as the numbers of men likely to act on the new insight that experimental science can yield larger profits as well as enhanced power for the state. Against the background of these reinforcing interconnections, the concept of the preconditions for takeoff serves here an important purpose, by holding out in reasonable clarity the functional changes required to prepare the way for and to sustain the industrialization process. Its functional headings also provide rough measures for the progress achieved in the various European states caught up in this transitional process.

As for the takeoff, it remains my judgment that this concept catches well the kind of experience through which Britain passed in the generation after 1783 and which many other nations have subsequently experienced as they entered sustained growth.

I conclude with a sense that I understand well enough how it all began to proceed with the analysis of how the story unfolded in the century and a half beyond 1820. I hope the reader shares some of that sense of clarification. But, more important, I hope this essay stimulates others to probe deeper into the great bundle and seek to disentangle it in their own ways.

Notes

Chapter 1.
Why Traditional Societies Did Not Generate
Self-Sustained Growth

1. For a review of the debate, see especially, Harry W. Pearson, "The Secular Debate on Economic Primitivism," in Karl Polanyi, Conrad M. Arensberg, and Harry W. Pearson, eds., *Trade and Market in the Early Empires* (Chicago: Henry Regnery, 1957, 1971).

2. E. F. Heckscher, "Swedish Population Trends before the Industrial Revolution," *Economic History Review*, 2d ser., vol. 2, no. 3 (1950), pp. 266–77. The surges in death rates in Sweden of the 1740s, 1770s, and toward the close of the first decade of the nineteenth century suggest the Chinese proverb that "in every thirty years there is a small upheaval. . . ." (Ssu-yu Teng, *New Light on the History of the Taiping Rebellion* [Cambridge, Mass.: Harvard University Press, 1950], p. 38.) The explanation for this (roughly) generational cyclical tendency may lie in the fact that a demographic crisis (due, say, to war, disastrous harvests, or plague) yielded in its aftermath a surge in the birth rate and an echo about a quarter-century later as those born in the recovery period themselves formed families. The consequent population expansion then would again exert Malthusian pressure on the constrained economic environment. For a discussion of this rhythm, see, for example, E. A. Wrigley, *Population and History*, (New York: McGraw-Hill, 1969), pp. 68–76.

3. For some fragmentary but suggestive data on income and its fluctuations in traditional empires, see "Excursus: Economic Comparisons with the Ancient World," in Colin Clark, *The Conditions of Economic Progress*, 2d ed., (London: Macmillan, 1951), pp. 542–67.

4. The dynamics of cycles similar to those described here have been formalized in the study of certain natural phenomena; c.g., fluctuations in the populations of two species of fish, one of which feeds off the other; and in the cyclical interplay between plants and their parasites. See especially, V. Volterra, *Leçons sur la Théorie Mathématique de la Lutte*

pour la Vie (Paris: Gauthier-Villars et Cie., 1931); and A. J. Lotka, *Elements of Physical Biology* (Baltimore: Williams & Wilkins, 1925).

5. M. M. Postan, "Some Economic Evidence of Declining Population in the Later Middle Ages," *Economic History Review,* 2d ser., vol. 2, no. 3 (1950), p. 246.

6. Idem.

7. The concept of politics as this eternal triangle of problems is developed in the author's *Politics and the Stages of Growth* (Cambridge: At the University Press, 1971), Chapter 1.

8. Charles P. Curtis, Jr., ed., *The Practical Cogitator,* rev. ed. (Boston: Houghton Mifflin, 1950), p. 87.

9. Quoted in R. E. Ward and D. A. Rustow, eds., *Political Modernization in Japan and Turkey* (Princeton: Princeton University Press, 1964), p. 43.

10. In the case of Mogul India, at least, the land was not owned by the aristocracy. It reverted, along with traceable accumulated wealth, to the king, on the death of the holder—a system conducive to high living and concealment, but not agricultural investment, as W. H. Moreland notes in *India at the Death of Akbar* (London: Macmillan, 1920), pp. 256–63.

11. See especially, Alexander Gerschenkron, "Agrarian Policies and Industrialisation: Russia 1861–1917," in H. J. Habakkuk and M. M. Postan, eds., *The Cambridge Economic History of Europe,* vol. 6, pt. II (Cambridge: At the University Press, 1966).

12. S. N. Eisenstadt, *The Political Systems of Empires* (New York: Free Press, 1963), p. 349.

13. Ping-ti Ho, *Studies on the Population of China, 1368–1953,* (Cambridge, Mass.: Harvard University Press, 1959), pp. 271–72.

14. M. M. Postan, "Evidence of Declining Population."

15. M. Rostovtzeff, *The Social and Economic History of the Roman Empire,* vol. 1, 2d ed. (Oxford: Oxford University Press, 1957), p. 538.

16. Pt. 3, bk. 1, ch. 11 (London: George Routledge, 1890), p. 165. The observation is made in passing as part of Smith's explanation of why, with lower money wages in the East, roughly equal technology and cheaper inland transport, both the real and nominal price of most manufactures was less than in Europe, and, therefore, it paid to export bullion, notably silver, where the gold-silver ratio was ten or twelve to one rather than fourteen or fifteen to one.

17. Ibid., b. 4, ch. 9, pp. 534–5.

18. Dwight H. Perkins, "Government as an Obstacle to Industrialization: The Case of Nineteenth-Century China," *Journal of Economic History,* vol. 27, no. 4 (December 1967), p. 485.

19. *The Cambridge Ancient History,* vol. 5 (Cambridge: At the University Press, 1927), p. 16.

20. Smith, *Wealth of Nations,* pt. 3, bk. 1, ch. 11, pp. 196–200. The

water-driven fulling mill apparently made its first appearance as early as the middle of the eleventh century in the north of France, according to Angelo Olivieri, from a paper of E. Carus-Wilson, "Productivity and Technologies in the 12th to the 17th Centuries," *The Journal of European Economic History*, vol. 1, no. 1 (Spring 1972), p. 176.

21. Moreland, *India*, p. 125.

22. *Men, Machines and History* (New York: International Publishers, 1965), especially pp. 20–24; 32–34; 39–41; 43–4.

23. M. I. Finley, "Technical Innovation and Economic Progress in the Ancient World," *Economic History Review*, 2d. ser., vol. 18, no. 1 (August 1965), p. 43.

24. Moreland, *India*, p. 94.

25. Dwight H. Perkins et al., *Agricultural Development in China, 1368–1968* (Chicago: Aldine Publishing, 1969), p. 86. Perkins notes that even when the state nominally owned all the land, much, in fact, was privately owned, bought, and sold. On Indian land tenure, see Moreland, *India*, pp. 96–100.

26. See, notably, Ping-ti Ho, *The Ladder of Success in Imperial China, Aspects of Social Mobility, 1368–1911* (New York: Columbia University Press, 1962).

27. Joseph Needham et al., *Clerks and Craftsmen in China and the West* (Cambridge: At the University Press, 1970), pp. 81–2.

28. See especially, Perkins, "Obstacle to Industrialization," pp. 478–92. A similar conventional view of the limited power and influence of the Indian merchant has also been challenged. See, for example, Brij Narain, *Indian Economic Life* (Lahore: Uttar Chand Kapur, 1929), chs. 3, 4; also M. N. Pearson, "Merchants and Rulers in Mughal India," and Howard Spodek, "Rulers, Merchants and Other Elites in the City-States of Saurashtra, India" (Papers delivered before Twenty-Fifth Annual Meeting of the Association of Asian Studies, Chicago, Ill., March 30–April 1, 1973). Perkins goes beyond a reassessment of the social status of the Chinese merchant to challenge (in my view, correctly) the Smithian proposition that underlies so much of the conventional analysis of modernization: "There is no natural or irresistible movement from commercial development to industrialization. The experience of China is alone testimony to this." (P. 485.)

29. M. M. Postan, "Why Was Science Backward in the Middle Ages?" in *The History of Science, A Symposium* (Glencoe, Ill.: Free Press, 1951), pp. 29–30.

30. Mark Elvin, *The Pattern of the Chinese Past* (Stanford, Ca: Stanford University Press, 1973), especially Chapter 17, "Quantitative Growth, Qualitative Standstill," pp. 285–316. Elvin's approach as a whole bears a family relation to that used in the present book. He notes (p. 7) that his objective is "to compare the Chinese experience of social and economic

development (and non-development) in a systematic fashion with what
had happened in Europe and elsewhere." He was led (p. 317) "to make
the changing pattern of the economics of technology . . . [the] central
point of reference." He uses this approach to get at three large issues, in
particular: "the size and survival of the Chinese Empire, the Chinese
medieval economic revolution [and its waning], China's failure to create
an industrial/mechanical revolution on her own initiative in late traditional times. . . ." The method also permits him to present the sequence
of Chinese dynasties not as oscillations about a static norm but as the
irregular but progressive evolution of a national society and culture. In
this Elvin belongs in the tradition of the Japanese scholar Naitō Torajirō
(1886–1934). See, for example, Hisayuki Miyakawa, "An Outline of the
Naitō Hypothesis and Its Effects on Japanese Studies of China," *Far
Eastern Quarterly,* August 1955, pp. 533–52. Elvin's references indicate
clearly his debt to modern Japanese scholarship on Chinese history.
31. Elvin, *Chinese Past,* pp. 297–8.
32. Without pretending to pronounce definitively on the Chinese case, it
may be that the answer to the question posed by Elvin—why "nobody
tried"—lies in another section of his book. After describing the impressive technological changes in China from the tenth to the fourteenth
century, he addresses himself to the question of why the scientific and
inventive impulse waned. He notes, among other factors, a profound
change around 1300 in painting and philosophy (pp. 225–9). The essence
of the change appears to be from a view that the study (and exact
representation) of nature was a correct route to identifying "the morally
correct principles for human society" to the more subjective and
impressionistic view that "Nature was . . . simply a derivative of man's
consciousness." Elvin concludes (pp. 226–7): "There was thus a shift
. . . away from the conceptual mastery of external nature and towards
introspection, intuition, and subjectivity. The new emphasis on Mind
devalued the philosophical significance of scientific research. . . . This
hindered the growth of a mechanistic and quantitative approach to
phenomena. . . ." Given the importance of the philosophic impact of the
scientific revolution in Europe and the Faustian perspective it fostered
(see pp. 151–157), this element in the Chinese equation might well have
been reexamined and weighed in Elvin's summation in Chapter 17.
33. The role of scientists in these societies and the quality of their results
were, of course, not uniform. George Sarton, for example, evokes
vividly the scientific genius of the Greeks, the severe utilitarianism of the
Romans, the damping effect of the rise of Christianity, the burgeoning of
Arab science from 750 to 1100, the restraints of scholasticism on science
in mediaeval Europe. For a summary of Sarton's view, see his introduc-
tory chapter in *Introduction to the History of Science,* vol. I, Carnegie
Institution of Washington Publication no. 376 (Baltimore: Williams &
Wilkins, 1927).

34. Postan, "Why Was Science Backward," p 28.
35. Giorgio de Santillana, ed., *Galileo Galilei, Dialogue on the Great World Systems,* Abr. txt. ed. (Chicago: University of Chicago Press, 1955), p. xv.
36. For Needham's principal findings, see Needham et al., *Clerks and Craftsmen.*
37. See especially, Brajendranath Seal, *The Positive Sciences of the Ancient Hindus* (London: Longmans, Green, 1915). Also, John Bentley, *Historical View of the Indian Astronomy* (Osnabruck, 1970) (reprint of the 1825 edition); Bibhutibhusan Datta and Avadhesh Narayan Singh, *History of Hindu Mathematics,* Pts. 1 and 2, single vol. ed. (Lucknow: Asia Publishing House, 1962); Satya Prakash, *Founders of Science in Ancient India* (New Delhi: Research Institute of Ancient Scientific Studies, 1965).
38. B. Seal, *Positive Sciences,* pp. 56–85 ("Chemistry in the Medical Schools of Ancient India"); 202–43 ("Hindu Physiology and Biology"). For further references to Indian medical knowledge and practice, see also, Needham, *Clerks and Craftsmen,* pp. 19–20, 60, 267, 269, 303, 340, 342. Moreland, *India,* p. 85, notes that doctors were typically available only for "kings and princes; the common people doctored themselves with herbs which they gathered, while a large town might contain one man—or possibly two—with some practice in medicine."
39. Needham, *Clerks and Craftsmen,* p. 16.
40. Ibid., p. 20.
41. Ibid., pp. 19–20.
42. A possible exception was Lucretius' invocation to Epicuros, quoted by George Sarton, *Introduction,* vol. I, p. 9: ". . . a kind of godlike delight mixed with shuddering awe comes over me to think that nature by thy power is laid thus visibly open, is thus unveiled on every side." But unlike the reaction to Newton in Europe of the late seventeenth and eighteenth centuries, the potentialities of Greek science did not fire the imagination of the active world and its potential inventors and private innovators. As Sarton notes p. 10): ". . . even in her days of greatest prosperity, Rome gave but little encouragement to science. Lucretius was preaching in the desert." Newton, in an age prepared by all that had transpired from Copernicus to, say, Francis Bacon, was not preaching in a desert. As noted in note 32, above, a more general exception may be the abortive expansion of Chinese science and invention from the tenth to the fourteenth century.
43. Acknowledging the debate on this issue, Finley notes in "Technical Innovation," pp. 32–5, that the early Ionian philosophers, even when dealing with cosmology, ". . . did not hesitate to draw analogies and clues from the potter's wheel, the fulling-mill, the smith's bellows, and other objects of craft and industry," whereas Aristotle and Archimedes (the latter with a few famous exceptions) rigorously avoided the con-

tamination of science with lesser concerns. Finley finds in Vitruvius a symmetrical reserve. In considering Vitruvius' wide-ranging study of civil engineering, *De Architectura,* Finley observes (p. 35): "Quite the reverse of Aristotle, he discussed only practical matters and referred the reader who wished to bother with 'things which are not for use but for the purpose of our own delight' . . . to the available literature."

44. Finley, "Technical Innovation," p. 32. In February 1962, R. V. Jones makes this point as follows ("Science, Technology, and Civilization," the 1962 Brunel Lecture, given at the Brunel College of Technology, mimeographed, p. 2): "Recourse to experiment [among the Greeks] was in their view a sign of an inferior mind, a view which was no doubt reinforced by the fact that in Greece most of the manual work was done by the helots, an inferior class, so that the manual work of an experiment would be well below the dignity of a philosopher. This mistake . . . crippled Greek science." On this point, see also Daniel Bell, "Technology, Nature and Society: The Vicissitudes of Three World Views and the Confusion of Realism," *The American Scholar,* vol. 42, no. 3 (Summer of 1973), p. 388: "Equally important was the contrast with the classical Aristotelian view that Thomas Aquinas had enlarged upon in medieval thought. Then, the object of science was to discover the different purposes of things, their essences, their 'whatness' and their qualitative distinction. But little attention was paid to the exactly measured *relations* between events or to the *how* of things. In this first break with the past [Galileo], measurement and relation became the mode."

45. Postan, "Why Was Science Backward," p. 31.
46. Finley, "Technical Innovation," p. 29.
47. Ibid., p. 37.
48. Idem.
49. Quoted in George Sarton, *The History of Science and the New Humanism* (Cambridge, Mass.: Harvard University Press, 1937), pp. 37–8.
50. Quoted in Oliveri, "Productivity and Technologies," p. 171.
51. Finley, "Technical Innovation," p. 44, says: "Not even that extraordinary but anonymous man, who in the fourth century wrote a short work, *De rebus bellicis,* begging the emperor (probably Valentinian I) to adopt a number of military inventions which would save both money and manpower, had any idea that inventions might also be applied to civilian purposes. He poured out his indignation at the misery and poverty of the people, at excessive taxes, at the idleness and hoarded wealth of the aristocracy. He praised the inventiveness of the barbarians. But he had none himself outside the traditional field of military technology."
52. Jones, Brunel Lecture, p. 2. Jones' specific reference is to the traditional Chinese state and the collective mind of its civil servants.
53. See especially, Hans Sachs, "The Delay of the Machine Age," *Psychoanalytic Quarterly,* vol. 2 (1933), pp. 404–24.

54. Quoted (as recorded by Simplicius) by C. A. Doxiadis, *Architectural Space in Ancient Greece,* Jaqueline Tyrwhitt ed. and trans., (Cambridge, MA: M.I.T. Press, 1972), p. 15.
55. Joseph Ben-David makes a similar point in concluding his discussion of "Science in Comparative Perspective," in *The Scientist's Role in Society* (Englewood Cliffs, NJ: Prentice-Hall, 1971), pp. 31–2. In analyzing the place of science in traditional societies, he argues that the "slow and irregular patterns of scientific growth" that marked their history resulted from the "nonacceptance of science as a social goal in its own right" and the consequent "absence of a specialized role" for the scientist. Thus, science "was something that was not 'needed.'" He then observes: "Actually, the question can be turned around. What needs explanation is the fact that science ever emerged at all. Students of traditional societies may argue that there is something pathological in the rapid growth of science which has occurred in the West."

Chapter 2.
The Politics of Modernization

1. Charles Wilson, *The Dutch Republic* (New York: McGraw-Hill, Inc. 1968), p. 233.
2. Richard Bean, "War and the Birth of the Nation State," *Journal of Economic History,* vol. 23, no. 1 (March 1973), especially pp. 210–17.
3. Using data drawn, in part, from colleagues who shared in an Oxford lecture series on "War and Economic Change," I once put together the following table (p. 236) for estimated peak wartime mobilization (including naval forces) in Britain over the centuries. It exhibits a rise beginning in the sixteenth century and persisting down to the twentieth. W. W. Rostow, *The Process of Economic Growth,* 2d ed. (Oxford: Clarendon Press, 1960), p. 150.
4. These calculations yield a somewhat different overall assessment of the net short-run impact of the eighteenth-century wars than those of A. H. John in his "War and the English Economy, 1700–1763," *Economic History Review,* vol. 7, no. 3 (1955), pp. 329–44. I would fully agree, however, with several of John's basic points: the wars of this period helped stimulate the new technology in metallurgy; they expanded demand for woolens and ships; and, above all, their impact must be assessed in terms of their effect on the relative trading and economic position of the competing national states, rather than in absolute terms.
5. For purposes of rough calculation, I used the total net public expenditure figures provided by B. R. Mitchell, with Phyllis Deane, in *Abstract of British Historical Statistics* (Cambridge: At the University Press, 1962), pp. 389–391, and extrapolations from the national income estimates of Gregory King (1688), Joseph Massie (1759–60), and Arthur

PEAK WARTIME MOBILIZATION: BRITAIN,
THIRTEENTH–TWENTIETH CENTURIES

War	Est. population	Est. peak mobilization (British forces)	Proportion of population mobilized, %
Richard and John	1,750,000 (Eng.)	25,000	1.4
100 Years' War	2,500,000 (Eng.)	35,000	1.4
16th century	4,000,000 (Eng. & Wales)	75,000	1.9
Spanish Succession	5,475,000 (1700, Eng. & Wales)	130,000	2.4
Early 18th century	8,000,000 (1760, Eng. & Wales)	240,000	3.0
Revolutionary and Napoleonic	15,700,000 (1801, U.K.)	500,000	3.2*
World War I	45,222,000 (1911, U.K.)	6,000,000	13.3
World War II	47,900,000 (1941, U.K.)	5,000,000	10.4

*If estimated peak mobilization is measured against England, Wales, and Scotland in 1801 (10.5 million), the proportion mobilized would be as high as 4.8 percent.

Young (1770). The outcome, to be used for only the crudest purposes of approximation, is to be found on page 237.

Jan Marczewski's data on French central government expenditure in relation to gross physical product (at current prices) fall in the same range ("Some Aspects of the Economic Growth of France, 1660–1958," *Economic Development and Cultural Change*, vol. 9, no. 3 [April 1961], p. 372). See Table on p. 238.

French GNP per capita, in a less urbanized society, was probably 20 percent below that of Britain down to the 1780s, when the gap widened. On the other hand, French GNP was absolutely much larger, given the difference in population between the two countries of about three to one,

BRITISH PUBLIC EXPENDITURE
AND GROSS NATIONAL PRODUCT: 1711–1782

	Peak Year	Total Net Public Expenditure (1)	Approximate GNP (2)	Col. 1 Col. 2
		(in £ millions)		
War of Spanish Succession	1711	15	60	25%
War of Austrian Succession	1749	12.5	84	15
Seven Years' War	1761	21	106	20
War of American Independence	1782	29	150	20

FRENCH GOVERNMENT EXPENDITURE
AND GROSS PHYSICAL PRODUCT: 1701–1779

	Central Government Expenditure (1)	Gross Physical Product (2)	Col. 1 Col. 2
	(annual averages in millions of francs at current prices)		
1701–10	200	1485	13%
1758	237	(2350)	(10%)
1774	400	(3300)	(12%)
1777–9	613	(3500)	(17%)

NOTE: ( ) indicates interpolated estimates.

for most of the eighteenth century. The absolute levels of French expenditures were, therefore, much larger than those for Britain, despite the lower proportion they bear to national product.

6. J. F. Bosher, *French Finances, 1770–1795* (Cambridge: At the University Press, 1970), pp. 23–24.

7. Quoted in Alexander Gerschenkron, *Europe in the Russian Mirror* (Cambridge: At the University Press, 1970), p. 85. Kliuchevskii's phrase refers to Russia in the seventeenth century, under pressure from Peter's predecessors. Gerschenkron notes it as a peculiarly apt evocation of the impact of Peter's reign.

8. The classic summary of mercantilist policies is, of course, that of Eli F. Heckscher, *Mercantilism,* Mendel Shapiro, trans., rev. ed., E. F. Söderlund, ed., 2 vols. (London: George Allen & Unwin, New York: Macmillan, 1955). Heckscher's work, organized functionally, is centered on a comparison of British and French policy and thought, with lesser references to German, Dutch, and Scandinavian experience. Spain and the Austrian Empire are dealt with only occasionally, and Russia is almost wholly neglected, a point strongly made by Gerschenkron, *Europe,* pp. 62–9.

9. Gerschenkron, *Europe,* p. 71.

10. For an account of the economic modernization of Spain in the eighteenth century, see especially, Jaime Vicens Vives, with Jorge Nadal Oller, *An Economic History of Spain,* Frances M. López-Morillas, trans. (Princeton: Princeton University Press, 1969), pp. 471–604. For a lively attack on the notion of uniquely French inspiration of the Bourbon reforms, see "The Spanish Enlightenment," H. R. Trevor-Roper, in *Men and Events* (New York: Harper and Brothers), pp. 260–72.

11. Given the limited effects of the Spanish railroad system of-the nineteenth century and the persistence of major areas of rural poverty,

there is even a case for the view that only with the automobile age in the 1960s and 1970s was Spain rendered an efficient national market.

12. Jan deVries, "On the Modernity of the Dutch Republic," *Journal of Economic History,* vol. 33, no. 1 (March 1973), p. 199. For a more complete account of the special characteristics of Dutch society and politics, including persistent strands from the feudal past, see "Political and Cultural Origins of the Republic" in Wilson, *Dutch Republic.*

13. L. A. Clarkson, *The Pre-Industrial Economy in England, 1500–1750* (London: B. T. Batsford, 1971), p. 192.

14. The list is from S. B. Clough and C. W. Cole, *Economic History of Europe,* 3d ed. (Boston: D. C. Heath, 1952), p. 218. For a full account of Colbert and his predecessors, including Laffemas, see especially, C. W. Cole, *Colbert and a Century of French Mercantilism* (New York: Columbia University Press, 1939).

15. J. Clayburn La Force, "Spanish Royal Textile Factories, 1700–1800," *Journal of Economic History,* vol. 24, no. 3 (September 1964), p. 338.

16. Ibid., pp. 356–63, for La Force's summary of the reasons for this failure. See also the evaluation of J. Vicens Vives, *Spain,* pp. 526–8.

17. Quoted from F. Hartung, *Studien zur Geschichte der preussischen Verwaltung* (Berlin, 1942), p. 23, in J. O. Lindsay, ed., *The New Cambridge Modern History,* vol. 7, *The Old Regime, 1713–63* (Cambridge: At the University Press, 1957), p. 313.

18. Joseph T. Fuhrmann, *The Origins of Capitalism in Russia* (Chicago: Quadrangle, 1972), pp. 243–4.

19. Ibid., p. 262.

20. See particularly, Arcadius Kahan, "Continuity in Economic Activity and Policy during the Post-Petrine Period in Russia," *Journal of Economic History,* vol. 25, no. 1 (March 1965), pp. 61ff. Also, Peter I. Lyaschenko, *History of the National Economy of Russia,* L. M. Herman, trans. (New York: Macmillan, 1949), especially pp. 299–304. In addition to documenting the rise of private enterprise during the eighteenth century, Lyaschenko provides (pp. 302–3) several estimates of the expansion of industrial plants. These diverge with respect to definition, but suggest an increase of about four times between 1725 and 1762 (the ascension of Catherine II), and, perhaps, a further three-fold increase by the last decade of the century. Lyaschenko gives (p. 273) census data for 1722, 1762, and 1796 including the rural-urban breakdown.

21. Gerschenkron, *Europe,* pp. 71–73.

22. See, for example, Theodore A. Wertime, *The Coming of the Age of Steel* (Chicago: University of Chicago Press, 1962), p. 101 and footnote 2, pp. 101–2, for sources. Other sources suggest Russia may have become the largest pig iron producer in Europe by 1725 (Fuhrmann, *Origins,* p. 263). Wertime gives a figure of 10–15,000 tons for Russian production in 1725–50; Fuhrmann, 31,975 tons for 1740. Consistent with the latter

figure, Kahan ("Continuity in Economic Activity," p. 73) provides (from Strumilin) an annual production series exhibiting a rise from 9,271 tons in 1718 to 13,350 tons in 1725 (at Peter's death) to 22,956 tons in 1735.
23. Gerschenkron, *Europe*, p. 80.
24. P. J. Thomas, *Mercantilism and the East India Trade* (London: Frank Cass, 1963), p. 32.
25. Paul Mantoux, *The Industrial Revolution in the Eighteenth Century*, rev. ed. (New York: Harper & Row, 1961), p. 198.
26. Thomas, *Mercantilism*, pp. 48–117 and 138–65, provides an excellent account of the intellectual and political struggles leading to the prohibitions of 1700 and 1720.
27. Thomas argues (ibid., pp. 171–3) that the author of this pamphlet was Henry Martyn, Inspector-General of Exports and Imports. See also, Paul Mantoux, *Industrial Revolution*, pp. 133.
28. Heckscher, *Mercantilism*, vol. 1, pp. 172–5, offers a useful summary of French calico policy. See also Thomas, *Mercantilism*, pp.160–1. The most complete account is to be found in C. W. Cole, *French Mercantilism, 1683–1700* (New York: Columbia University Press, 1943), pp. 36–40, 164–77.
29. Heckscher, *Mercantilism*, vol. 1, p. 173.
30. Phyllis Deane and W. A. Cole, *British Economic Growth, 1688–1959*, 2d ed. (Cambridge: At the University Press, 1967), p. 127. In his detailed study of the English village Colyton, Wrigley (*Population and History*, pp. 82–3) found a subsidence of burials in the period 1730–50; a sharp rise in marriages in the 1740s; a slow rise of births in the 1750s, set back during the late 1760s, but markedly accelerating in the period 1770–1810. Burials rose in the late 1760s, but fell away to the 1790s. In general, Wrigley (p. 87) finds a return in Colyton to the demographic pattern of the period 1538–1624 in the period 1700–74, after the demographic setback of the seventeenth century. In the argument that follows, Habakkuk (*Cambridge Economic History*, pp. 25–33) has developed the case most lucidly for the role of agricultural expansion in increasing European population in the second half of the century through early marriages and a rise in birth rates. Thomas McKeown and R. G. Brown, "English Population Changes in the Eighteenth Century," *Population Studies* 9 (1955–56), pp. 119–41, have responded to Habakkuk's argument with a sophisticated rationale for ascribing the increase to a fall in death rates due to "improvements in the environment." Since data are not adequate, the argument remains unresolved, as McKeown and Brown make clear. They note, however, a basic point of agreement in the two views (p. 140): ". . . it [eighteenth-century population increase] resulted from an improvement in economic and social conditions. This is true whether we attribute more importance to the death rate or the birth rate; for in the latter case the only conceivable explanation is a substantial

decrease in the mean age at marriage of women in consequence of the economic development of the period."

31. See especially, A. H. John, "Aspects of English Economic Growth in the First Half of the Eighteenth Century," *Economica*, n.s., vol. 28, no. 110 (May 1961), and "Agricultural Productivity and Economic Growth in England 1700–1760," *Journal of Economic History*, vol. 25, no. 1 (March 1965), reprinted with a postscript in E. L. Jones, ed., *Agriculture and Economic Growth in England 1650–1815* (London: Methuen & Co., 1967), pp. 172–93. John's postscript is a response to a critique of his hypothesis by M. W. Flinn, "Agricultural Productivity and Economic Growth in England, 1700–1760: A Comment," *Journal of Economic History*, vol. 26 (March 1966). For British growth rates relative to Prussia and Russia in the second half of the eighteenth century, see table 2. Wrigley (*Population and History*, p. 153) estimates the annual average rate of growth for England and Wales at 0.80 percent, East Prussia (1700–1800) at 0.84 percent, Pomerania (1740–1800) at 0.80 percent, as opposed to 0.45 percent for France (1740–89), 0.45 percent for Italy (1700–1800), 0.56 percent for Württemberg (1740–1800).

32. Perkins, *Agricultural Development* p. 24. See also, p. 209.

33. Ping-ti Ho, *Population of China*, pp. 264, 266, 270.

34. Perkins, *Agricultural Development*, p. 24.

35. Ibid., p. 267.

36. *Population of China*, p. 270.

37. See especially, Kozo Yamamura, "Toward a Reexamination of the Economic History of Tokugawa Japan, 1600–1867," *Journal of Economic History*, vol. 33, no. 3 (September 1973), pp. 509–41, including footnote references to other revisionist studies.

38. On Japanese population in this earlier period, see especially, Irene B. Taeuber, *The Population of Japan* (Princeton: Princeton University Press, 1958), pp. 3–34.

39. Ibid., pp. 24–5.

40. Herbert Heaton, *Economic History of Europe* (New York: Harper and Brothers, 1948), pp. 428–29.

41. There is a double point to be made about R. H. Tawney's famous calculations on the distribution of the ownership of manors and his debate with Hugh Trevor-Roper ("The Rise of the Gentry, 1558–1640," in E. M. Carus-Wilson, ed., *Essays in Economic History* [London: Edward Arnold, 1954], pp. 173–214, reprinted from *Economic History Review*, vol. 11, no. 1 [1941]; "Postscript," *Economic History Review*, 2d ser., vol. 7, no. 1 [1954]). The important tables are on p. 242. Trevor-Roper objected to Tawney's exclusion, in table 2a, of manors owned by peers who were created between 1561 and 1640. Tawney, therefore, produced table 2b. For present purposes, and especially to dramatize the difference between England and the Continent, the two critical points

THE OWNERSHIP OF 2,547 MANORS IN SEVEN COUNTIES IN 1561 AND 1640

(1) 1561

Total	Crown	Peers	Gentry	Ecclesiastical	Colleges, Hospitals and Schools	Other
2,547	242 (9.5%)	335 (13.1%)	1,709 (67.1%)	185 (7.2%)	67 (2.6%)	9

(2) 1640

(a) Assigning to gentry manors owned by families ennobled 1561–1640

Total	Crown	Peers	Gentry	Ecclesiastical	Colleges, Hospitals and Schools	Other
2,547	53 (2.0%)	157 (6.1%)	2,051 (80.5%)	179 (7.0%)	76 (3.0%)	31

(b) Assigning to peers manors owned by families ennobled 1561–1640

Total	Crown	Peers	Gentry	Ecclesiastical	Colleges, Hospitals and Schools	Other
2,547	53 (2.0%)	343 (13.4%)	1,865 (73.3)	179 (7.0%)	76 (3.0%)	31

are: the dominating and rising role of the gentry, in both tables (from 67 percent in 1561 to 81 percent or 73 percent in 1640); and the high proportion of manors owned by newly created peers, mainly rising from the gentry, reflecting the flexibility of the English class of nobles at this time (186 out of 343, or 54 percent in seventy-nine years).

42. B. Behrens, "Nobles, Privileges and Taxes in France at the End of the Ancien Regime," *Economic History Review,* 2d ser., vol. 15, no. 3 (April 1963), p. 459, provides the following breakdown of landownership in France in the later eighteenth century: clergy, 10 percent; nobility, 20 percent; bourgeoisie (property-owners in town), 30 percent; peasantry, 35 percent; commons, etc., 5 percent. "Peasantry" includes all those who held land from which they could not be arbitrarily removed, even if they still owed some feudal dues.

43. Marczewski, "Some Aspects," p. 375. The decade before the French Revolution was marked by a sharp deceleration. These calculations have been criticized as showing an exaggerated increase in French agricultural production. The fact is, however, that after 1740 the French no longer experienced famine in the face of an expanding population and increased urbanization.

44. In an imaginative essay, Robert Forster seeks to specify the sources of the long-observed lack of entrepreneurial zeal in French as opposed to English agriculture of the eighteenth century ("Obstacles to Agricultural Growth in Eighteenth-Century France," *American Historical Review,* vol. 75, no. 6 [October 1970], pp. 1600ff.). Technically, he finds the root of the matter in the unwillingness of French landowners to plough their own capital into agriculture and, especially, to encourage their tenants to improve their land without wholly losing the increase in productivity in higher rents. He finds significant differences in English approaches to agricultural investment and rent-setting, and he finds confirmation of his hypothesis in the unpopular success of the French *gros fermier,* who leased large acreage to grow grain for the urban market in Paris and northeast France. The higher productivity of their commercial operations was acknowledged even by their critics. In Forster's view, the *gros fermier* virtually alone escaped the deeper weaknesses of French agriculture (p. 1613): the peasant's "governing passion" for a subsistence farm, and the "landlord's aversion to risk and his obsession with immediate return . . . closely related to the magnetic role of Paris as the focus of French social aspirations. Paris promised much—the marriage market, the money market, the sinecures, offices, preferments, and, of course, the magnificent setting, without which to be a gentleman was a poor thing indeed. The land was but a means, too often sucked dry to provide the cream of society the resources to consume, to buy regiments, to pay dowries, and to consume again. And when the landed revenues were not enough, the large landlords mortgaged the land and drew off the capital of others for more conspicuous consumption on the rue Saint Honoré or

to pay family portions and dowries that were in turn 'consumed' for status. How much of this capital was diverted from productive industry is another issue, but that little flowed back to the land for capital improvement there seems no doubt."

45. Vicens Vives, *Spain,* 509–10. Raymond Carr has drawn a vivid portrait of the stifling effects on agricultural productivity of the higher Spanish nobility of the eighteenth century in Albert Goodwin, ed., *The European Nobility in the Eighteenth Century* (London: Adam and Charles Black, 1953), especially pp. 48–54. A system of strict entail led to the concentration of land ownership in progressively fewer noble families, but the nobility were oriented toward the court and their role in urban life, collecting great incomes from vast landholdings but exhibiting no interest in the economics of their holdings, let alone increases in productivity. Unlike the nobility of Prussia, Sweden, and Russia—and, to a degree, even France—the Spanish nobility played no significant positive role in the modernizing enterprises initiated by the Bourbon governments of the eighteenth century.

46. See, for example, W. O. Henderson, *Studies in the Economic Policy of Frederick the Great* (Liverpool and London: Frank Cass, 1963), p. 126 and note 2, for sources and alternative estimates.

47. See, especially, Robert V. Eagly, ed., *The Swedish Bullionist Controversy, P. N. Christiernin's "Lectures on the High Price of Foreign Exchange in Sweden (1761)"* (Philadelphia: American Philosophical Society, 1971), especially pp. 13–21. Briefly, the Hats pursued an expansionist economic and military policy that yielded inflation and military stalemate in the period 1739–65. But the Caps, once in power, pursued a rigid deflationary policy that culminated in their ouster in 1769.

48. For English public finance data from 1688–91, see Elizabeth Boody Schumpeter, "English Prices and Public Finance, 1660–1822," *The Review of Economic Statistics,* vol. 20, no. 1 (February 1938), pp. 36–7; and Mitchell, with Deane, *British Historical Statistics,* pp. 386–91. For the state of the British fiscal system at the end of the eighteenth century, including significant administrative reforms, see, especially, J. E. D. Binney, *British Public Finance and Administration, 1774–92* (Oxford: Clarendon Press, 1958). On the role of the sale of Crown lands in the seventeenth century in setting the stage for parliamentary control over British finance and the formal ordering of the fiscal system, see Ian Gentles, "The Sales of Crown Lands during the English Revolution," *Economic History Review,* vol. 26, no. 4 (November 1973).

49. This antiseptic statement of the right of the English king to seek advice outside the formal cabinet and parliamentary structure does not fully reflect the extent, in England and elsewhere, to which influence on policy at the court might be informally exercised. The Duke of Buckingham's statement (quoted by Winston S. Churchill, *Marlborough: His Life and Times,* Vol. 2, p. 1008) on his dismissal from office in 1714 is

perhaps exaggerated but it is germane: "Good God, how has this poor Nation been governed in my time! During the reign of King Charles the Second we were governed by a parcel of French whores; in King James the Second's time by a parcel of Popish Priests; in King William's time by a parcel of Dutch Footmen; and now we are governed by a dirty chambermaid, a Welsh attorney, and a profligate wretch that has neither honour nor honesty."

50. Data quoted from P. G. M. Dickson and John Sperling, "War Finance, 1689–1714," in J. S. Bromley, ed., *The New Cambridge Modern History*, vol. 6, *The Rise of Great Britain and Russia, 1688–1715/25* (Cambridge: At the University Press, 1970), p. 299. This chapter relates, in an original and useful way, war finance to the administrative and constitutional changes in Europe over the period.

51. French naval strength was maintained well until 1693; it fell off, relatively, down to 1707, when naval construction virtually ceased until the postwar period. Although precise comparison is difficult, England emerged with an advantage over France of, say, ten to seven, consisting of relatively newer vessels. Starting in the 1720s, the French fleet was again expanded, but for a century and more Britain did not lose the primacy first clearly gained in the generation before 1713.

52. See, especially, Behrens, "Nobles, Privileges and Taxes," especially pp. 470–2. Miss. Behrens argues persuasively that the French nobility were hard pressed by the land taxes; that other groups enjoyed equal or greater privileges in France; and that the burden of war taxes rather than excessive privilege was at the root of the French problem. Her analysis underlines the greater French than British reliance on direct taxes, but, I believe, overstates the average income differential between the two countries.

53. Like Binney's study of British public finance and administration for the period 1774–92, Bosher documents for France this significant process in his *French Finances.*

54. For a detailed account of the emergence of the Prussian bureaucracy, its social constitution, and its evolution in the period after Frederick the Great, see Hans Rosenberg, *Bureaucracy, Aristocracy, and Autocracy: The Prussian Experience, 1660–1815* (Cambridge, Mass: Harvard University Press, 1958).

55. Gerschenkron, *Europe*, p. 75. W. H. Bruford notes in "The Organization and Rise of Prussia," in J. O. Lindsay, ed., *The New Cambridge Modern History*, vol. 7, *The Old Regime, 1713–63* (Cambridge: At the University Press), p. 297, that under Frederick the Great, the burden of the Contribution on the Prussian peasantry averaged about 40 percent of the net yield of his holdings: "In addition . . . the peasant had to pay in many cases quite as much to his landlord also." Whatever the exact figures might be, both Russian and Prussian peasants were evidently taxed to a point that brought them close to minimum subsistence standards.

56. Max Beloff provides a useful brief account of the changing status of the Russian nobility in Albert Goodwin, ed., *The European Nobility,* especially pp. 177–89. Beloff emphasizes the limited nature of the increased authority gained by the nobility in the post-Petrine period, concluding (p. 189): ". . . the nobility, at the end of the eighteenth century, was no less a subservient element in the Russian State than it had been under the masterful Peter one hundred years before."

Chapter 3.
The Commercial Revolution

1. For the role of the Italian cities and Italians in orienting Spain and Portugal towards the Atlantic, from the twelfth century forward, see Charles Verlinden, "From the Mediterranean to the Atlantic, Aspects of an Economic Shift (12th–18th Century)," *Journal of European Economic History,* vol. 1, no. 3 (Winter 1972), pp. 625–46.
2. Charles Wilson, *Profit and Power, A Study of England and the Dutch Wars* (London, New York, Toronto: Longmans, Green, 1957), pp. 143–4.
3. William Cunningham, *The Growth of English Industry and Commerce, The Mercantile System* (Cambridge: At the University Press, 1925), p. 332, provides a useful table of English colonial acquisitions in the seventeenth century, suggesting how much was owed to initiative under the Stuarts. See p. 247.
4. See, especially, F. J. Fisher, "London's Export Trade in the Early Seventeenth Century," in W. E. Minchinton, ed., *The Growth of English Overseas Trade in the Seventeenth and Eighteenth Centuries* (London: Methuen, 1969), reprinted from *Economic History Review,* 2d. ser., vol. 3, (1950), pp. 64–77.
5. Cole, *Colbert,* vol. 1, pp. 383, 436.
6. For this period see, especially, Ralph Davis, "English Foreign Trade, 1660–1700," in Minchinton, ed., *English Overseas Trade,* reprinted from *Economic History Review,* 2d. ser., vol. 6, no. 2, (1954), pp. 78–98.
7. See Table 1, p. 43, above.
8. See, especially, H. E. S. Fisher, "Anglo-Portuguese Trade, 1700–1770," in Minchinton, *English Overseas Trade,* especially pp. 158–63, reprinted from *Economic History Review,* 2d. ser., vol. 16, no. 2, (1963).
9. Emory R. Johnson et al., *History of Domestic and Foreign Commerce of the United States,* vol. 1 (Washington, D.C.: Carnegie Institution, 1915), p. 89, table 3.
10. E. Levasseur, *Histoire du Commerce de la France, Première Partie: Avant 1789* (Paris: Libraire Nouvelle de Droit et de Jurisprudence, 1911), pp. 515–31, with important table on p. 518.

PLANTATIONS IN AMERICA AND THE WEST INDIES		
Newfoundland	1583	Sir H. Gilbert
Barbados	1605	
Virginia	1607	Company
Bermudas	1614	Company
New England	1620	Company
Nova Scotia	1621	Sir W. Alexander
Guiana	1627	Duke of Buckingham
Antigua, etc.	1627	Earl of Carlisle
Trinidad, etc.	1627	Earl of Montgomery
Carolina	1629	General Heath
Bahamas	1630	Company
Maryland	1632	Lord Baltimore
Long Island	1635	Sir W. Alexander
Jamaica	1655	
New York, etc.	1664	Duke of York
Hudson's Bay	1670	Company
Pennsylvania	1682	W. Penn

FACTORIES AND POSSESSIONS OF AFRICAN COMPANY

Gambia	1631
Gold Coast	1660
Lagos	1661

FACTORIES AND POSSESSIONS OF EAST INDIA COMPANY

Surat	1609
Madras	1639
Hooghly	1650
S. Helena	1651
Bombay	1665

11. François Crouzet, "England and France in the Eighteenth Century: A Comparative Analysis of Two Economic Growths," J. Sondheimer, trans., in R. M. Hartwell, ed., *The Causes of the Industrial Revolution in England* (London: Methuen, 1967), pp. 146–7, edited from an article in *Annales,* vol. 21, no. 2 (1966).
12. For a discussion of this failure, see R. Koebner, "Adam Smith and the Industrial Revolution," *Economic History Review,* 2d. ser., volume 11, no. 3 (1959), pp. 381–91. Koebner attributes Smith's failure to deal

with technological change and its possibilities to his focusing on the need to break the power of policies and institutions that restricted competition at home and abroad.

13. T. S. Ashton, *The Industrial Revolution, 1760–1830* (London: Oxford University Press, 1948), p. 57.

14. E. Baines, *History of Cotton Manufacture* (London, 1835), p. 115.

15. For a useful summary of the broader economic consequences in England of commercial expansion during this period, see Minchinton's Introduction to *English Overseas Trade,* pp. 36–52. Minchinton does not make sharply the distinction here between effects on economic expansion and those related to technological change.

16. Minchinton (p. 47) notes by way of example: "In Bristol itself merchants invested in iron, glass, pottery, soap, sugar, brass and copper, and other metal-working industries while Bristol capital is also to be found in South Wales iron, tinplate and brass and copper industries."

17. François Crouzet, "Wars, Blockade, and Economic Change in Europe, 1792–1815," *Journal of Economic History,* vol. 24, no. 4, (December 1964), pp. 568–9.

18. Deane and Cole, *British Economic Growth,* p. 7. The basis for these calculations is not clear from the text, but they appear to derive from estimates of population increase in the major cities and towns.

19. For a parallel argument that the commercial revolution was not a sufficient condition for the industrial revolution, see Paul Bairoch, "Commerce international et genèse de la révolution industrielle anglaise," *Annales Economies Sociétés Civilisation,* vol. 28, no. 2 (March–April 1973). In its commercial expansion without the effective absorption of major new technologies, western Europe's experience was similar to that of some later developing nations that entered into periods of rapid export expansion, but generated an industrial revolution only after considerable delay. See, for example, Nathaniel H. Leff, "Tropical Trade and Development in the Nineteenth Century: The Brazilian Experience," *Journal of Political Economy,* vol. 81, no. 3 (May/June 1973), pp. 678–96.

Chapter 4.
Science, Invention, and Innovation

1. A. N. Whitehead, *Science and the Modern World* (New York: Macmillan, 1925), p. 3.

2. H. Butterfield, *The Origins of Modern Science, 1300–1800* (New York: Macmillan, 1952), p. 149.

3. This way of looking at science, invention, and innovation is developed in the author's *Economic Growth,* especially chs. 2 and 3.

4. In one of the few efforts of which I am aware to assess explictly the motives of inventors, Shelby T. McCloy, *French Inventions of the*

Eighteenth Century (Lexington, Ky: University of Kentucky Press, 1952), p. 189, has this to say about French inventors of the eighteenth century: "The question of the motives or incentives of the inventors is much more difficult to solve. In our own century, due in no small degree to the writings of Karl Marx, a reader might easily jump to the conclusion that the economic motive was paramount. With not a few of the inventors it must have been. It is probable, in fact, that most of them hoped to realize some financial benefit from their inventions. This is far from saying that the hope of economic gain was the paramount motive, or indeed that it was the original driving force. Few inventors benefited appreciably from their inventions; a much greater number squandered their inheritance and savings on their inventive activity. The largest return to most of them was a government pension, usually modest. Some received no reward whatever. As a matter of fact, some inventors were so indifferent to monetary returns that they renounced claim to economic exploitation of their inventions. In this category were Berthollet, Berthelot, Camus, and Saint-Sauveur. With difficulty the friends of Conté persuaded him not to do likewise, and only the consideration of the other members of his family moved him. Vaucanson bequeathed his collection of machines, on which he had spent much of his earnings, to the king for public display. With these men patriotism and humanitarianism burned brightly. Even more brightly burned the desire for achievement and fame; this was the dominant motive of the French inventors. Economic returns were of secondary consideration, and humanitarianism and patriotism were seldom absent."

5. A curve of this kind is implicit in the analysis of Thomas S. Kuhn, *The Structure of Scientific Revolutions*, 2d. ed., enl. (Chicago: University of Chicago Press, 1962 and 1970). For a sustained debate on Kuhn's propositions and his response, see Imre Lakatos and Alan Musgrave, eds., *Criticism and the Growth of Knowledge* (Cambridge: At the University Press, 1970). For formulation of a similar sequence, see the author's *Economic Growth*, pp. 62–3, including the relevant footnotes, where the difficulty of defining the economic yield from fundamental science is discussed.

6. For the author's view of the sectoral pattern of investment in modern growing economies, see *Economic Growth,* especially pp. 96–103, as well as *The Stages of Economic Growth*, 2d. ed. (Cambridge: At the University Press, 1971), especially pp. ix–xiv; 12–16; 174–6; 184–6.

7. See especially, Jacob Schmookler, *Invention and Economic Growth* (Cambridge, MA: Harvard University Press, 1966). For earlier discussions of invention as an economically induced phenomenon, see A. P. Usher, *A History of Mechanical Inventions* (New York: McGraw-Hill, 1929); S. C. Gilfillan, *The Sociology of Invention* (Chicago: Follett, 1935); also R. S. Sayers, "The Springs of Technical Progress in Britain, 1919–39," *Economic Journal*, vol. 60, no. 238 (June 1950), especially pp.

282 ff.; and Ashton, *Industrial Revolution,* pp. 91–92. J. Schumpeter's indecisive discussion of this question should also be noted *(Business Cycles,* vol. 1, p.85n.) (New York: McGraw-Hill, 1939). Schumpeter allows for the existence of inventions and innovations induced by necessity, but also for inventions not related to any particular requirement or not related to the requirement met by the particular innovation that incorporates them. Schumpeter states: "It might be thought that innovation can never be anything else but an effort to cope with a given economic situation. In a sense this is true. For a given innovation to become possible, there must always be some 'objective needs' to be satisfied and certain 'objective conditions'; but they rarely, if ever, uniquely determine what kind of innovation will satisfy them, and as a rule they can be satisfied in many different ways. Most important of all, they may remain unsatisfied for an indefinite time, which shows that they are not in themselves sufficient to produce an innovation." This issue is discussed in the author's *Economic Growth,* pp. 83–6.

8. Nathan Rosenberg has thoughtfully discussed this point—and the limits it sets on Schmookler's basic thesis—in "Science, Technology, and Economic Growth," *The Economic Journal,* vol. 84, no. 333 (March 1974).

9. *Economic Growth,* p. 67, makes a further modification in the conventional presentation of the Keynesian determination of the investment level: ". . . one can envisage as deducted from the marginal efficiency of capital curve, as a cost, a risk premium; that is, the difference between the safe rate of interest and the interest appropriate to the degree of risk attached by the given society to the particular act of investment." With that additional modification, the level of investment appears as the exhaustion of profit possibilities above the safe rate of interest.

10. See, especially, I. D. Burnet, "An Interpretation of Take-off," *The Economic Record,* September 1972 pp. 424–8; and Nicholas Kaldor, "The Irrelevance of Equilibrium Economics," *Economic Journal,* vol. 82, no. 328 (December 1972), pp. 1237–1255. Both authors refer to the famous article of A. A. Young, "Increasing Returns and Economic Progress," *Economic Journal,* vol. 38 (December 1928), pp. 528–42. For Alfred Marshall's puzzlement with the case of increasing returns, see, especially, Appendix H in his *Principles of Economics* and Appendix J, paragraphs 8 and 10, of *Money, Credit, and Commerce.* Burnet's article represents a sharp break with previous theoretical treatments of increasing returns in that he applies the concept to major innovative breakthroughs, creating new industries, rather than incremental improvements in technology and organization, within existing industries.

11. New York, 1930, pp. 4–5.

12. Herbert Dingle, "Copernicus and the Planets," in *The History of Science, A Symposium* (Glencoe, IL.: Free Press, 1951), p. 37. For a sociological analysis of the scientific ferment in Italy, which influenced

Copernicus, see Ben-David, *The Scientist's Role,* especially pp. 55–69. Ben-David argues that the basic thrust of early Italian science came from a group "that was trying to displace the official university philosophers and modernize the intellectual outlook of the Catholic church" (p. 63). It lacked, therefore, the linkage to the concept of material progress that emerged in northern Europe.

13. See, especially, "Scientific Societies in Eighteenth Century America," in Ralph S. Bates, *Scientific Societies in the United States,* 2d. ed. (New York: Columbia University Press, 1958), pp. 1–27.

14. "Social and Economic Aspects of Science," in G. N. Clark, *Science and Social Welfare in the Age of Newton* (Oxford: Clarendon Press, 1937), pp. 60–91, and B. Hessen, "The Social and Economic Roots of Newton's 'Principia'" in *Science at the Cross Roads* (Papers presented before the International Congress on the History of Science and Technology, London, June 29–July 3, 1931, by the Delegates of the U.S.S.R). Ben-David adds an additional element to the equation linking seventeenth-century English science to the society (*The Scientist's Role,* p. 74). He argues that in the period of intense ideological conflict, from the Puritan Revolution to the Glorious Revolution, experimental natural science "served as the symbol of a neutral meeting ground for the useful pursuit of common intellectual goals." Science became "the paradigm for the philosophy of an open and plural society." In this view, the Resolution of 1688 deflated this philosophical role for science in Britain (p. 79), but science assumed a similar function in eighteenth-century France (pp. 82–3). Ben-David would thus explain the greater vitality of the French Academy than the Royal Society in the eighteenth century.

15. B. Hessen, "Newton's 'Principia,'" pp. 182–3.

16. Ibid., p. 167.

17. Ibid., p. 176.

18. Ibid., pp. 183, 191.

19. Clark, *Science and Social Welfare,* p. 86.

20. Sir James Jeans, *The Growth of Physical Science* (Cambridge: At the University Press, 1947), p. 160.

21. For an explicit discussion of the bases for the concentration of talent in painting in seventeenth century Holland, see Wilson, *Dutch Republic,* ch. 7.

22. Ibid., p. 123.

23. See, especially, Donald Fleming, "Latent Heat and the Invention of the Watt Engine," *Isis,* vol. 43, Pt. 1, no. 131 (April 1952), pp. 3–5.

24. Charles C. Gillispie, "The Natural History of Industry," *Isis,* vol. 48, 1957, reprinted in A. E. Musson, ed., *Science, Technology, and Economic Growth in the Eighteenth Century* (London: Methuen, 1972), p. 126.

25. Quoted in Whitehead, *Science and the Modern World,* pp. 2–3.

26. Ibid., p. 14.

27. Samuel Lilley, "The Development of Scientific Instruments in the

Seventeenth Century," in *The History of Science,* pp. 74–5. See also Lilley's *Men, Machines and History.*

28. Ashton, *Industrial Revolution,* p. 16.

29. Robert E. Schofield, "The Industrial Orientation of Science in the Lunar Society of Birmingham," *Isis,* vol. 48 (1957), pp. 408–15, reprinted as in Musson, *Science, Technology and Economic Growth,* pp. 136–147. See also, Schofield's *The Lunar Society of Birmingham* (Oxford: Clarendon Press, 1963).

30. See, especially, A. E. Musson and Eric Robinson, *Science and Technology in the Industrial Revolution* (Manchester: Manchester: University Press, 1969). Peter Mathias has also explored the complexities of the linkage between science and innovation in "Who Unbound Prometheus? Science and Technical Change, 1600–1800," in Peter Mathias, ed., *Science and Society, 1600–1900* (Cambridge: At the University Press, 1972), reprinted in Musson, *Science, Technology and Economic Growth,* pp. 69–96. This chapter, in an earlier version, was published in the *Yorkshire Bulletin of Economic and Social Research,* vol. 21, 1969.

31. Quoted in Fleming, "Latent Heat," p. 5.

32. Schmookler, *Invention and Economic Growth,* p. 200.

33. Quoted from W. Radcliffe, *The Origin of Power Loom Weaving,* 1828, p. 62, in Phyllis Deane, *The First Industrial Revolution* (Cambridge: At the University Press, 1965), p. 87.

34. Edward Baines, *History of the Cotton Manufacture* (London, 1835), p. 357.

35. For a retelling of this story on the basis of new evidence, see Charles K. Hyde, "The Adoption of Coke-Smelting in the British Iron Industry, 1709–1790" (Mimeographed paper presented to the Conference on the "New" Economic History of Britain, Cambridge, 1972). Hyde's analysis, in terms of the rising cost of charcoal, fits well the important revisionist article of G. Hammersley, "The Charcoal Iron Industry and Its Fuel, 1540–1750," *Economic History Review,* vol. 26, no. 4 (November 1973). Hammersley argues persuasively that the claims on the British woodlands of the charcoal-fueled iron industry were modest, but the price of charcoal about tripled during the seventeenth century, rising slowly thereafter (p. 609). This pressure on price arose not from increasing demand from the iron industry but from the need for more farmland and the fuel requirements of industries other than iron. The upshot was a competitive disadvantage versus Sweden, involving factors beyond fuel costs, and the kind of growing economic incentive to shift from charcoal to coke that Hyde presents.

36. Baines, *Cotton Manufacture,* p. 220.

37. Quoted in Mantoux, *Industrial Revolution,* p. 320.

38. H. J. Habakkuk, "Population, Commerce and Economic Ideas," p. 42.

39. See, especially, Crouzet, "England and France." In three famous

articles, "A Comparison of Industrial Growth in France and England from 1540 to 1640," Pts. 1, 2 and 3, *Journal of Political Economy*, vol. 44, nos. 3, 4, and 5 (1936), John N. Nef compares French and English industrial growth in earlier times. He argues that there was, in this century, a surge in English mining, metallurgy, shipbuilding, brewing, and chemical manufacture (alum and copperas) not matched in France; that these industries lent themselves to capitalist factory production; and that the "Industrial Revolution of the late eighteenth and nineteenth centuries only increased a lead England had long held in the volume of industrial output and the progress of industrial capitalism" (p. 666). The initial industrial advantage of Britain in the late seventeenth and early eighteenth centuries is incontestable, although, as Nef notes, it was least marked in the most important of all branches of manufacture, textiles. It is not satisfactory, however, to jump, as Nef does, from 1660 to 1783 and beyond. France did a good deal of catching up in the second and third quarters of the eighteenth century.

40. For discussion of relative income per capita levels in eighteenth-century Europe, see Cole and Deane, "The Growth of National Incomes," in Habakkuk and Postan, eds., *Cambridge Economic History*, vol. 6, especially pp. 3–6.

41. Deane and Cole, *British Economic Growth,* especially pp. 82–97.

42. Ibid., p. 92.

43. Mathias, "Who Unbound Prometheus?" p. 81.

44. From the anonymous author of *A Treatise on Taxes and Contributions,* 1679, p. 53, deposited in the British Museum, quoted in Alfred P. Wadsworth and Julia De Lacy Mann, *The Cotton Trade and Industrial Lancashire, 1600–1780* (Manchester: Manchester University Press, 1931), pp. 113–4.

45. Ibid., p. 413.

46. The interplay between French inventors and the public authorities can be best traced in McCloy, *French Inventions,* which examines the evolution of French inventions in eleven major fields, summing up the role of the government in Chapter 12, "Patents and Encouragement." The history of French inventions and efforts to generate them in the eighteenth century underlines the inadequacy of the argument centered on private property rights used by D. C. North and R. P. Thomas to explain the relative pace of modernization in Britain and France in *The Rise of the Western World* (Cambridge: At the University Press, 1973), especially ch. 10.

47. McCloy, *French Inventions,* p. 191.

48. The best exposition of this argument is that of Crouzet, "England and France," pp. 168–72.

49. J. R. Harris, *Industry and Technology in the Eighteenth Century: Britain and France* (Birmingham, England: University of Birmingham Press, 1972).

50. Quoted in Thomas, *Mercantilism,* p. 161.
51. Crouzet, "England and France," . 170–71.
52. Wadsworth and Mann, *The Cotton Trade,* p. 204.
53. See, for example, ibid., pp. 416–19.
54. Baines, *Cotton Manufacture,* p. 115.
55. Ibid., p. 116.
56. Ashton, *Industrial Revolution,* pp. 16–19.
57. Everett E. Hagen, *On the Theory of Social Change* (Homewood, IL: Dorsey Press, 1962), pp. 294–309. See also, "The Puritan Spur to Science," in Robert K. Merton, *The Sociology of Science,* Norman W. Storer, ed. (Chicago: University of Chicago Press, 1973) pp. 228–253 (originally published 1938).
58. Charles Henry Hull, ed., *The Economic Writings of Sir William Petty,* vol. 1 (Cambridge: At the University Press, 1899), pp. 263–4.
59. McCloy, *French Inventions,* pp. 186–88.
60. On the shift of Holland to a *rentier* economy, see Wilson, *Dutch Republic,* pp. 230–42. For a more detailed analysis, see Wilson's *Anglo-Dutch Commerce and Finance in the Eighteenth Century* (Cambridge: At the University Press, 1941).

Chapter 5.
The World Economy, 1783–1820: An Epilogue

1. Gillispie, "Natural History of Industry," p. 125.
2. For a discussion of this proposition, see Arthur D. Gayer et al., *The Growth and Fluctuation of the British Economy, 1790–1850,* vol. 2 (Oxford: Clarendon Press, 1953), chs. 4, 5, especially pp. 646–9.
3. For a pioneering analysis of eighteenth-century fluctuations, see T. S. Ashton, *Economic Fluctuations in England, 1700–1800* (Oxford: Clarendon Press, 1959).
4. The latter stages of this expansion and its crisis are chronicled in Gayer et al., *Growth and Fluctuation,* vol. 1, pp. 7–27.
5. David Macpherson, *Annals of Commerce,* vol. 4 (London, 1805), pp. 387–8.
6. For an analysis of the economic impact on the Continent of the war years emphasizing the "de-Americanization" of European trade, see especially, Crouzet, "Wars, Blockade, and Economic Change."
7. Ibid., p. 578.
8. Ibid., pp. 579–80.
9. Ibid., p. 585.
10. Jan Marczewski, "Economic Growth of France," p. 380, estimates French cotton spinning and weaving as having the highest rate of growth among French industries for both the period 1781–90 to 1803–12 (5.14 percent) and 1803–12 to 1825–34 (4.73 percent). Cotton fabrics show similar rates for the two periods.

11. For a brief account of the Belgian takeoff, see the exposition of Prof. Léon Dupriez in W. W. Rostow, ed., *The Economics of Take-Off into Sustained Growth* (New York: St. Martin's Press, 1963), pp. 375–8. Dupriez notes that, in Belgium, also, the textile industry was an insufficient basis for takeoff. For an interesting comparison of the long-term evolution of Belgium and the Netherlands, emphasizing the bias towards industry in the former, see Jan A. Van Houtte, "Economic Development of Belgium and the Netherlands from the Beginning of the Modern Era," *Journal of European Economic History,* vol. 1, no. 1 (Spring 1972), pp. 100–20.

12. Vicens Vives, *Spain,* p. 580.

13. Wilson, *Anglo-Dutch Commerce,* p. 204.

14. For an account of British-Russian frictions of this period and the evolution of the British iron industry, see especially, T. S. Ashton, *Iron and Steel in the Industrial Revolution* (Manchester: University of Manchester Press, 1924), pp. 142–56.

15. For an account of Russian industry in this period, see Lyaschenko, *National Economy of Russia,* pp. 327–39.

16. See, especially, C. Northcote Parkinson, *Trade in the Eastern Seas, 1793–1813* (Cambridge: At the University Press, 1937), especially, pp. 69–97, 357–65.

17. R. Mukerjee, *The Economic History of India, 1600–1800* (Allahabad: Kitab Mahal, 1967), pp. 193–4.

18. Baines, *Cotton Manufacture,* p. 416, for a detailed breakdown of British cotton exports in 1832, showing total exports to Germany of £3.3 million; to China, East India Company's territories, and Ceylon of £1.6 million.

19. C. C. Chang, *An Estimate of China's Farms and Crops, 1932,* pp. 11–14, quoted in A. K. Chiu, "Agriculture," in H. F. MacNair, ed., *China* (Berkeley and Los Angeles: University of California Press, 1946), p. 469.

20. Parkinson, *Eastern Seas,* p. 94. On tea smuggling as well as the change in the British tea drinking habit, see especially, W. A. Cole, "Trends in Eighteenth-Century Smuggling," ch. 4 in Minchinton, ed., *Growth of English Trade,* pp. 121–43, reprinted from *Economic History Review,* vol. 10, no. 3 (1958).

21. Cole, p. 128.

22. See Gayer et al., *Growth and Fluctuation,* p. 69, for the first railroads of 1801–4. For a brief but useful account of the pre-1829 British railroads, see H. J. Dyos and D. H. Aldcroft, *British Transport* (Leicester: Leicester University Press, 1969), pp. 111–8.

23. McCloy tells this tale in *French Inventions,* pp. 32–5.

Index